PUBLIC
GUARDIANSHIP

In the Best Interests of
Incapacitated People?

Pamela B. Teaster, Winsor C. Schmidt Jr.,
Erica F. Wood, Susan A. Lawrence,
and Marta S. Mendiondo

 PRAEGER

AN IMPRINT OF ABC-CLIO, LLC
Santa Barbara, California • Denver, Colorado • Oxford, England

Library of Congress Cataloging-in-Publication Data

Public guardianship : in the best interests of incapacitated people? / Pamela B. Teaster . . . [et al.].
   p. ; cm.
   Includes bibliographical references and index.
   ISBN 978-0-313-37827-0 (hardcover : alk. paper) — ISBN 978-0-313-37828-7 (ebook)
   1. Guardian and ward—United States.   2. Capacity and disability—United States.
3. People with disabilities—Legal status, laws, etc.—United States.   4. People with disabilities—Services for—Government policy—United States.   5. People with disabilities—Care—Government policy—United States.   I. Teaster, Pamela B. (Pamela Booth).
   [DNLM: 1. Legal Guardians—legislation & jurisprudence—United States.   2. Disabled Persons—legislation & jurisprudence—United States.   3. Patient Advocacy—legislation & jurisprudence—United States.   4. Public Policy—United States.
W 32.5 AA1 P976   2010]
   KF553.P83   2010
   346.7301'8—dc22   2009037035

14   13   12   11   10   1   2   3   4   5

This book is also available on the World Wide Web as an eBook.
Visit www.abc-clio.com for details.

ABC-CLIO, LLC
130 Cremona Drive, P.O. Box 1911
Santa Barbara, California 93116-1911

This book is printed on acid-free paper ∞

Manufactured in the United States of America

CONTENTS

PREFACE

The purpose of this book, which is based on two phases of research conducted in 2004 and 2007, is to advance public understanding about the operation and impact of state public guardianship laws and programs, including a comparison of public guardianship today with public guardianship in 1981. The anticipated audience is not only the aging public, but also attorneys, judges, policy makers, public administrators, researchers, aging and disability advocates, social workers, long-term care facility staff, gerontology and social work students, law enforcement officials, professional guardians, and family and friend guardians. There are private, professional, and public guardians all over the country, and the number of persons performing this function is increasing in terms of both size and national visibility. There is a growing body of research on this topic and the related issues of elder abuse, elder rights, and ethics. For individuals who are public and professional guardians, this text will serve as an essential tool for the job. Our book is useful both as a primary and as a supplemental textbook in law schools, and for undergraduate and graduate programs that focus on gerontology, disability, social work, psychology, public health, public administration, nursing, and health care management and policy.

ACKNOWLEDGMENTS

The views expressed herein have not been approved by the House of Delegates or the Board of Governors of the American Bar Association and should not be construed as representing the policy of the American Bar Association.

Preparation of this book was supported in part by The Retirement Research Foundation.

The authors are grateful for the support they received throughout this project. The public guardianship staff, judges, lawyers, adult protective services workers, aging and disability advocates, and incapacitated persons who participated in our site visit interviews contributed greatly to our findings.

In particular, we thank the following people who assisted with the project: Anita Royal, Pima County, Arizona, Office of the Public Fiduciary; Richard Vanderheiden, Phoenix, Arizona, Maricopa County Office of the Public Fiduciary; Jane Adams, San Bernardino County, California, Office of the Public Guardian; Christopher Fierro, Los Angeles County, California, Office of the Public Guardian; Robin Williams-Bruner, Delaware, Office of the Public Guardian; Michelle Hollister, Florida, Florida Statewide Public Guardianship Office; John Wank, Illinois, Office of the State Guardian; Patrick Murphy, Cook County, Illinois, Office of the Public Guardian; and Valarie Colmore, Suzanne Lord, and Sue Vaeth, the Maryland Adult Public Guardianship Program.

We thank the Virginia Public Guardians for helping us with case examples.

Our advisory committee offered valuable perspectives that improved our report: Karen Roberto, Virginia Polytechnic Institute and State University; Joy Duke, Virginia Guardianship Association; David English, University of Missouri-Columbia School of Law; Naomi Karp, AARP Public Policy Institute; Sally Hurme, AARP Financial Security; and Marty Ford of the Arc of the United States.

We appreciate the assistance of Julie Kaufman at The Retirement Research Foundation and the grant from the Foundation that made this project possible.

We acknowledge all of the incapacitated persons served by the public guardians and hope this report will contribute to their quality of life.

We thank Jamie Philpotts of the ABA Commission on Law and Aging for her excellent editorial assistance. We gratefully acknowledge the help of Debra Dunn and Francis Vorksy, graduate students at the University of Kentucky Graduate Center for Gerontology, as well as that of Post-Doctoral Scholar, Dr. Tenzin Wangmo.

Finally, we thank our colleagues, friends, and families for supporting us as we worked on this project.

Pamela B. Teaster
Winsor C. Schmidt Jr.
Susan A. Lawrence
Marta S. Mendiondo
Erica F. Wood

Chapter 1

INTRODUCTION

Mrs. K, at age 89, has lived in a small group home for over 20 years. During early adulthood, Mrs. K was diagnosed with schizophrenia and depression, and her sister had served as her guardian, but has recently died. Mrs. K never married, and had no relatives except a distant cousin in another state who expressed little interest. Now she is slowly losing mobility, has significant hearing loss, and is at risk for a stroke. Mrs. K has fallen and broken her shoulder. Moreover, the group home where she resides has not been paid for many months due to a Medicaid problem. Social services recommended that Mrs. K be served by the state's public guardianship program.

This book aims to shed light on how governments are carrying out their basic *parens patriae* role for those who have no one else. *Parens patriae* literally means "parent of the country" and refers to the vital role of a state as the sovereign and guardian of people with legal disabilities.[1]

OVERVIEW

This chapter provides an introduction and overview of adult guardianship and public guardianship, including key studies, news stories, and cases affecting the evolution of guardianship. It also briefly describes the design, methods, and procedures used to collect the data that serve as the foundation for this book.

BACKGROUND

Noted bioethicist Nancy Dubler observes that:

The single greatest category of problems we encounter are those that address the care of decisionally incapable [individuals] . . . who have no living relative or friend who can be involved in the decision-making process. These are the most vulnerable . . . because no one cares deeply if they live or die, no one's life will be fundamentally changed by the death of the resident. We owe these [individuals] the highest level of ethical and medical scrutiny; we owe it to them to protect them from over-treatment and from under-treatment; we owe it to them to help them to live better or to die in comfort and not alone.[2]

These unbefriended incapacitated people are the clients of public guardianship programs. The unbefriended are persons who are unable to care for themselves and are typically poor, alone, and often different[3] persons with no other recourse than to become wards of the state. Serving them well is a challenge for any government, especially one under budgetary constraints. Their lives have remained largely unexamined, a part of the backwater of the governmental social service and welfare machinery. A legal services advocate observes, "When examined in the larger context of social programming through which we purport to help the less advantaged, involuntary guardianship emerges as an official initiation rite for the entry of the poor and the inept into the managed society."[4] When Schmidt and colleagues conducted the landmark national study of public guardianship[5] in the late 1970s, it was a fairly new phenomenon and public guardianship practices were highly uneven. The purpose of that study was to assess the extent to which public guardianship assists or hinders older persons in securing access to their rights, benefits, and entitlements. No further study was conducted on a national level until 2005.[6] In the intervening period of over 25 years, converging trends escalated the need for guardianship: the graying of the population (with a sudden upward spike anticipated around 2010, when the Baby Boomers begin to come of age), the aging of individuals with disabilities and the aging of their caregivers, the advancements in medical technologies affording new choices for chronic conditions and end-of-life care, the rising incidence of elder abuse, and the growing mobility that has pulled families apart. In response, most states have reformed their adult guardianship laws and many have enacted public guardianship programs.

Against this backdrop, it was imperative to conduct a new national study. This new and second national study of public guardianship funded by The Retirement Research Foundation was conducted from 2004–2007. It aimed for a direct comparison over time with the pioneering 1981 work, as well as to update statutory analysis, produce a model statute, and develop detailed profiles of each state's public guardianship situation. It provides a compelling snapshot based on a national survey, as well as in-depth case studies of nine programs in six states (e.g., Arizona, California, Delaware, Florida, Illinois, and Maryland), as did the previous work.[7]

The purpose of this book, based on the latter research, is to advance public understanding about the operation and impact of state public guardianship laws and programs, including a comparison of public guardianship today with public guardianship in 1981. The book seeks to aid both the interested and aging public, as well as policy makers, public guardianship practitioners, and advocates in promoting better public guardianship programs and, thus, more meaningful lives for unbefriended incapacitated persons (IPs) under the care of the state.

ADULT GUARDIANSHIP

Overview of Reform

Guardianship is a relationship created by state law in which a court gives one person (the guardian) the duty and power to make personal and/or property decisions for another (the ward or legally incapacitated person).[8] The appointment of a guardian occurs when a judge decides that an individual lacks the legal capacity to make decisions on his or her own behalf. Adult guardianship protects legally incapacitated individuals and provides for their decisional needs while simultaneously removing fundamental rights.[9] Guardianship can "unperson" individuals and make them "legally dead."[10] Guardianship can be a double-edged sword, "half Santa and half ogre."[11]

Early studies of protective proceedings, including guardianship, found little benefit for the legally incapacitated person (IP) and concluded that many petitions were filed for the benefit of third parties, or based on well-meaning but ineffective motivations to aid vulnerable groups.[12] Despite the initial reform efforts of the 1970s and 1980s, state guardianship remained an unexamined area governed by archaic terms, inconsistent practices, drastic paternalistic interventions, little attention to rights, and meager accountability.[13]

In 1986, the Associated Press undertook a one-year investigation of adult guardianship in all 51 jurisdictions, including more than 2,200 randomly selected guardianship court files and multiple interviews with a range of informants. The resulting six-part national series presented in 1987, *Guardians of the Elderly: An Ailing System,* described a troubled process: "a crucial last line of protection for the ailing elderly, [that] is failing many of those it is designed to protect."[14] In quick response, the U.S. House Select Committee on Aging convened a hearing,[15] which, in turn, triggered an interdisciplinary National Guardianship Symposium in 1988 (the Wingspread Conference) that resulted in recommendations covering procedural issues, capacity assessment, and guardian accountability.[16]

These events precipitated a rush to reform state guardianship laws, highlighted by five marked trends: (1) enhanced procedural due process in the appointment of a guardian; (2) a more robust determination of capacity based not only on medical condition, but also on functional ability, cognitive impairments, risks, and values; (3) an emphasis on limited orders that were more tailored to the specific capacities of the individual; (4) bolstered court monitoring of guardians; and (5) the development of public guardianship programs.[17] A Uniform Guardianship and Protective Proceedings Act (UGPPA) was developed in 1982 and updated in 1997.[18]

However, guardianship practices by judges, attorneys, guardians, and other actors did not automatically follow statutory reforms. Guardianship experts contend that although many legislative changes have occurred, commensurate changes to guardianship proceedings in practice and in effect on the lives of vulnerable respondents have been uneven or difficult to determine.[19]

Empirical Research

Few empirical studies of guardianship exist. In 1972, Alexander and Lewin studied over 400 guardianships and concluded that as a device of surrogate management, third parties use it to protect their own interests:

> Under the present system of "Estate Management by Preemption" we divest the incompetent of control of his property upon the finding of the existence of serious mental illness whenever divestiture is in the interest of some third person or institution. The theory of incompetency is to protect the debilitated from their own financial foolishness or from the fraud of others who would prey upon their mental weaknesses. In practice, however, we seek to protect the interest of others. The state hospital commences incompetency proceedings to facilitate reimbursement for costs incurred in the care, treatment, and maintenance of its patients. Dependents institute proceedings to secure their needs. Co-owners of property find incompetency proceedings convenient ways to secure the sale of realty. Heirs institute actions to preserve their dwindling inheritances. Beneficiaries of trusts or estates seek incompetency as an expedient method of removing as trustee one who is managing the trust or estate in a manner adverse to their interests. All of these motives may be honest and without any intent to cheat the aged, but none of the proceedings are commenced to assist the debilitated.[20]

A quasi-experimental study conducted through the Benjamin Rose Institute addressed the risks of well-meaning intervention, including guardianship, in the lives of vulnerable older persons, finding that intervention resulted in a higher rate of institutionalization than for the control group.[21] The significant contribution of elder protective referrals, including guardianship, to institutionalization, specifically nursing home placement, was revisited in an epidemiologically rigorous fashion and re-confirmed in 2002.[22]

In 1994, the University of Michigan Center for Social Gerontology conducted a national study that examined the guardianship process intensively in 10 states, finding that: only about 1/3 of respondents are represented by an attorney during the guardianship process; medical evidence is present in the court file in most cases, but medical testimony is rarely presented at the hearing; the majority of hearings are very brief, with 25 percent being less than 5 minutes long; some 94 percent of guardianship requests are granted by the court; and only 13 percent of the orders place limits on the guardian's authority.[23]

Recent Developments

Significant events over the past several years have refocused public attention on the nation's adult guardianship system. In 2001, seven national groups convened a second national guardianship conference (the Wingspan Conference) to assess progress on reform. The conference resulted in recommendations for action on mediation, the role of counsel, the use of limited guardianship, fiduciary and lawyer liability, and guardian accountability.[24] In 2004, many groups reconvened to develop specific steps for the implementation of selected Wingspan recommendations.[25]

Meanwhile, in 2002, a District of Columbia court of appeals overturned a lower court decision, *In re Orshansky*,[26] that highlighted critical guardianship issues. This case and other guardianship rumblings prompted a U.S. Senate Committee on Aging hearing in 2003, "Guardianships Over the Elderly: Security Provided or Freedoms Denied,"[27] which, in turn, prompted a study by the U.S. Government Accountability Office (GAO). The GAO study, *Guardianship: Collaboration Needed to Protect Incapacitated Elderly People*, included findings on variations in guardianship oversight, lack of data on guardianship proceedings and IPs, problematic interstate guardianship issues, and lack of coordination between state courts handling guardianship and federal representative payment programs.[28]

In 2005, Quinn produced a comprehensive text about guardianship for community health and social services practitioners.[29] Also in 2005, the *Los Angeles Times* published a comprehensive series titled *Guardians for Profit*, highlighting problems with professional conservators in Southern California,[30] which sparked state legislative action in 2006. A survey by Karp and Wood in 2006 found continued wide variation in guardianship monitoring practices, a frequent lack of guardian report and accounts verification, limited visitation of individuals under guardianship, and minimal use of technology in monitoring.[31] In 2007, the National Conference of Commissioners on Uniform State Laws produced the UGPPA.[32] States continued to make changes in their laws, with at least 14 states passing a total of 27 adult guardianship bills in 2007, and 15 states passing 18 adult guardianship bills in 2008.[33]

PUBLIC GUARDIANSHIP

Definition and Overview

An important subset of guardianship is public guardianship, which provides a last resort when there is no one willing or appropriate to help—usually for some at-risk, low-income incapacitated adults. A public guardian is an entity that receives most, if not all, of its funding from a governmental entity. Public guardianship programs are funded through state appropriations, Medicaid funds, county monies, legislated fees from the IP, or some combination of these. Public guardianship programs may serve several distinct populations: (1) older IPs who have lost decisional capacity, (2) individuals with mental retardation and/or developmental disabilities who may never have had decisional capacity, and (3) adults of all ages with mental illness or brain injury.

State public guardianship programs are operated from a single statewide office, or have local or regional components. They are either entirely staff-based or may operate using both staff and volunteers. Public guardians may serve as guardian of the property, guardian of the person, and sometimes as a representative payee or other surrogate decision-maker. They can also provide case management, financial planning, public education, social services, adult protective services (APS), or serve as guardian *ad litem* (GAL), court investigators, and/or advisors to private guardians.

Empirical Research

As with private guardianship, few published studies exist on the need for public guardianship and on the operation of public guardianship programs. In 1987, Schmidt and Peters studied the unmet need for guardians in Florida and found over 11,000 individuals in need, typically female, elderly, and predominantly white, with many having both medical and psychiatric conditions.[34] In 1990, Hightower, Heckert, and Schmidt assessed the need for public limited guardianship, conservator, and other surrogate mechanisms among elderly nursing home residents in Tennessee and found over 1,000 residents needing a surrogate decision maker.[35] A 2000 report by Florida's Statewide Public Guardianship Office stated that the need for public guardianship was approaching crisis proportions and estimated that 1.5 guardianships were needed per 1,000 people in the population.[36]

In comparison, Schmidt reported that the overall guardianship annual filing rate ranged from 1 of every 1,785 (.056 percent) for Florida in 1977, to 1 of every 1,706 (.059 percent) for 6 states (Delaware, Minnesota, North Carolina, Ohio, Washington, and Wisconsin) in 1979,[37] and half a million people total under guardianship in the United States in 1995.[38] Kroch most recently reported the ratios of the international population adjudicated with guardianship and trusteeship orders ranging from 0.444 in Alberta, Canada in 2003, to 0.459 for Israel, 0.625 for Austria, 0.721 for Ontario, Canada, 0.850 in Switzerland, and 1.345 in Germany.[39]

Schmidt and colleagues conducted the landmark national study of public guardianship, published in 1981. The study sought to "assess the extent to which public guardianship assists or hinders older persons in securing access to their rights, benefits, and entitlements."[40] The study reviewed existing and proposed public guardianship laws in all states and focused intensively on the most active and experienced states (Arizona, California, Delaware, Maryland, and Illinois), as well as one state without public guardianship (Florida, which has since enacted a public guardianship statute). Using Regan and Springer's taxonomy, Schmidt classified public guardianship programs into the following models: (1) court, (2) independent state office, (3) division of a social service agency, and (4) county.

The study findings focused on the individuals served, program characteristics (staff size and qualifications), funding, legal basis, due process safeguards, oversight, and other areas. The study confirmed the need for public guardianship. However, it stated that "public guardianship offices seem to be understaffed and underfunded, and many of them are approaching the saturation point in numbers."[41] The study found that, consequently, many IPs received little personal attention, and noted that there were identified instances of abuse. A core conclusion for the extent to which public guardianship assists or hinders legally incapacitated people in securing access to their rights, benefits, and entitlements was expressed as follows:

> The success of public guardianship is dependent upon several clear considerations. The public guardian must be independent of any service providing agency (no conflict of interest), and the public guardian must not be responsible for both serving as guardian, and petitioning for adjudication of incompetence (no self-aggrandizement). The public guardian must be adequately staffed and funded to the extent that no office is responsible for more than 500 wards, and each professional in the office is responsible for no more than thirty wards. A public guardian is also only as good as the guardianship statute governing adjudication of incompetence and appointment. Failure of any of these considerations will tip the benefit burden ratio against the individual ward, and the ward would be better off with no guardian at all.[42]

In 1995, Schmidt followed this seminal research with a focused examination of public guardianship, collected in *Guardianship: Court of Last Resort for the Elderly and Disabled.*[43] In 2003, Teaster studied the role of the public guardian from the viewpoint of public administration through contact with public guardian offices in four states (Delaware, Maryland, Tennessee, and Virginia).[44]

Evaluative studies of public guardianship were conducted in three states: Florida, Virginia, and Utah. First, in 1988, Schmidt examined the evolution of public guardianship in Florida and found that the volunteer model required significant staff time for volunteer management, at the cost of providing direct service to IPs.[45] Second, in the mid-1990s, the Virginia Department for the Aging contracted for two pilot public guardianship programs. A program evaluation compared the staff versus volunteer models and collected information on public guardianship functions and clients, using much the same model pioneered by Schmidt in Florida.[46] The evaluation found the pilots to be viable.[47] Third, in 2002, a legislatively mandated evaluation of 10 Virginia projects by Teaster and Roberto collected detailed information on program administration, client characteristics, and needs. The study determined that the programs were performing reasonably well and recommended an extension of the geographic reach to cover all areas of the state. Other recommendations addressed the need for rigorous standardized procedures and forms for client assessment, care plans, guardian time accounting, regular program review of these documents, the need for an established guardian-to-client ratio, increased fiscal support, and greater attention to meeting the needs outlined in the care plans. Importantly, the study determined that the public guardianship program saved the state a total of over $2,600,000 for each year of the evaluation period through placements in less restrictive settings and the recovery of assets (at a total program cost of $600,000).[48] Fourth, when the Utah legislature created a public guardian office in 1999, it required an independent program evaluation by 2001. The evaluation included on-site visits, interviews, and case file reviews. The study recommended additional resources and staff, a continued location within the Department of Human Services, the development of a unified statewide system, and a system in which the office would not act as petitioner, as well as additional record-keeping, and educational suggestions.[49]

JUSTIFICATION

As this national public guardianship study was being proposed, there was widespread agreement among experts in the aging and disability fields regarding the need for increased attention to guardianship practices in general and public guardianship in particular. The 2001 national Wingspan Conference on guardianship[50] recommended that "research be undertaken to measure successful practices and to examine how the guardianship process is enhancing the well-being of persons with diminished capacity." Specifically concerning public guardianship, the recommendations urged that "states provide public guardianship services when other qualified fiduciaries are not available;" that "the public guardianship function [should] include broad-based information and training; " that "guardianship agencies [. . .] should not directly provide services, such as housing, medical care, and social services to their own wards, absent court approval and monitoring;" and that "funding for development and improvement of public [. . .] guardianship services should be identified and generated."

Despite substantial social and demographic changes since the 1981 Schmidt study, only a handful of state and local studies had examined the institution of public guardianship until the 2005 national study.

RESEARCH METHODS

A detailed elaboration of the research methods used for the first national study of public guardianship in 25 years is beyond the scope of this book. Specific descriptions of the research methods are available elsewhere.[51]

The purpose of the 2005 national public guardianship study was to update the 1981 study conducted by Schmidt and colleagues, which assessed the extent to which public guardianship assists or hinders older persons in securing access to their rights, benefits, and entitlements. Like its 1981 predecessor, this study used multiple case studies to clarify the face of public guardianship. To improve the science of the study, the original data-gathering instruments (i.e., surveys) were refined, and disciplines from which the pool of informants was gathered were increased. This approach is consistent with the iterative nature of qualitative inquiry.[52] Using Schmidt's 1981 effectiveness criteria as a baseline against which to measure, this study attempted to discover how public guardianship had changed since the original study.

To replicate the original study, the public guardianship programs in Arizona (Maricopa and Pima counties), California (Los Angeles and San Bernardino counties), Delaware, Florida, Illinois, and Maryland were investigated. Deviation from the original study occurred in one instance; the original study included Alameda County in California. Although letters of support were obtained from the public guardianship program in Alameda County, Alameda withdrew after funding was awarded.[53]

Before presenting the examination of the individual states, Chapter 2 analyzes the legal basis for public guardianship and the state public guardianship statutes.

NOTES

1. *Parens patriae* is the alleged authority of a sovereign to act as "the general guardian of all infants, idiots and lunatics" (English common law terminology). Hawaii v. Standard Oil Co. of California, 405 U.S. 251, 257 (1972) (quoting three W. Blackstone, *Commentaries* *47). For a more detailed note on the etiology for *parens patriae*, ranging from a 17th-century printer's error, to a rationalization to exclude juveniles from constitutional protection, to the confinement of persons with mental illness and protective services for the elderly, see, for example, Winsor Schmidt, "A Critique of the American Psychiatric Association's Guidelines for Legislation on Civil Commitment of the Mentally Ill," *New England Journal on Criminal and Civil Confinement* 11, no. 1 (1985): 14–15, note 20. Cf. O'Connor v. Donaldson, 422 U.S. 563, 583–584 (1975) (Burger, C. J., concurring) ("The existence of some due process limitations on the *parens patriae* power does not justify the further conclusion that it may be exercised to confine a mentally ill person only if the purpose of the confinement is treatment").

2. Nancy Dubler quoted in Naomi Karp and Erica Wood, *Incapacitated and Alone: Health Care Decision-Making for the Unbefriended Elderly* (Washington, DC: American Bar Association Commission on Law and Aging, 2003), 1.

3. Cf. Peter Conrad and Joseph Schneider, *Deviance and Medicalization: From Badness to Sickness* (Philadelphia: Temple University Press, 1992); Nicholas Kittrie, *The Right to Be Different: Deviance and Enforced Therapy* (Baltimore: Johns Hopkins Press, 1971). See also Sandra Reynolds, "Guardianship Primavera: A First Look at Factors Associated with Having a Legal Guardian Using a Nationally Representative Sample of

Community-Dwelling Adults," *Aging and Mental Health* 6, no. 2 (2002): 109 ("Particularly for older adults, increasing age, having physical or emotional limitations, a small family network, and not living with a spouse are associated with having a guardian").

4. Annina Mitchell, "Involuntary Guardianship for Incompetents: A Strategy for Legal Services Advocates," *Clearinghouse Review* 12, no. 8 (1978): 466. See also Kent Miller, *Managing Madness: The Case Against Civil Commitment* (New York: Free Press, 1976).

5. Winsor Schmidt et al., *Public Guardianship and the Elderly* (Cambridge, MA: Ballinger Publishing Company, 1981).

6. Pamela Teaster et al., *Wards of the State: A National Study of Public Guardianship* (Lexington, KY: University of Kentucky Graduate Center for Gerontology, 2005). The data for the study were collected in 2004.

7. Ibid.

8. Portions of this section are based on Pamela Teaster et al., "Wards of the State: A National Study of Public Guardianship," *Stetson Law Review* 37, no. 1 (2007): 193–241 (describes the Phase I national study and results). Courtesy of the *Stetson Law Review*.

9. In most states, a finding of legal incapacity restricts or takes away the right to: make contracts; sell, purchase, mortgage, or lease property; initiate or defend against suits; make a will, or revoke one; engage in certain professions; lend or borrow money; appoint agents; divorce, or marry; refuse medical treatment; keep and care for children; serve on a jury; be a witness to any legal document; drive a car; pay or collect debts; and manage or run a business. Robert Brown, *The Rights of Older Persons* (New York: Avon Books, 1979), 286.

10. Fred Bayles and Scott McCartney, *Guardians of the Elderly: An Ailing System* (Associated Press Special Report, Sept. 1987). See also Winsor Schmidt, "Guardianship of the Elderly in Florida: Social Bankruptcy and the Need for Reform," in Winsor Schmidt, ed., *Court of Last Resort for the Elderly and Disabled* 6 (Durham, NC: Carolina Academic Press, 1995), 6: "The loss of any one of these rights can have a disastrous result, but taken together, their effect is to reduce the status of an individual to that of a child, or a nonperson. The process can be characterized as legal infantalization."

11. John Regan and Georgia Springer, U.S. Senate Special Committee on Aging, *Protective Services for the Elderly: A Working Paper.* (Washington, DC: GPO, 1977), 27.

12. George Alexander and Travis Lewin, *The Aged and the Need for Surrogate Management* (Ithaca, NY: Cornell University Press, 1972); Margaret Blenkner, Martin Bloom, and Margaret Nielsen, "A Research and Demonstration Project of Protective Services," *Social Casework* 52, no. 8 (1971): 483–499; Margaret Blenkner et al., *Final Report: Protective Services for Older People: Findings from the Benjamin Rose Institute Study* (Cleveland, OH: Benjamin Rose Institute, 1974). Cf., for example, "Experience should teach us to be most on our guard to protect liberty when the Government's purposes are beneficent. Men born to freedom are naturally alert to repel invasion of their liberty by evil-minded rulers. The greatest dangers to liberty lurk in insidious encroachment by men of zeal, well-meaning but without understanding." *Olmstead v. United States*, 277 U.S. 479 (1928) (Brandeis, J., dissenting).

13. Peter Horstman, "Protective Services for the Elderly: The Limits of *Parens Patriae*," *Missouri Law Review* 40, no. 2 (1975): 215–236; Mitchell, 451–468; Roger Peters, Winsor Schmidt, and Kent Miller, "Guardianship of the Elderly in Tallahassee, Florida," *The Gerontologist* 25, no. 5 (1985): 532–538; Regan and Springer, *op. cit.*; Win-

sor Schmidt, "Guardianship of the Elderly in Florida: Social Bankruptcy and the Need for Reform," *Florida Bar Journal* 55, no. 3 (1981): 189–195; Erica Wood, *Statement of Recommended Judicial Practices on Guardianship Proceedings for the Aging* (Washington, DC: American Bar Association Commission on Legal Problems of the Elderly and National Judicial College: 1986); National Conference of Commissioners on Uniform State Laws, *Uniform Guardianship and Protective Proceedings Act* (1982); The Center for Social Gerontology, *Guidelines for Guardianship Service Programs* (Ann Arbor, MI: Center for Social Gerontology: 1986).

14. Bayles and McCartney, *Guardians of the Elderly.*

15. U.S. House of Representatives, Select Committee on Aging, *Abuses in Guardianship of the Elderly and Infirm: A National Disgrace* (GPO Committee Publication No. 100-641: 1987).

16. American Bar Association Commission on the Mentally Disabled and Commission on Legal Problems of the Elderly, *Guardianship: An Agenda for Reform—Recommendations of the National Guardianship Symposium and Policy of the American Bar Association* (Washington, DC: American Bar Association: 1989).

17. See state statutory charts on adult guardianship, as well as the annual update, on the Web site of the ABA Commission on Law and Aging at http://www.abanet.org/aging/legislativeupdates/home.shtml.

18. National Conference of Commissioners on Uniform State Laws, http://www.law.upenn.edu/bll/archives/ulc/ugppa/guardsh2.htm.

19. For example, Frank Johns, "Guardianship Folly: The Misgovernment of Parens Patriae and the Forecast of Its Crumbing Linkage to Unprotected Older Americans in the Twenty-First Century—A March of Folly? Or Just a Mask of Virtual Reality," *Stetson Law Review* 27, no. 1 (1997): 1–93.

20. Alexander and Lewin, *The Aged and the Need for Surrogate Management,* 136.

21. Blenkner, Bloom, and Nielsen, "A Research and Demonstration Project"; Blenkner, Bloom, Nielsen, and Weber, *Protective Services for Older People.*

22. Mark Lachs, Christianna Williams, Shelly O'Brien, and Karl Pillemer, "Adult Protective Service Use and Nursing Home Placement," *The Gerontologist* 42, no. 6 (2002): 734–739 ("[I]t is remarkable that controlled studies of differential outcomes of APS have not been conducted. A review of the literature shows no systematic attempt to evaluate program outcomes or to examine unintended consequences of APS intervention"). See also Sandra Reynolds and L. Carson, "Dependent on the Kindness of Strangers: Professional Guardians for Older Adults Who Lack Decisional Capacity," *Aging and Mental Health* 3, no. 4 (1999): 301–310 ("Wards with family guardians were more likely to be living in the community than those with professional guardians").

Cf., for example, Robert Davis and Juanjo Medina-Ariza, *Results from an Elder Abuse Prevention Experiment in New York City* (National Institute of Justice: Sept. 2001) ("New incidents of abuse were more frequent among households that both received home visits and were in housing projects that received public education") at http://www.ojp.usdoj.gov/nij. See also Winsor Schmidt, "Quantitative Information About the Quality of the Guardianship System: Toward a Next Generation of Guardianship Research," *Probate Law Journal* 10 (1990): 61–80.

23. Lauren Lisi, Anne Burns, and Kathleen Lussenden, *National Study of Guardianship Systems: Findings and Recommendations* (Ann Arbor, MI: Center for Social Gerontology: 1994).

24. Symposium, "Wingspan—The Second National Guardianship Conference," *Stetson Law Review* 31, no. 3 (2002): 573–1055.

25. National Academy of Elder Law Attorneys, National Guardianship Association, and National College of Probate Judges, *2004 National Wingspan Implementation Session: Action Steps on Adult Guardianship Reform* (2004): http://www.guardianship.org/associations/2543/files/WingspanReport.pdf.

26. *In re Orshansky*, 804 A. 2d 1077 (D.C. 2002).

27. U.S. Senate Special Committee on Aging, *Guardianship Over the Elderly: Security Provided or Freedom Denied?* (GPO Serial No. 108-3: 2003).

28. U.S. Government Accountability Office, *Guardianships: Collaboration Needed to Protect Incapacitated Elderly People* (GAO-04-655: 2004).

29. Mary Joy Quinn, *Guardianships of Adults: Achieving Justice, Autonomy and Safety* (New York: Springer Publishing, 2005).

30. Robin Fields, Evelyn Larrubia, and Jack Leonard, "Guardians for Profit" (a four-part series), *Los Angeles Times* (November 13–16, 2005). See also Winsor Schmidt, Fevzi Akinci, and Sarah Wagner, "The Relationship Between Guardian Certification Requirements and Guardian Sanctioning: A Research Issue in Elder Law and Policy," *Behavioral Sciences and the Law* 25, no. 5 (2007): 641 ("83.3% of [General Equivalency Diploma] or [high school] graduates are likely to have more severe sanctions compared to 76.4% undergraduate or higher education, and 47.7% with an [Associate of Arts] or [Technical] degree, respectively. Guardians with an A.A. or Tech degree are 0.28 times less likely to have more severe sanctions than guardians with an undergraduate degree or higher education ($p < 0.01$).") Cf. Carol Leoning, "Misplaced Trust: Special Report," *Washington Post*, June 15–16, 2003; Lise Olsen, "New Payment Guidelines Ease Strain Probate Fees Put on Elderly, Disabled," *Houston Chronicle*, September 4, 2007; Cheryl Phillips, "Secrecy Hides Cozy Ties in Guardianship Cases," *Seattle Times*, December 4, 2006; Denise Topolnicki, "The Gulag of Guardianship," *Money Magazine*, March 1, 1989; Barry Yeoman, "Stolen Lives," *AARP: The Magazine*, January–February, 2004.

31. Naomi Karp and Erica Wood, *Guardianship Monitoring: A National Survey of Court Practices* (American Association of Retired Persons [AARP] Public Policy Institute: 2006); Naomi Karp and Erica Wood, *Guarding the Guardians: Promising Practices for Court Monitoring* (AARP Public Policy Institute: 2007).

32. National Conference of Commissioners on Uniform State Laws, *Uniform Adult Guardianship and Protective Proceedings Jurisdiction Act* (2007).

33. Erica Wood, *State Adult Guardianship Legislation: Directions of Reform—2006*, http://www.abanet.org/aging/docs/gdlegisupdate0106.doc; Erica Wood, *State Adult Guardianship Legislation: Directions of Reform—2008*, http://www.abanet.org/aging/legislative updates/home.shtml.

34. Winsor Schmidt and Roger Peters, "Legal Incompetents' Need for Guardians in Florida," *Bulletin of the American Academy of Psychiatry and Law* 15, no. 1 (1987): 69–83.

35. David Hightower, Alex Heckert, and Winsor Schmidt, "Elderly Nursing Home Residents: Need for Public Guardianship Services in Tennessee," *Journal of Elder Abuse and Neglect* 2, no. 3/4 (1990): 105–122.

36. Florida Statewide Public Guardianship Office, *Forgotten Faces of Florida* (2000).

37. Schmidt, "Guardianship of the Elderly in Florida," 189.

38. Schmidt, *Guardianship: Court of Last Resort*, xiii.

39. Uri Kroch, "The Experience of Being A Dependent Adult (Ward)-A Hermeneutic Phenomenological Study" (Ph.D. thesis, University of Calgary, 2009), 57.

40. Schmidt et al., *Public Guardianship and the Elderly*, 3.

41. Ibid., 172.

42. Schmidt, "Guardianship of the Elderly in Florida," 192. See also Schmidt et al., *Public Guardianship and the Elderly*, 16–17, 34, 38, 170, 174–175, 183–184, 193.

43. Schmidt, *Guardianship: Court of Last Resort*.

44. Pamela Teaster, "When the State Takes Over a Life: The Public Guardian as Public Administrator," *Public Administration Review* 63, no. 4 (2003): 396–404.

45. Winsor Schmidt et al., "A Descriptive Analysis of Professional and Volunteer Programs for the Delivery of Guardianship Services," *Probate Law Journal* 8, no. 2 (1988): 125–156 (1988); Winsor Schmidt, "The Evolution of a Public Guardianship Program," *Journal of Psychiatry and Law* 12, no. 3 (1984): 349–372.

46. Winsor Schmidt et al., *Second Year Evaluation of the Virginia Guardian of Last Resort and Guardianship Alternatives Demonstration Project* (Memphis: The University of Memphis Center for Health Services Research, 1997).

47. Pamela Teaster et al., "Staff Service and Volunteer Staff Service Models for Public Guardianship and 'Alternatives' Services: Who Is Served and With What Outcomes?" *Journal of Ethics, Law, and Aging* 5, no. 2 (1999): 131–151.

48. Pamela Teaster and Karen Roberto, Virginia Public Guardian and Conservator Programs: Summary of the First Year Evaluation (Virginia Department for the Aging, 2002). See also Pamela Teaster and Karen Roberto, *Virginia Public Guardian and Conservator Programs: Evaluation of Program Status and Outcomes* (Blacksburg: The Center for Gerontology, Virginia Polytechnic Institute and State University, 2003), pp. 11–16; Pamela Teaster, et al., *The Florida Public Guardian Programs: An Evaluation of Program Status and Outcomes* (Lexington: University of Kentucky Graduate Center for Gerontology, 2009)(cost savings to Florida of over $1.8 million in one year from public guardianship), http://www.panhandleparade.com/index.php/mbb/article/study_public_guardianship_programs_save_florida_taxpayers_1.9_million/mbb7718858/.

49. Center for Social Gerontology, *Utah Office of Public Guardian: Program Evaluation* (Ann Arbor, MI: Center for Social Gerontology, 2001).

50. Symposium, Wingspan Conference.

51. Teaster et al., *Wards of the State* (2005): i–ii, 6, 61–62; Teaster et al., *Public Guardianship After 25 Years*: 5, 21–26.

52. John Creswell, *Research Design: Qualitative and Quantitative Approaches* (Thousand Oaks, California: Sage Publications, 1994); Matthew Miles and A. Michael Huberman, *An Expanded Sourcebook: Qualitative Data Analysis*, 2nd ed. (Thousand Oaks, California: Sage Publications, 1994).

53. The following is the verbatim e-mail response from Alameda County. "I'm sorry, but our County Counsel indicated to you previously that Alameda County will not be participating in this survey. Sorry the information did not reach you!" The research team never received such information from the county counsel. Subsequent entreaties by the principal investigator and project manager to conduct a limited version of the site visit went unanswered.

Chapter 2

State Statutory Analysis: Adult Guardianship and Public Guardianship Law

T
wo adult daughters clashed over the care of their mother. One claimed that her sister drained the mother's bank account and neglected her care. Without checking with anyone, she brought her mother to live with her. The second daughter disputed the allegations and contended that the move was abusive. APS filed a petition naming the public guardianship program as the proposed guardian. What would be the process for appointment? Would the mother receive notice? Have an attorney? Have rights at the hearing? What would be the court's criteria for determining whether the mother is incapacitated and requires a guardian? What would be the criteria for selecting the public guardianship program? If appointed, what accountability would the program have to the court? If the mother receives insufficient care and services, to what extent can the program challenge care providers and zealously advocate for her interests?

Overview

This chapter provides a summary analysis of state adult guardianship statutes, highlighting public guardianship provisions. It includes eligibility, scope, petitioners, investigation and examination, due process protections, rights, powers, costs, and review and monitoring, and outlines key statutory changes over time.

Background

As with the 1981 study, one of the first tasks of the national public guardianship study was to research state statutes to identify jurisdictions with provisions for public guardianship. In addition, the new study's practitioners conducted statutory research and analysis, constructing a table matching the one established in the original 1981 work.[1] (The 2007 table is broken into five sub-tables for ease of reading.) The tables (Appendix A), as well as the commentary below (updated to 2007 unless otherwise indicated), generally use the framework of the 1981 table, thus providing two directly comparative snapshots across 26 years. (However, the 1981 Schmidt table includes only the 34 states with statutory provisions for public guardianship, whereas the current table includes all states.) Both tables integrate basic elements of state adult guardianship and conservatorship statutes with more specific provisions concerning public guardianship, as an understanding of public guardianship statutes requires a close look at the state guardianship codes on which they are based. Indeed,

> the public guardian, and the public guardian process, do not exist in isolation . . . [but are] an end point in the process of guardianship, which itself seems to exist in a continuum of protective services and civil commitment. In fact, the success of a public guardian seems to be quite dependent upon the quality of the state's guardianship statute.[2]

Public guardianship programs are shaped by the overall contours of the state guardianship codes that determine the procedures for appointment, the definition of incapacity, the powers and duties of guardians, and the mechanisms for judicial oversight. For updated state adult guardianship tables with citations for each provision, see the Web site of the ABA Commission on Law and Aging at http://www.abanet.org/aging/guardianship/lawandpractice/home.html.

STATUTORY PROVISIONS

Adult guardianship is a state, rather than a federal, function. All states have a general guardianship code. These laws have undergone significant change in the past two decades, with particular emphasis on procedural protections, the determination of capacity, limited guardianship, and court oversight.[3] These state laws provide the foundation for public guardianship.

As of 2007, a total of 44 states[4] had specific statutory provisions on public guardianship. Seven states included no such reference in their code. Public guardianship provisions are most frequently included as a section of the state guardianship code. But in some states, the public guardianship provisions are located in separate statutory sections, such as, for example, services for the aging, APS, or services for individuals with disabilities.[5]

In 1981, Schmidt distinguished between "explicit" and "implicit" public guardianship provisions:

> One can distinguish between explicit public guardianship statutes that specifically refer to a "public guardian" and implicit statutes that seem to provide for a mechanism equivalent to public guardianship without actually denominating the mechanism as "public guardian." The distinction is often nominal at best. Although an explicit scheme often indicates a progressive trend in this field, this is not always true. Indeed, several of the implicit schemes are even more progressive than the typical explicit statute.[6]

Twenty-six years ago, Schmidt found 26 implicit statutory schemes in 26 states, and 14 explicit schemes in 13 states, with some states having more than one scheme. In 2007, research shows a total of 18 implicit statutory schemes in 18 states, and 28 explicit schemes in 27 states (with one state having both an implicit and explicit scheme). Implicit schemes often name a state agency or employee as a guardian of last resort when there are no willing and responsible family members or friends to serve.

ELIGIBILITY FOR PUBLIC GUARDIANSHIP

The 1981 Schmidt study found that of the 34 states under analysis, 20 generally provided public guardianship services for incompetents, 17 provided services specifically for individuals with mental retardation who needed a guardian, 19 targeted incapacitated elderly persons, and 11 provided a form of public guardianship for minors. The majority of public guardianship schemes served limited categories of beneficiaries. Fewer than half of the 34 states had provisions to aid 3 or more targeted groups. Schmidt noted that the specific needs of individuals with mental retardation and elders had "come into focus only recently," and that the needs of minors are temporary and could perhaps receive adequate service through private resources.

In 2005, the overwhelming majority of the state statutes provided for services to incapacitated individuals who were determined to require guardians under the adult guardianship law, but who had no person or private entity qualified and willing to serve. Modern guardianship codes rely more on a functional determination of incapacity and less on specific clinical conditions. Thus, states are less likely to segregate specific categories of individuals for service, instead filling the void created when a judge determines a person is incapacitated but no one is there to act as guardian.

However, a few statutory provisions do target specific groups of IPs. Four state statutes limit public guardianship services to IPs who are elderly. Connecticut, New Jersey, Tennessee, and Vermont serve only those who are 60 years of age or older. Four states (Arkansas, Maryland, New York, and Texas) limit services to those requiring APS, or to those in a state of abuse, neglect, or exploitation.

Four statutory schemes are designed to aid persons with specific mental disabilities. In California, a specific provision enables the appointment of the county public guardian for "any person who is gravely disabled as a result of mental disorder or impairment by chronic alcoholism." In Maine, one state agency serves as the public guardian for persons with mental retardation and another agency serves for other IPs in need. The Ohio public guardianship statutory scheme solely targets persons who have mental retardation or developmental disabilities. In South Carolina, the director of the mental health department or the director's designee may serve as the conservator for patients of mental health facilities whose fees do not exceed $10,000 per year.

In addition, a number of state statutes specify services for persons with financial limitations. Connecticut limits services to those with assets that do not surpass $1,500. Florida indicates that services are primarily for those of "limited financial means." In Indiana, services are for indigent adults, as defined administratively. In Illinois, one scheme serves individuals with estates of $25,000 or less and another serves individuals whose estates are over $25,000. In Virginia, the public guardianship program serves IPs whose resources are insufficient to fully compensate a private guardian or pay court costs and fees. In the state of Washington, under a law enacted in 2007, the office of public guardianship serves individuals whose incomes do not exceed 200 percent of the federal poverty level and who are receiving Medicaid long-term care services. On the other hand, Mississippi law specifies that the appointment of a clerk as guardian is only for "a ward who has property."

SCOPE OF PUBLIC GUARDIANSHIP PROVISIONS

As Schmidt explained, guardianship terminology differed by state in 1981, and still does, creating confusion in terms of statutory comparisons. The Schmidt study cautions that a careful reading of state guardianship code definitions is required to determine the scope of public guardianship services. Today, the UGPPA[7] makes a clear distinction between "guardianship" of a person and "conservatorship" of property, and close to 20 states have adopted this distinction. But state terminology still varies considerably.

In Schmidt's study, only one state with public guardianship provisions, Wyoming, did not clearly provide for public guardianship of both person and property. Today, all but four state laws specify that the public guardian program can provide services as both the guardian of the person and the estate. Two states appear to cover property only: Alabama provides for the appointment of a general county conservator or sheriff; and South Carolina allows the director of the mental health department to serve as the conservator for limited amounts. One state, Arkansas, authorizes APS to provide "custodian" services of the person only and to identify a guardian for the estate if necessary.

In many states, there is no specific provision in the public guardianship statute granting or restricting services, but reliance on the overall guardianship code affords coverage of both. (In some states, program services are limited by rule or by practice. For example, in Maryland, the area agencies on aging serve as public guardians of the person only.) Schmidt observed that in many states, there was only a cursory mention of guardianship of the person: the emphasis was on providing for property management. This is less true today (at least on paper), as guardianship codes have changed to more clearly delineate the duties of the guardian of the person in procuring services and benefits, as well as in maximizing autonomy.

Potential Petitioners in Guardianship Proceedings

The process of appointing a public guardian generally begins with the filing of a petition in the court of appropriate jurisdiction. The 1981 study found that at least 26 of 34 states studied permitted a relative or interested person to petition, and that 12 states allowed the proposed ward to file.

Today, virtually all states allow any person, including the alleged IP, to file, with many listing a string of categories of potential filers ending with the catch-all "or any person", in some cases, "any interested person." Such provisions are in line with the UGPPA, which allows "an individual or a person interested in the individual's welfare" to file. This could include both public and private guardianship agencies, raising the specter of possible conflict of interest.

Indeed, a question central to the operation of any public guardianship program is whether the program can petition to have itself appointed guardian. Such petitioning could present several conflicts of interest.[8] First, if the program relies on fees for its operation, or if its budget is dependent on the number of individuals served, the program might petition more frequently, regardless of individual needs. On the other hand, the program might, as Schmidt points out, "only petition for as many guardianships as it desires, perhaps omitting some persons in need of such services." It could also cherry pick, petitioning only for those individuals who are the easiest or least costly and time-consuming to serve. The Schmidt study did not specifically address statutory provisions that allow the public guardianship agency to petition for its own wards. Today, statutes in 12 states explicitly allow this. Only two states (Vermont and Washington) explicitly prohibit the public guardianship agency from petitioning for its own IPS; the remaining statutes do not address the issue.

Investigation of Individuals in Need

The 1981 study included a section on state approaches toward "discovering the identity of those individuals who are in need of public guardianship services."[9] The study pointed out that this problem was addressed in "only a handful of states" through an investigative body or professional reporting laws.

Today, the landscape has changed completely. Every state has enacted and administers an APS law[10] with: reporting requirements for various professions; investigation of possible abuse, neglect, or exploitation; and mechanisms to address the problems of at-risk adults, including the initiation of a guardianship. Indeed, in many cases, APS programs are a primary referral source for public guardianship programs. Because of these developments in APS, as well as the aging of the population, many more cases are likely to come to the attention of public guardians than in 1981. (Note that the APS laws are not shown in Table 1, but statutory charts are available on the Web site of the ABA Commission on Law and Aging at: http://www.abanet.org/aging/about/elderabuse.shtml.)

Due Process Protections
in Guardianship Proceedings

In the quarter century since the Schmidt study, state procedural protections for respondents in guardianship proceedings have undergone a paradigm shift, with virtually all states bolstering the requirements for due process protections. Schmidt discovered that 5 of the 34 states studied made no provision for a hearing. Today, all states provide for a hearing. In 1981, 29 of the states studied required notice to the respondent, as well as to family members and other interested parties. Today, all states require notice. Moreover, many state notice provisions now require large print and plain language, as well as information about hearing rights and the rights potentially lost as the result of the hearing. In addition, states generally maintain that the respondent has a right to be present at the hearing. An increasing number go beyond this entitlement to require the respondent's presence unless it would be harmful or there is other good cause for his or her absence. Courts today are subject to the provisions of the Americans with Disabilities Act, which call for reasonable accommodations at the person's request.

Right to counsel. A key to providing procedural due process for respondents in guardianship proceedings is representation by counsel. Approximately 22 of the states studied in 1981 provided a right to counsel during guardianship proceedings. Today, there is a growing recognition of the right to counsel as an empty promise for a vulnerable indigent individual. Thus, over 25 states require the appointment of counsel, generally making counsel available without charge to indigent respondents. The remaining states allow a right to counsel or, in a few instances, do not address the issue. Some states require appointment only under designated circumstances: if the respondent requests counsel, if the GAL recommends it, or if the judge determines that counsel is necessary.

Free counsel for indigents. In 1981, 17 states made counsel available free of charge to indigent persons. Today, over 20 states provide for such free counsel in their guardianship statutes, and there may be additional states with relevant provisions in other parts of the code.

Right to jury trial. Eleven of the states studied in 1981 gave the individual the opportunity to have a trial by jury. Today, 27 states provide for trial by jury if the respondent requests it. It is particularly notable that Kentucky makes a jury trial mandatory in every adult guardianship case.

Right to cross-examine. In 1981, only nine states made explicit provisions for the respondent or counsel to cross-examine any witnesses who testify against the alleged IP. This is critical in preserving the integrity of the hearing process.

Today, 35 state guardianship statutes provide for this important right, and there are probably additional states with relevant provisions in the rules of evidence or civil procedure.

Standard of proof. The Schmidt study found only a couple of states that used a "clear and convincing evidence" standard of proof. Today, a total of 36 states require clear and convincing proof that the respondent lacks decisional capacity and requires a guardian. One state (New Hampshire) uses a standard of "beyond a reasonable doubt"; two (North Carolina and Washington) use a standard of "clear, cogent, and convincing evidence"; one (Wyoming) uses a mere "preponderance of the evidence"; two (Idaho and South Carolina) state that the court must be "satisfied" that a guardian is necessary; and the remaining eight states provide no statutory standard.

Appeal/review. In 1981, only three of the states provided a direct and immediate review of the findings of a guardianship proceeding. Today, some 29 states refer to an appeal or review within their guardianship statutes. However, there may be additional states with relevant provisions in the rules of civil procedure.

EXAMINATION OF THE ALLEGED INCAPACITATED INDIVIDUAL

Clinical examinations provide important evidence for judicial determinations.[11] Schmidt found that in 1981, over half of the 34 states studied required a medical examination prior to the determination of the need for a guardian, 14 provided for a psychological examination, and 10 provided for other examinations. He also noted that some states required a more comprehensive capacity-specific assessment.

Today, at least 40 states refer to examination by a physician and 31 specifically include a psychologist. Other examiners named by state statutes include psychiatrists, mental health professionals, social workers, nurses, and "other qualified professionals." The UGPPA calls for examination by "a physician, psychologist, or other individual appointed by the court who is qualified to evaluate the respondent's alleged impairment." A growing number of states provide a comprehensive, interdisciplinary team approach. For instance, Florida uses a three-member examining committee; Kentucky calls for an interdisciplinary evaluation by a physician, psychologist, and social worker; North Carolina alludes to a "multi-disciplinary evaluation;" and Rhode Island sets out a detailed clinical assessment tool.[12]

THE RIGHTS OF INCAPACITATED PERSONS

One aspect examined by Schmidt et al. in 1981 was the preservation of individual civil rights under guardianship. Some fundamental rights (such as the right to vote) are personal in nature and not delegable to the guardian. Thus, they are either retained or lost under guardianship, but not transferred. Other fundamental rights are delegable, but state law may include a presumption that the individual retains them unless they are specifically removed in the court order (see the section on limited guardianship below). Schmidt found that only 10 state statutes explicitly preserved the civil liberties of IPs.

Today, 27 state laws include a provision designed to preserving basic rights. For example, such a provision may state that the individual under guardianship "retains all legal and civil rights except those which have been expressly limited by court order or have been specifically granted by order to the guardian by the court." Florida has one of the most extensive provisions, setting out the rights retained by the individual (such as the right to retain counsel, to receive visitors and communicate with others, to privacy); rights that may be removed by court order, but not delegated to the guardian (such as the right to marry, vote, have a driver's license); and rights that are removable and delegable to the guardian (such as the right to contract, to sue, and to defend against lawsuits).

WHO SERVES AS GUARDIAN

Guardians are family members, other individuals, professionals, private non-profit or for-profit agencies, or public guardianship entities. In 1981, Schmidt found that about one-third of the states used "the usual probate priority scheme," that is, a hierarchy that provides for the appointment of a spouse, adult child, parent, or other relative. Such a list often states that any suitable person or institution may serve, and that the court should make the selection in the best interest of the incapacitated individual.

Today, most states continue to offer such a hierarchical scheme, building sufficient court discretion to act in the IP's best interest. In addition, 43 states include a mechanism for the input of the IP in the form of advance nomination of a guardian, the most recent nomination of an agent under a durable power of attorney "in accordance with the IP's stated wishes," or the "person preferred by IP."

A recent examination of APS laws found that approximately 11 states specifically allow the APS agency to serve as the guardian of an APS client, either on a temporary or permanent basis.[13]

GOVERNMENTAL LOCATION OF PUBLIC GUARDIANSHIP

Perhaps the most fundamental issue that arises in analyzing public guardianship statutes is: where in the governmental administrative structure is the public guardianship function placed? This question was a basic element of both the

1981 study and the project's national survey. As explained above, an important distinction evident in comparing the statutory schemes is between states that merely name a state agency or employee as a last resort guardian (generally, implicit schemes) and states that establish an office with the sole mandate of serving as public guardian (generally, explicit schemes). States that establish a public guardianship office (such as Delaware, Florida, Virginia, New Jersey, Utah, and a number of others), have detailed statutory provisions on powers and duties, staffing, funding, record keeping, and review.

Schmidt relied on an earlier classification by Regan and Springer using four models: (1) a court model; (2) an independent state office; (3) a division of a social service agency; and (4) a county agency. He noted, however, that while the four models "at first appeared to provide a useful classification," upon further analysis, there were "many exceptions and variations" and that "few states fit the exact organization described in the models." This study uses the same classification, with the same caveat.

Court model. The court model establishes the public guardianship office as an arm of the court that has jurisdiction over guardianship and conservatorship. In 1981, there were six states with a court model for public guardianship. In 2007, statutory provisions revealed five. In Delaware, Hawaii, Mississippi, and Washington, the public guardian is located in the judiciary. In Georgia, recent legislation created a public guardianship program in which qualified and trained individuals are approved and registered by the county probate court to serve as public guardians, yet the training, administration, and funding of the program is conducted through the Division of Aging in the Department of Human Resources, which must maintain a master list of registered public guardians.

Independent agency model. The independent state office model is one in which the public guardianship office is established in an executive branch of the government that does not provide direct services for IPs or potential IPs. Schmidt found three independent state offices. Today, statutory provisions show four states that approximate this model: Alaska, in which the office is located in the Department of Administration; Illinois, in which the Office of State Guardian (one of the state's two schemes) is located in the guardianship and advocacy commission; Kansas, in which the Kansas Guardianship Program is independent, with a board appointed by the governor; and New Mexico, in which the office of guardianship is in the developmental disabilities planning council.

Social service agency. The placement of the public guardianship function in an agency providing direct services to IPs presents a clear conflict of interest. The 1981 study explained that:

The agency's primary priority may be expedient and efficient dispersal of its various forms of financial and social assistance. This can be detrimental to the effectiveness of the agency's role as guardian. If the ward is allocated insufficient assistance, if payment is lost or delayed, if assistance is denied altogether, or if the ward does not want mental health service, it is unlikely that the providing agency will as zealously advocate the interests of that ward.[14]

Schmidt found that over one-half of the states studied configured the public guardianship function in a manner that presented a conflict of interest between the role of guardian (deciding on, monitoring, and advocating for services) and the role of the social services agency (providing services). That is largely still true today. The percentage of states with statutes providing a potential for conflict appears to have increased. More than half of the 44 states with public guardianship statutory provisions name a social service, mental health, disability, or aging services agency as guardian, or as the entity to coordinate or contract for guardianship services. For example, Connecticut names the Commissioner of Social Services. New Hampshire authorizes the Department of Health and Human Services to contract for public guardianship services. Vermont, Virginia, Florida, and other states charge the Department on Aging with the administration of the public guardianship program.

Schmidt noted that some of the states with potential conflicts of interest had sought to alleviate the problem within the statutory scheme, for example, by stating that the agency is not to serve unless there is no other alternative available. The majority of statutes include such language today. Moreover, most specify that a key duty of the public guardian is to attempt to find suitable alternative guardians. In Florida, the statewide Office of Public Guardian must report on efforts to find others to serve within six months of appointment. A few statutes include more specific language addressing conflict of interest. For instance, the Illinois Office of State Guardian may not provide direct residential services to legally IPs. North Dakota allows the appointment of any appropriate government agency, unless the agency provides direct care and has custody of the IP (except if the court offers the specific finding of no substantial risk). Indiana requires that regional guardianship programs have procedures to avoid conflict of interest in providing services. Montana prohibits the appointment of guardians who provide direct services to the IP, but makes an exception for the agency serving in the public guardianship role.

County model. Approximately 13 of the statutory schemes place the public guardianship function at the county level, and a number of others have designed programs coordinated at the state level but carried out administratively or by contract at the local or regional level. For example, in Arizona, the county board of supervisors appoints a public fiduciary, and in California, the county board creates an office of public guardian. In Idaho, the board of county commissioners creates a "board of community guardian." In Missouri, the county public administrators serve as public guardians.

THE POWERS OF THE GUARDIAN AND PUBLIC GUARDIAN

Every state guardianship code sets out an array of duties and powers for the guardians of the person and the estate. In some states, guardians have a great deal of flexibility in their authority to sell property, invest assets, make major health care or end-of-life decisions, or relocate the individual, while in other states, guardians must obtain a court order to take some of these actions.

Public guardianship statutes generally provide that the public guardian has the same duties and powers as any other guardian. However, many of the statutes list additional duties and powers for public guardianship programs. For example, mandatory duties may include specifications about visits to the IP. At least eight states dictate the frequency of public guardianship IP visits or contacts. A few states require the public guardianship program to take other actions, such as developing individualized service plans, making periodic reassessments, visiting the facility of proposed placement, and attempting to secure public benefits.

Most of the additional listed duties, though, are programmatic in nature. Statutes may require the public guardianship entity to maintain professional staff; contract with local or regional providers; assist petitioners, private guardians, or the court; provide public information about guardianship and alternatives; contract for evaluations and audits; and maintain records and statistics. Public guardianship statutes frequently set out additional powers, as well as duties, for example, the authority to contract for services, recruit and manage volunteers, and intervene in private guardianship proceedings, if necessary.

TERMINATION OF GUARDIANSHIP AND RESTORATION

The Schmidt study discussed guardianship termination, indicating that 20 of the states studied had an explicit termination mechanism. The most common reason for termination, of course, is the death of the IP. Additional reasons cited by Schmidt include restoration to capacity or, in some cases, other changes, such as exhaustion of the person's estate or the institutionalization of the IP.

Today, the UGPPA provides that a guardianship may terminate upon the death of the ward or upon the order of the court "if the ward no longer needs the assistance or protection of a guardian."[15] The Uniform Act established a procedure for terminating a guardianship. Virtually all states provide a termination procedure, including one for the restoration of the rights of the individual. At least 45 states allow the IP to petition for restoration if a guardian is no longer needed.

COSTS OF PUBLIC GUARDIANSHIP

In 1981, the Schmidt study observed that the funding of public guardianship programs "has not been given much mention in the statutory schemes" and that the lack of explicit funding may leave programs subject to "the vicissitudes of an annual budget." Equally unclear, the study noted, was whether the ward's estate or the governmental agency must bear the cost of guardianship services. This lack of clarity could result in hardship for wards with few resources. The study found that statutes in 11 of the states said that the agency must bear the cost, and statutes in 15 states noted that the ward must pay for public guardianship services.

Today, some 31 of the 44 states with statutory provisions make some mention of cost. At least 10 states include references to state appropriations. Some states may have separate statutory provisions for appropriations, but others may not have made any provisions, leaving the public guardianship program financially at risk. Florida has especially elaborate provisions, referencing the inclusion of the program's annual budget as a separate item in the budget of the Department of Elderly Affairs' legislative request; the establishment of a "direct support organization" to raise funds for the program; and the establishment of a matching grant program to assist counties in supporting public guardianship. Utah allows for the acceptance of private donations and Virginia allows local or regional programs to accept private funds for supplemental services for IPs. At least four states (Idaho, Illinois in its county program, Nevada, and Oregon) specifically enable the county to budget for the public guardianship program.

Twenty-four states identify the governmental agency (state or county) as being responsible for the payment of costs, while 22 reference the estate of the IP. Seventeen hold both the governmental agency and the estate accountable for the payment of guardianship services, as well as for the costs and fees associated with the initiation of the guardianship. A common scenario is that the IP's estate pays, but if the IP is unable to pay, the county or state makes up the difference. A number of states mention recovery from the estate after death, and two states (Indiana and New Jersey) allow for a lien on the estate. Washington facilitates the payment of guardianship fees from Medicaid funds. Statutes in seven states (Idaho, New Jersey, Ohio, Oregon, Tennessee, Utah, and Washington) provide either that the court may, or must, waive filing fees and court costs, at least for indigent IPs.

COURT REVIEW OF GUARDIANSHIP

At the time of the 1981 study, guardianship monitoring was fairly rudimentary. Schmidt maintained that "a greater emphasis upon improved review might effect a significant improvement in the guardianship scheme as a whole." Schmidt reported that 20 of the 34 states studied had some provision for review, with 16 providing for an annual report to the court. He also noted that the review provided focused primarily on property, neglecting any examination of the ward's condition.

Currently, all states provide for regular financial accountings and, as of 2007, all but two states (Delaware and Massachusetts) provided regular status reports on the personal well being of the IP (but in 2009, Massachusetts law required a report). In some 40 states, the accounting or personal status report is submitted to the court on an annual basis. Most states set levy sanctions for the failure to report. Some 18 states provide for post-hearing investigators to visit the IP and verify the accuracy of the report, at least if the judge finds this necessary. California has the most comprehensive model of review, with a regular visit to each IP by a court investigator six months after appointment and every year thereafter. Unfortunately, in practice, state courts often lack sufficient resources to fully implement a monitoring scheme.[16]

Public guardianship programs are subject to the same provisions for guardianship accountability and monitoring as other guardians. However, in close to 20 states, the public guardianship statute either specifically mentions that the program must report to court and abide by state requirements for guardian review, or provides for special additional oversight. States such as Maine, Minnesota, and New Hampshire call for an annual report to the court on each public guardianship case, and one state (Delaware) requires court review of public guardianship cases every six months. In Florida, the public guardianship office must report to court on its efforts to locate a successor guardian and on potential restoration within six months of appointment.

In addition to requiring court reports, several statutes call for annual reports on the program or on cases to governmental entities. For instance, in Hawaii, the office must submit an annual report to the chief justice and in Kansas, the program must report annually to the governor, legislature, judiciary, and the public. Five state statutes (Florida, Indiana, Kansas, Tennessee, and Vermont) call for an annual audit of the program. Several states call for local or regional programs to report annually to the coordinating state agency. Maryland has a unique oversight mechanism, providing county review boards to conduct biannual reviews of each public guardianship case, including face-to-face hearings by volunteer multidisciplinary panels. Two states (Utah and Virginia) require an independent evaluation of the program. Finally, a majority of the state statutes specify bonding requirements for the public guardianship program.

EMERGENCY PROCEDURES

The Schmidt study also referred to the need for emergency procedures when the "needs of an individual may be so acute as to require immediate aid." This is particularly relevant for public guardianship, as frequently vulnerable individuals without societal contacts (candidates for public guardianship appointment) experience crises that put them in jeopardy. Schmidt discovered that in 1981, only "a handful of states" had emergency procedures, and that these were outlined in APS legislation and emergency guardianship procedures in "some states."

Currently, as reported above, all states have APS legislation and programs in place, which frequently funnel cases to public guardianship programs. In addition, virtually all states have provisions for emergency guardianships. One issue is that due process safeguards for emergency guardianship are typically less stringent than for permanent guardianship, yet emergency guardianship often functions as a gateway to the more permanent status. Thus, some individuals may end up in a guardianship with less than full due process protection.[17]

LIMITED GUARDIANSHIP

In 1981, the Schmidt study touched on the issue of limited guardianship, which at that time was "becoming more prevalent of late." The principle underlying limited guardianship is that there is no "bright line" of capacity; incapacity is not all or nothing. A limited guardian has powers only in those areas in which the person lacks capacity, allowing the IP to retain as much independence and autonomy as possible. This is in accordance with the principle of using the "least restrictive alternative."

In 1982, the UGPPA incorporated limited guardianship provisions, giving a major boost to the adoption of the concept in state law. Today, virtually all state guardianship statutes include provisions for limiting or tailoring the court order (in some cases, stating a preference for limited over plenary guardianship), and most include language acknowledging the importance of "maximizing [the] self-determination and independence" of the individual.[18] Such language on limited guardianship, however, is difficult to put into practice. A 1994 study found that nationwide, the overall use rate for limited guardianships (excluding one high-use state) was about 5 percent.[19]

In nine states, statutory language specifically mentions that the public guardianship program may serve as a limited guardian, thus emphasizing the legislative intent. In some of these states (such as California and Illinois), the public guardianship program may petition to serve, and could thus petition for a limited order. The recent Washington legislation states that the public guardianship providers must annually certify that they have reviewed the need for continued public guardianship services and the appropriateness of limiting or further limiting the scope of the order.

APPRAISAL OF STATUTORY CHANGES

Clearly, much has changed since the statutory review conducted in 1981. Schmidt remarked on the variability of state guardianship law and the need for "renewed impetus for uniform state laws" on public guardianship specifically and guardianship generally. Since that time, the UGPPA has undergone two revisions and is adopted in whole or piecemeal in a number of states. However, as shown by the ABA Commission on Law and Aging statutory tables, state guardianship law remains variable, causing particular problems when guardianship jurisdiction issues arise. The Uniform Law Commission has developed the UGPPA, which is being enacted by state legislatures. State statutes have reflected significant progress in affording procedural protections, including a more functional determination of incapacity, promoting limited orders, and bolstering court oversight procedures.

State public guardianship statutes are markedly variable, as well. There is no uniform public guardianship law. A now-and-then statutory comparison shows that some nine additional states have adopted explicit public guardianship legislation. Explicit provisions provide for an actual program, rather than a governmental entity to serve as guardian of last resort, and can articulate standards with much greater specificity. These explicit provisions are more likely to provide for budgetary appropriations and to establish greater oversight than that required for private guardians. Finally, it is important to note that seven states now reference staffing ratios. This is a great leap forward, which is probably attributable to the 1981 study's emphasis on adequate staffing. However, a substantial portion of states still place public guardianship programs in a governmental agency with the potential for conflicts of interest. While some attempt to mitigate these potential conflicts with statutory language, the conflicting agency roles remain problematic.

NOTES

Portions of this chapter are based on Teaster, Pamela, Erica Wood, Susan Lawrence, and Winsor Schmidt. "Wards of the State: A National Study of Public Guardianship." *Stetson Law Review* 37, no. 1 (2007): 193–241. Courtesy of the *Stetson Law Review*.

1. Schmidt et al., *Public Guardianship and the Elderly*.

2. Ibid., 179.

3. See state statutory charts on adult guardianship, as well as the annual update, on the Web site of the ABA Commission on Law and Aging at http://www.abanet.org/aging/legislativeupdates/home.shtml. See also Teaster et al., *Public Guardianship After 25 Years*, 33–37; and Erica Wood in Quinn, *Guardianships of Adults*.

4. In mid-2007, Arkansas passed a public guardianship bill, S.B. 820, creating an office of public guardian for adults within the Division of Aging and Adult Services. The Act does not take effect until and unless the director of the division determines that adequate appropriations or other funding are available and appoints a public guardian.

5. This project did not include a systematic search of all state adult protective services statutes, which might reveal additional guardianship provisions. See ABA Commission on Law and Aging, *Adult Protective Services Agency Authority to Act As Guardian of A Client: Guidance and Provisions from Adult Protective Services Law, By State*, http://www.abanet.org/aging/elderabuse.shtml. Throughout this chapter, the District of Columbia is counted as a state.

6. Schmidt et al., *Public Guardianship and the Elderly*, 26.

7. National Conference of Commissioners on Uniform State Laws, *Uniform Guardianship and Protective Proceedings Act* (1982).

8. Cf. Washington Certified Professional Guardian Board, Ethics Advisory Opinion 2005-001-Professional Guardian Petitioning for Appointment, http://www.courts.

wa.gov/committee/?fa=committee.display&item_id=644&committee_id=127 ("The practice of nominating oneself as guardian automatically raises the appearance of self-dealing.")

   9. Schmidt et al., *Public Guardianship and the Elderly*, 34.

   10. See http://www.ncea.aoa.gov/NCEAroot/Main_Site/Find_Help/APS/Analys is_State_Laws.aspx. Cf. Winsor Schmidt, "Adult Protective Services and the Therapeutic State," *Law and Psychology Review* 10 (1986): 101–121; Winsor Schmidt and Kent Miller, "Improving the Social Treatment Model in Protective Services for the Elderly: False Needs in the Therapeutic State," *Journal of Comparative Social Welfare* 1, no. 1 (1984): 90–106.

   11. See ABA Commission on Law and Aging, American Psychological Association, and National College of Probate Judges, *Judicial Determination of Capacity of Older Adults in Guardianship Proceedings* (ABA and APA, 2006).

   12. Michael Mayhew, "Survey of State Guardianship Laws: Statutory Provisions for Clinical Evaluations," BIFOCAL 27, no. 1 (2005): 1–2, 13–19. See also Jennifer Moye, Stacey Wood, et al., "Clinical Evidence in Guardianship of Older Adults Is Inadequate: Findings From a Tri-State Study," *The Gerontologist* 47, no. 5 (2007): 604–612; Jennifer Moye, Steven Butz, et al., "A Conceptual; Model and Assessment Template for Capacity Evaluation in Adult Guardianship," *The Gerontologist* 45, no. 5 (2007): 591–603.

   13. ABA Commission on Law and Aging, *Adult Protective Services Agency Authority to Act As Guardian of A Client: Guidance and Provisions from Adult Protective Services Law, By State*, http://www.abanet.org/aging/elderabuse.shtml.

   14. Schmidt et al., *Public Guardianship and the Elderly*, 38.

   15. U.G.P.P.A. section 318.

   16. Karp and Wood, *Guardianship Monitoring: A National Survey of Court Practices*; Karp and Wood, *Guarding the Guardians: Promising Practices for Court Monitoring*. See also Sally Hurme and Erica Wood, "Guardian Accountability Then and Now: Tracing Tenets for an Active Court Role," *Stetson Law Review* 31, no. 3 (2002): 867–940. A recent Guardianship Task Force report in the state of Washington not only recommends that adequate public funding should be allocated to the guardianship system, but also advocates that courts should actively, and not just passively, monitor guardianship cases. Elder Law Section, Washington State Bar Association, *Report of the Guardianship Task Force to the WSBA Elder Law Section Executive Committee* (Seattle, WA: Washington State Bar Association, 2009), http://www.wsba.org/lawyers/groups/elderlaw/

   17. See Peter Barrett, "Temporary/Emergency Guardianships: The Clash Between Due Process and Irreparable Harm," BIFOCAL 13 (1992–1993): 3. See also Grant v. Johnson, 757 F. Supp. 1127 (D. Or., 1991), ruling a state emergency guardianship statute unconstitutional because it lacked sufficient due process protection.

   18. See the state-specific chart of statutory provisions on limited guardianship by the AARP Public Policy Institute, on the Web site of the ABA Commission on Law and Aging, http://www.abanet.org/aging/guardianship/lawandpractice/home.html.

   19. Lisi, et al., *National Study of Guardianship Systems: Findings and Recommendations*. See also Sally Hurme, "Current Trends in Guardianship Reform," *Maryland Journal of Contemporary Legal Issues* 7, no. 1 (1995–1996): 143–189; Lawrence Frolik, "Promoting Judicial Acceptance and Use of Limited Guardianship," *Stetson Law Review* 31, no. 3 (2002): 735–755; Winsor Schmidt, "Assessing the Guardianship Reform of Limited Guardianship: Tailoring Guardianship or Expanding Inappropriate Guardianships?," *Journal of Ethics, Law and Aging* 2, no. 1 (1996): 5–14.

Chapter 3

CASE STUDIES

Helen is an 87-year old woman with a history of mental illness. Two years ago, the group home sought the payment of fees that were six months in arrears. The courts found that there were no family members and no one able and/or willing to serve as guardian. As a result, Helen was made a ward of the state. ABC Services was named to provide guardianship services. ABC staff resolved the financial confusion and Helen was delighted to be able to stay in the place she calls her home. Several months later, Helen fell and broke her shoulder. Again, ABC stepped in and sought her input and was able to ensure that physical therapy services were provided and Helen was able to regain most of her mobility. Six months ago, Helen was diagnosed with inoperable cancer. Yet again, ABC stepped in and, with its knowledge of Helen's values, ensured that she would be provided hospice care, in keeping with her wishes.

OVERVIEW

Chapter 3 presents information about and an assessment of site visits to nine public guardianship programs in six states. Florida and Illinois were studied using focus groups composed of key stakeholders, while individual interviews were utilized in the other four states. Thus, the headings for Florida and Illinois differ from those for California, Arizona, Maryland, and Delaware. Programs are presented within the context of how stakeholders regard them, as well as consideration of the programs' strengths, weaknesses, opportunities, and threats. Cases that either made the newspapers in each state or were described during the site visit are also included.

THE FLORIDA STATEWIDE PUBLIC GUARDIANSHIP OFFICE

The state interview contact for the Florida Statewide Public Guardianship Office (SPGO), which falls under the administrative umbrella of the Florida Department of Elder Affairs in Tallahassee, was Michelle Hollister, Executive

Director. She had occupied this position for nearly a year at the time of the interview. Previously, she worked for the court system in Broward County, overseeing the probate, guardianship, and mental health divisions for court administration and, for a brief period, represented the public guardian. Karen Campbell, Director of the Office of the Public Guardian, Inc., the public guardian for the Second Judicial Circuit, also attended the interview.

Administrative Structure and Location in Government

In the 1980s, Florida's public guardianship consisted of three pilot projects in three distinct parts of the state. They remained pilots for over 15 years. As a result of legislation passed in 1999, there are now 16 public guardianship programs. The SPGO must appoint every public guardian, and the Executive Director may both approve and rescind the appointment of the public guardianship offices. SPGO appoints the program for a four-year term and awards contracts that range from $15,000 to $438,000. Most programs receive state SPGO dollars. In addition to state monies, local programs receive funding from United Way and charitable donations.

The office appointment is granted to a single individual or to a non-profit entity. By statute, more than one public guardianship program can serve a geographic area. Local offices have varying models of operation and cover 23 of 67 counties in Florida. The public programs serve individuals 18 years of age and over who require public guardianship services.

Local programs offer uniform annual reports, but at the time of the site visit, the other reports were not standardized. Programs also use performance measures in the newly instituted annual report. National Guardianship Association (NGA) standards inform the annual report and performance measures. SPGO holds quarterly meetings with all offices and the programs take turns hosting meetings. Only the executive director's travel is funded, however.

Changes in funding are of great concern. Until July 1, 2004, many of the programs received a portion of their funding from civil filing fees. However, a recent change in the Florida Constitution resulted in the rescinding of counties' authority to direct filing fees toward public guardianship. The public programs then tried to find a substitute funding mechanism, and Governor Jeb Bush recommended a five million dollar matching grant program at the outset of the legislative session. The matching grant program passed (S.B. 1782), but the funding was subject to appropriation, which was not approved. Thus, the Office began assisting the local programs to identify alternative sources of funding. The total budget for the SPGO in fiscal year (FY) 2003 was $2,399,569, in statewide dollars that were funneled to the Department of Elder Affairs. Ms. Hollister reported that there are serious threats to their ability to maintain funds on an everyday basis. Under S.B. 1782, the SPGO will have a direct support organization that will enable a fund raising mechanism. A non-profit mechanism with the ability to take funds would then be implemented.

The program hopes to acquire additional monies by using an administrative claims model, based on a practice conducted by the Illinois public guardian. Administrative dollars fund Medicaid eligibility, but an incapacitated person can only access Medicaid funds through a guardian. If the individual has no means of obtaining a guardian, the public guardian steps in to fill the void. If the state provides public guardianship services, it incurs a cost so that the incapacitated individual receives a Medicaid payment. The state can ask the federal government to share that cost and receive 50 percent in matching funds. The request for a Medicaid claims model, however, had been pending federal approval for over a year when this research was conducted and, was still pending. With this initiative, the state files an application to pay for assisting an incapacitated person with accessing Medicaid funds, not for guardianship service provision.

Functions of the Public Guardianship Program

A policies and procedures manual provides guidelines on making IP decisions, but most decisions are left to individual programs. There are very few limited guardianships, and so the local programs generally have full decision-making authority. However, some programs sought court approval even when it was not strictly necessary, such as when an IP is traveling out of the county for more than two weeks. Decisions concerning whether to settle real estate or abandon property must come before a judge.

Institutionalization. There are no special procedures for institutionalizing IPs. Ms. Campbell reported that, in reality, very few IPs were living in the community when they were referred to the public guardian, stating, "By the time the person is referred to my program, they have either been institutionalized most of their lives or they are in an institution."

Illnesses and end-of life decision making. When IPs have illnesses, such as Alzheimer's disease, programs make every attempt to match resources with clients' special needs. Due to the volume of IPs with developmental disabilities, some programs are active in the mental disability advocacy community. End-of-life decisions are given special attention because the state developed a written procedure authorizing the guardian of a person, when the wishes of an IP are not known, to make decisions to withhold or withdraw life-prolonging procedures under certain circumstances.[1] The procedures, grounded in Florida statute, specify what a case manager must do, including who to notify and what letters to submit for approval. Though the statute does not require it, one local program will submit a motion to the court seeking the authority to act in the best interest of the IP. Under this procedure, the director of the local program must personally visit the IP 24 hours before making a decision to withhold or withdraw treatment.

Based on the statute, when an IP dies, the public guardian office must close out the guardianship absolutely. It notifies any family, if possible. The public guardian offers the family the opportunity to make final arrangements and gathers up all personal belongings and stores them at cost to the program, not to the IP. Then, a final report is made to the court, but the guardians do not have to file for probate. Typically, a report is made to the court, and the remaining dollars from the IP's estate are sent to the Registry of the Court. The family of the IP is notified of the death in writing and is given the opportunity to probate the estate. After a reasonable amount of time, if the family has not made any filings, then the program seeks to abandon the personal belongings and leave them to a charitable organization.

Representative payee. The local public guardianship offices serve as representative payees and were exploring having public guardianship programs serve as organizational representative payees. (Organizational representative payees are allowed by Social Security to have 10 percent of the ward's benefit or $28 per month, whichever is less.) Though this is not a great deal of money, it is more than an individual representative payee receives, which is no compensation whatsoever. Social Security does not recognize an appointed guardian and requires guardians to apply to become representative payees to manage an IP's Social Security funds. The programs serve as representative payees because they often deal with an IP's Social Security income. Programs only serve as representative payees for their own IPs.

Petitioning. Under Florida law, an individual must be declared incapacitated before a petition is filed for the appointment of a guardian. The public guardian programs sometimes petition for incapacity. Most other interested parties (e.g., nursing homes, hospitals) do not want to bear the costs of petitioning. An attorney on contract or on staff represents the programs in court. In one county, the program is housed in Legal Aid.

One of the public guardianship programs was attempting to avoid the conflict inherent in petitioning for its own IPs by having the individual making the report on the proposed IP swear in an affidavit that he or she reasonably believes that the proposed IP is incapacitated. This information is attached to the public guardian's petition. A case manager from the public guardian's office will meet with the alleged IP for the purpose of stating that there is no contradiction with the affidavit, and this statement appears in the petition. Then, a judge is presented with a petition from the public guardian's office that indicates the presence of a concerned individual in the community who swears that he or she has reason to believe the individual is incapacitated and that the public guardian has met with the person and finds no reason to contradict what said individual has sworn. For that particular public guardian office, the judge will shift the work of preparing the case to the county attorney, who will set up the examining committee and schedule the hearing.

Coordination with other entities. All programs maintain a relationship with APS, and many have a relationship with area agencies on aging. The most frequent scenario for triggering a guardianship is when an individual is in the hospital, the hospital does not know his or her identity, and family members cannot be identified. In this case, the hospital needs some entity to grant informed consent for treatment. Other common scenarios include a hospital needing to authorize transfer to a nursing home, or a nursing home caring for an incapacitated individual who cannot receive Medicaid benefits.

Special initiatives. The state office was in the process of receiving the results of a statewide needs assessment conducted by the Department for Elder Affairs to gauge the unmet need for public guardianship.

Local Public Guardian Staff

Composition. The education levels of local staff range from B.A. to Ph.D. Attorneys run several offices. Case managers with social work backgrounds staff many programs. They reported very little staff turnover, although some changes in staffing occurred with a program that went from being part of a state agency to a non-profit. Program representatives said that they have a good relationship with the state office.

Caseloads and cases. Even though Florida has an unusually high number of older adults, most programs reported a fairly even split between older and younger IPs. Caseloads are divided by geographic location or by the facilities in which IPs reside. Most wards are visited monthly, although the statute requires quarterly visitation. IPs are included as much as possible in decision making, with at least one program focusing on the concept of self-determination to ensure IP inclusion. Case managers and IPs often set goals together. Many programs use standard forms for care planning purposes, but forms are not uniform across the state. Many entities join public guardians in care provision (e.g., developmental services, economic eligibility, Social Security, APS, hospitals, nursing homes).

Accountability. Program supervisors conduct random monthly file reviews. Programs are audited, in many cases, by their board, as well as by the state office. A state policies and procedures manual guides the programs and annual reports are given to the courts. Some programs bi-annually assess the work done on behalf of the IPs.

Education and training. In addition to coordinating the local public guardianship programs, the statewide office is also responsible for the registration, education, and training of professional guardians. Moreover, the office develops materials on educating the general public about guardianship and public guardianship.

Representatives from many programs attend the Florida State Guardianship Association Conference and receive continuing education from that entity, as well as through the SPGO. All guardians, including public guardians, are required to have 16 hours of continuing education every 2 years. The statewide office handles the paperwork for all professional guardianship training in the state. Staff members reported that they needed additional training in end-of-life decisions, Medicaid planning, and the management of investments and property. Staffers also wanted guidelines on guardianship practices from the state office.

Special issues. First, the filing fee change in Florida, discussed in detail above, was of great concern to the local programs, which stood to lose a substantial amount of their program income due to this change. Second, the diverse population in Florida requires sensitivity to cultural differences. Third, guardians reported testifying in court in Baker Act proceedings (Florida civil commitment proceedings). Public guardians are also often present at guardianship hearings.

Ratios. Based on the related statute, public guardians may only serve 40 IPs for every 1 professional. Waiting lists are common in most parts of the state with a public guardian program. The ratio is increased or decreased only by the state office. Most program staffers agreed that it was important to have the 40:1 ratio due to the complexity of cases. However, one staff person later wrote that she believed a 20:1 ratio would actually provide better services and cited the unpredictable nature of guardianship cases.

Promising practices. Barry University School of Social Work, one of the local programs, utilizes social work interns to help support public guardianship services.

Judges and Court Administrators

Composition. Most of the judges and court administrators interviewed had been in the judiciary for no less than 5 years and some had served there for as many as 25 years. This group had interactions with both the public guardian and private and corporate guardians. Approximately 8,000 persons are under guardianship in Miami. The main public guardianship program in Dade County has 804 IPs, as well another 40 IPs under the care of a secondary public guardianship program.

Cases. Most of the proposed IPs coming before the courts are living at home, but are unable to manage their finances, their health care, or both. Indigent cases are brought to the attention of the courts primarily though APS or by a facility. Pro bono attorneys are often appointed by the courts to serve as guardians because of the cap on IPs for the public programs.

Public guardianship cases seem to consume a higher percentage of administrative time than private guardianship cases due to their emergency nature. A General Master said that over 40 percent of cases were from the public guardianship program.

Petitioning. Typically, the public guardian office petitions for its own IPs, but that was not true for all jurisdictions. For example, Miami and Lee Counties use a "wheel" system to select attorneys to serve as petitioners. In many instances, an emergency temporary guardian is appointed at the same time that the petition for determination of incapacity and plenary guardianship is filed. There were very few limited guardianships granted, and when they were granted, they were typically for persons with mental illness. Restoration of capacity rarely occurs.

Accountability. A computerized system used to track IPs appeared to be problematic because it was dated and the data gathered were insufficient. A uniform computerized system would facilitate better tracking of the IPs.

In some courts, such as Miami, an initial guardianship plan is required and subsequent plans are required annually. The plan helps the court understand IPs' needs, particularly in the realm of finances. Plans are not uniform throughout the state. In addition, an exploration of filing plans via computers was underway.

Promising practices. At least one judge took an active role in public guardianship by personally going to county commissioners to secure additional funding. Judges were also active in helping to secure other community resources for the public programs. In one circuit, the judiciary even educated county board chairmen and budget directors from the county attorney's office. Judges were informed about guardianship and public guardianship at a conference of judges. Several large judicial circuits also have specific units for guardianship. One judge suggested that it would be useful to have a database of grants or alternative funding sources for which the courts and/or the public guardian could apply.

Strengths, weaknesses, opportunities, threats. A major threat is a lack of funding. One participant said, "It is very sad for everybody, including the workers at our public guardian office, to be living with the day-to-day threat that the doors could be closed for lack of funding." Related to this lack of funding is a lack of attention by policymakers. An opportunity for awareness of public guardianship exists in the form of additional training for all guardians, however. Judges and court administrators also cited the continuing and increasing need for public guardians.

Attorneys

Composition. The attorney group had a range of practice experiences, from private practice to working for the state. Some attorneys served as guardians, while others represented the petitioner or worked with public guardianship in an advisory capacity. The range of tenure in their current position was from 3 to 10 years. Attorneys stated that with the addition of the new public guardian programs, the need for guardians was somewhat alleviated.

Petitioning. The petitioning issue was regarded as a problem and not only was the change to the filing fee problematic, but, more broadly, the way cases arise in the first place was also viewed as problematic. Many cases emerge because a concerned neighbor or friend comes forward. One attorney said:

> We have to go out and draft petitioners sometimes. When it [petition] comes from facilities, there is an added conflict of interest issue. The facility has a resident whom they believe to be incapacitated. There are some ethical issues that we talk about in our Bar meetings for a facility to initiate the guardianship process. There are some potential areas for abuse. Having said that, again, when you are desperate for a petitioner to get this in front of the court, you are willing to do whatever it takes.

As of July 2004, a $400 filing fee was required, and fees could not be waived, even if there was an affidavit of indigency. It is possible for a petitioner to defer the $400 filing fee; however, in at least one circuit, if they are not paid, the deferment agreement becomes a judgment against the attorney. Nursing homes, assisted living facilities, and hospitals were apparently not a ready source of payment for the $400 filing fees, though, in some cases, they are willing to serve as petitioner.

Accountability. There is little guidance in the Florida statute or in case law regarding the responsibility of the court-appointed attorney for the alleged IP. Attorneys who are not immersed in guardianship presented potential failings in client advocacy. Some attorneys regard their job as defending the capacity of the individual in the same manner as a criminal defense proceeding. The attorneys said that bar consensus, however, is that a court-appointed attorney should act in the best interest of the alleged IP. The chance of having an attorney unfamiliar with guardianship is high. Court-appointed attorneys are not paid unless a guardianship is awarded. In some counties, the county selects the court-appointed attorney for the AIP, but in others, the petitioner selects the court-appointed attorney.

Appraisal. There is generally a positive appraisal of the public guardians, and the office was commended for educating the media about public guardianship. One attorney said that the public guardian program was excellent at securing grant dollars to fund the program. The public guardian's office is regarded as the first source for education on guardianship. There was some negative media coverage, and one of the attorneys stated that the public programs are, unfortunately, associated with the negative comments in the press on private guardianship.

Special issues. One issue was that non-profit entities were not totally under the jurisdiction of the state public guardian's office. Such private nonprofit guardianship agencies are assigned both indigent IPs and paying IPs, entities that are forming referral relationships with health care providers. For example, a hospital or a chain of skilled nursing faculties may form a relationship with a non-profit agency. The facility agrees, de facto, to call the non-profit when it has a guardianship case, whether it is fee-generating or not, if the non-profit agrees to take all the IPs. Because the non-profit has developed that relationship (and receives dollars, especially from fee-generating cases), there is a propensity to avoid confronting the facility if there is a problem with the IP later on, which compromises its ability to advocate for the IP. Attorneys did not believe that the problem had made its way into the public guardian system, but they did regard it as a potential problem.

Another problem cited was the potential risk of non-profit programs to charge a great deal for paying IPs in order to cover the costs of indigent IPs. Paying IPs may receive more zealous advocacy and oversight than indigent ones.

Promising practices. Broward County has a fairly sophisticated court monitoring system for guardianship, thanks to a judge who secured funding for the division.

In some counties, persons are not adjudicated as legally incapacitated if there is no one to serve. To overcome this problem, sometimes a person is willing to serve as a health-care proxy if the individual still has the capacity to execute an advance directive under Florida law. For example, a facility can hire a social worker (who must undergo 40 hours of guardianship training) to serve in the capacity of health-care proxy, while a local non-profit might serve as representative payee.

Strengths, weaknesses, opportunities, threats. First, programs are underfunded, and the unmet need for guardians is significant. When the public guardian obtains the maximum number of IPs, there is no provision for backup. Second, because local public guardianship programs differ across the state, there is not much uniformity and accountability suffers. Third, it would be helpful to enact provisions regulating the relationships of guardians to referral sources. Finally, some public programs can take both public and private cases, which may present a conflict of interest.

Adult Protective Services

Composition. The APS group included over 20 people from all over Florida. Most participated by telephone.

Cases. APS estimated that generally, between 10 percent and 25 percent of cases involved incapacitated persons or persons in need of public guardianship services. In a few instances, that number was as low as 1 percent. APS caseloads ranged from 80 to 120 cases per worker. APS can and does petition for public guardianship. Securing a public guardianship typically closes an APS case.

In some counties, APS works well with the public guardian, while other counties have no public guardian. Non-profits, such as Lutheran Family Services, filled this need in some instances and corporate, for-profit guardians addressed it in others. Rural counties appeared to have a difficult time securing guardianship services. In at least one district, the public guardian had such a waiting list that APS had not used the program in over 10 years, and at least one public guardian would not take cases unless the individual was in a skilled nursing facility or locked facility. In at least one district, the council on aging provides public guardianship services and does petitioning.

The majority of cases referred are self-neglect cases, although exploitation is also often involved. Most guardianships are initiated by APS for people in the community as opposed to facilities. In rare instances, guardianships are initiated to move people from one facility to another when, for example, the resident's needs are not met by the current facility. APS determines capacity by the use of a standard assessment tool called a "Life's Capacity to Consent" form. Psychological evaluations are generally contracted out. Some districts have limited dollars set aside for that purpose. Involuntary protective services, such as placing an individual in a state mental institution, may be provided by court order.

Appraisal. The APS appraisal of the public guardianship system was not positive in that public guardianship offices frequently could not accept cases or could serve only a fraction of APS cases in which a public guardian is needed. Respondents indicated that in some areas, 90–100 percent of the need for public guardians was unmet. For other jurisdictions, the need was met. In at least one area, when the need for public guardianship for adults was addressed, a local commissioner said, "If we had any money, we would give it to the children."

Strengths, weaknesses, opportunities, threats. The APS group identified the strengths of the program as being that its staff gets the job done and provides the appropriate and necessary services. The public guardianship program provides valuable resources when they are available. The weaknesses are the lack of funding and inadequate staffing. APS wanted a public guardian office in every county and to have the public guardians perform a full review of the annual reports that are submitted to the courts.

One potential solution was a guardian advocate program comprised of individuals who could just be responsible for the needs of the client, including medication and medical decisions. (Serving as a limited guardian for health care and financial decisions would meet that need).

Aging and Disability Advocates

Composition. Participants included representatives from area agencies on aging, the Advocacy Center for Persons with Disabilities, and the Local Long-Term Care Ombudsman.

Cases. A concern was expressed about the number of people who were without guardians and who were residing in nursing homes. An unmet need for public guardians was identified, but not quantified. The public guardian appears to be active in case planning and in facility complaints filed by the ombudsman.

Appraisal. Advocates stressed that the public guardianship program is underfunded and is not statewide. Public guardianship programs are already at their maximum capacity. Those who worked with the local offices were complimentary. The new Statewide Office Executive Director was positively regarded. Since the program was placed in the Department of Elder Affairs, there is more concern about the guardianships of older adults, but the respondents could not comment on the younger population. One person indicated that at one time and in one jurisdiction, the public guardian had over 60 IPs to 1 worker and a waiting list of well over 1,000 people.

Strengths, weaknesses, opportunities, threats. Strengths include that the program is more visible than it was under the previous administration and that it is generally regarded positively. Maintaining a high profile in government and with the media is important. This program's weaknesses include the lack of a statewide registry of people who need guardianship services. The public guardian offices could also provide more community and judicial education. The ratio of staff to IPs was regarded as too high.

Threats exist in the form of underfunding and staff burnout: "They're dealing with people who have enormous amounts of needs and are relying solely on them. That's like having 45 children." Medicare and Medicaid should alter reimbursement procedures so that funding for public guardianship services is allowed. Licensure for all guardians is also recommended.

Incapacitated People

The two IPs interviewed (a male and a female) were both aware that they were under the protection of a public guardian. They seemed generally satisfied with the help that the public guardian provided them. One said, "It's the best thing that ever happened to me," and that his guardian "knows [him] like a book." Both believed that their needs were attended to and that their wishes were respected.

Summary and Conclusions

The pilot projects in Florida existed when Schmidt and colleagues (also located in Florida) conducted the original study. That it took an additional 18 years from the time the authors' book was published to establish a potential statewide system of public guardianship is surprising, given that a clear foundation was established through an assessment of unmet need and scholarly and legislative activity prior to 1980. Nevertheless, the Florida programs are now established in the Department of Elder Affairs and cover approximately half the counties in the state. The established model is the social services agency model, which was discussed in greater detail in the previous chapter. Problems with advocacy for IPs are obviously inherent. Local programs, typically non-profit entities, have contracts with the SPGO and utilize a variety of operation methods. Sixteen entities had entered applications at the time of this study. The state program also has oversight of Florida's private professional guardians. At the time of this report, the state had just instituted a policy of certifying all guardians through a licensing examination.

The public programs serve adults 18 years of age and older, and serve as both guardian of the person and of the property. The programs also serve as representative payees and were exploring the possibility of serving as an organizational representative payee. Under this arrangement, if it is approved, the program could realize a slight fee for this service. Guardians, by statute, can authorize the withdrawal of an IP's nutrition and hydration, and the local program director must personally visit the IP within 24 hours prior to the program making this decision.

A change in the collection of court filing fees threatens the existence of the programs, and virtually all of the entities interviewed cited it. Programs had been partially funded by dollars realized by civil filing fees, but that funding stream was eliminated and programs were scrambling to recoup the loss. The governor proposed a source of funding using a matching program, and this was enacted, but dollars were not allocated. The executive director was seeking funding for the programs in a variety of ways, including a Medicaid administrative claims model and options for fundraising by a non-profit entity.

The programs can petition for guardianship, although they were reported as rarely doing so. Funding the filing of petitions from outside sources was regarded as a real impediment to establishing guardianships, as was the GAL system. The GAL system was noted to be highly uneven, offering little training for attorneys who elect to serve in this capacity and who, according to many, exhibit a lack of understanding of the role.

Notable, too, was a statutorily defined guardian-to-ward ratio of 40:1, which was the only statutory ratio in any of the site visit states. In some programs, this level was already reached. The result of the cap was that public guardian services were inaccessible in that service region and that when a public guardian was required, this last resort need was not met. One focus group participant later wrote investigators to say that the 40:1 ratio was too high to adequately serve the IPs. The use of volunteer guardians to fill the service gap was piloted, although it had been explored by the Schmidt study in Florida over 15 years earlier and its effectiveness was questioned.[2]

Programs were establishing some uniform procedures at the state level, but internal working forms were not standardized across programs. Efforts were undertaken to hold meetings of the local programs throughout the state, although funding was inadequate to provide for travel by local program staff. Staff members typically had social work backgrounds.

Early in their development, the programs were generally well regarded in the state. Focus group participants had high hopes for Ms. Hollister, who had recently assumed her position and had taken an aggressive stand on helping to secure funds, increasing the visibility of the office, and exploring relationships with other entities associated with public guardianship in the state.

OFFICE OF THE STATE (PUBLIC) GUARDIAN (OSG), ILLINOIS

After conducting the site visit in Florida, the research team travelled to Illinois. The state contact for OSG was John Wank, the Acting Director and General Counsel of the Illinois Guardianship and Advocacy Commission (the Commission). On paper, OSG is "as independent as a political entity can be in Illinois." The Commission's OSG is "beholden to the executive branch and the legislative branch. The executive branch controls . . . budget, and the legislative branch approves it." The Commission does not provide social services, and so the OSG does not fall into the conflict-of-interest trap that is inherent when social service providers supply guardianship services.

OSG has eight regional offices providing coverage for the entire state. Each office has a director, a manager, and caseworkers. Many, but not all, have an attorney. Each office handles caseloads with a cross section of IPs, including elders, as well as individuals with developmental disabilities, mental illnesses, and physical limitations that preclude engagement in meaningful decision making.

OSG is consistent with other state agencies with centralized programs for personnel and time keeping. In addition to standard oversight, OSG has an internal auditor who examines fiduciary operations on a regular basis. External auditors unaffiliated with the Commission perform biennial audits and file reports with the State of Illinois. Audits include a program audit that examines the compliance of OSG with mandates requiring periodic IP visits and periodic court accounting filings. Although some downstate courts excuse OSG from annual report filing requirements, such reports are filed in all counties.

Funding

The OSG budget for FY 2003 was approximately eight million dollars. Funding sources include assessments against the estates of the IPs and Medicaid funds (since 1998). OSG can assess fees against the estate of IPs, but because of the nature of the clientele (i.e., estates <$25,000) assets are likely to be limited, and so the yield from this source is minimal. The monies gleaned from Medicaid are matching funds and accrue to the benefit of the taxpayer (in the amount of $800,000 in FY 04), rather than directly to the Commission. The balance of funding is derived from general revenue fund dollars. Medicaid claims are made for administrative case management activities that are eligible for reimbursement through the federal financial participation (FFP) program. (This Medicaid claims program should be contrasted with targeted case management, which seems to be used by Ohio, upon whose practice Illinois based their pursuit of Medicaid funding. Through contacts with the National Guardianship Association (NGA), OSG received information that led to the pursuit of Medicaid funds to offset costs of guardianship. The cost per IP for FY 2003 was $672.00 [this only accounts for $3.6 million of budget].)

Procedures

Approximately four years ago, OSG centralized its intake process. OSG processes approximately 5,700 public service inquiries to the Commission per year (which has a staff of four), of which 2,600 are related to OSG services. Of the 2,600, approximately 500 become guardianship cases. A temporary or emergency guardianship can take from one to five days from referral to appointment. A plenary guardianship usually occurs within 30 days of a call. There are exceptions. For example, transitioning a minor IP to adult guardianship generally takes one year, but some may take as long as two and half years.

In general, OSG does not petition for itself as guardian. Most cases arise from hospitals and long-term care facilities. In many cases, the OSG is appointed temporary guardian for a person in need of medical treatment for which he or she cannot consent and is appointed temporary guardian specifically to cover the medical procedure. Sixty days later, OSG is appointed plenary guardian. Occasionally, the Attorney General of the State of Illinois will petition on behalf of the state department of human services, generally for persons who are institutionalized in a state-operated facility for persons with developmental disabilities or mental illnesses.

Interaction between the Office of the Public Guardian (OPG) and OSG is primarily limited to either an IP of the OPG having spent down to the point that his or her estate is worth less than $25,000, or an OSG IP who has come into a great deal of money. In a limited number of cases, the OSG and OPG may work in tandem: a parent with a sizable estate is served by OPG, while the adult child, whose estate is negligible, is served by OSG.

OSG does not serve as the agent under a power of attorney. It does serve as a representative payee for IPs under the program. Most live in supervised facilities, and the facilities may serve as representative payees. OSG does not assume a conflict of interest in such cases. Rather, it monitors for abuse, but does not assume that it will occur.

The events that trigger a guardianship include an individual's need for medical procedures or exploitation and poverty. Although the unmet need was undetermined, the staff indicated that there was a population of approximately 100,000 institutionalized adults in Illinois. OSG serves approximately 3,000 of these adults.

Staffing and Training

OSG has 48 caseworkers, 95 percent of whom are Registered Guardians certified by the Center for Guardianship Certification (CGC). The Office also supports staff, attorneys, and managers for a total staff of 73 full-time equivalent (FTE) employees. The number of IPs for FY 2003 was 5,383, for an IP-to-guardian ratio of 77:1. In terms of staff members who have actual IP contact, the ratios are 132:1 for person-only guardianship cases and 31:1 for estate cases.

In an attempt to address the issue of inadequate staff numbers, OSG made a conscious decision that its staff should be extremely well trained. In support, Commission staff members provide periodic training sessions. The training given to new staff members is intense and includes a training manual and introduction to the policy and procedures manual. In addition, new staff members shadow existing staff for about two weeks. OSG staff members indicated that this mentoring aspect was particularly effective, as illustrated by the following:

> I think at the time, the best way for individuals to truly learn, at that time, was to have someone in the Commission take your hand, and they supported you. They would go to you and you would go to them.

OSG provides staff with at least 10 hours of continuing education units each year, which can be applied to recertification as Registered Guardians with CGC. There is also some cross-training among the three branches of the Commission. Six staff attorneys and 2 managing attorneys cover approximately 100 of 102 counties and the entire OSG caseload (approximately 5,500 persons).

OSG has about one-third minority staff members, reflecting the diverse population it serves. The Office has a staff that is proficient in Spanish, Polish, and other Eastern European dialects. There are also staff members who can sign to hearing-impaired individuals. Staff members are sensitive to religious and cultural issues surrounding end-of-life decision-making. OSG remains involved with IPs after death regarding burial, autopsies if necessary, and, in some cases, with financial matters.

Volunteers

The Human Rights Authority branch of the Commission consists exclusively of volunteers, but only a handful of volunteers have worked consistently for OSG. OSG is beginning a pilot program that uses volunteers, which is intended to address understaffing. According to a key informant:

> That's one of those "necessity is the mother of invention" alternatives. When it becomes more and more evident that you're just not going to get staff that you may wish for or the funding, I think it creates greater impetus to look around and think creatively and come up with things like that.

Incapacitated Persons

Placement, health care, and the withdrawal of life-sustaining treatments are decisions made on behalf of IPs. Withdrawing or foregoing life-sustaining treatment is based on the Illinois Health Care Surrogate Act. Prior to this Act, a guardian was required to go to court on every end-of-life decision. Since its passage, guardians have rarely been required to seek court approval for end-of-life decisions. Ironically, the Probate Act still requires the review and approval by a judge of any transaction involving realty, reflecting what some Illinois practitioners see as an anomaly in the law.

OSG staff members visit IPs living in unlicensed community placement situations and those who live at home on a monthly basis, with some on a weekly basis. IPs in facilities are visited once every three months as mandated. OSG attempts to include IPs in placement decisions by arranging a pre-placement visit to the facility to provide an opportunity to meet facility staff and residents. With medical decisions, there are cases where the IP is not really capable of giving input, and so OSG makes the decision using substituted judgment where possible, consistent with the decision-making standard in the Probate Act.

If placement means relocating to another county or geographic area, any remaining family members are notified. This illustrates another ironic situation in that the OSG is the guardian of last resort, which in many cases means that the IP is "abandoned, abused or maligned in some way by family, but the OSG will, despite suspicions, bend over backwards to accommodate [the] interests of other persons"

(John Wank, personal communication). Key informants said that the greatest amount of contact with family occurs upon the IP's death, with contact concerning any residual estate.

Wards of the OSG live in many different settings in the community, such as in nursing homes, assisted living facilities, and other facilities. One respondent said, "I think our wards live in 1,600 different places," to which another respondent replied, "That's quite an adjustment for us. Twenty years ago, all of our wards could have been found in about 16 sites: state institution sites."

Every IP must be visited at least four times each year. This event is checked by the external audit, and OSG is 99 percent compliant. OSG staff members indicated that IPs placed in unlicensed community placements are visited at least monthly, which ensures an ongoing record of progress, medication compliance, and assessment. One respondent observed that this is because "we don't have the benefit of other staff and facilities to assist us to gather information, trying to assess how a particular person is doing."

Rural and Urban Differences

Not surprisingly, the differences between rural and urban guardianship are immense. In the Chicago metropolitan area, OSG has approximately 3,000 IPs. In other regions, 500 IPs are spread out over 14 counties, requiring overnight visits in order to meet the state mandate of quarterly visits. One important consideration is the expertise of the judiciary involved in guardianship. In the Chicago area, there may be five or six judges with whom the OSG interacts on a regular basis, while in a rural area, the judge is more likely to be a generalist who may see one or two guardianship cases in the course of an entire year.

IP Interview

Investigators interviewed one IP by telephone; a 68-year-old man served by both OPG and OSG, the latter of which was utilized when his funds declined due to exploitation. The gentleman had been under a guardian's care for over 15 years. He lived in Chicago in a special apartment for older adults. At the time of the interview, he was planning on going to court to discuss the possibility of having some of his rights restored, about which he seemed uncertain. He said that he had not always received his money from the public guardian in a timely fashion.

OFFICE OF THE PUBLIC GUARDIAN, COOK COUNTY, ILLINOIS

Schmidt and colleagues interviewed Patrick Murphy over 25 years ago. Mr. Murphy had just begun in the Cook County Office of Public Guardian (OPG), which was awash in scandal from the previous administration. At that time, Mr. Murphy had a staff of three people. A highly visible attorney both in

Illinois and nationally, Mr. Murphy had, at the time of the present interview, a staff of over 300. He knew the staffers he introduced us to by name and had personal remarks to make to most of them. Robert Harris, who later replaced Mr. Murphy (who received a judgeship), was also interviewed, as well as a social worker with the program.

OPG in Cook County serves approximately 650 older IPs and 12,000 children. The office has three divisions: a Juvenile Division, a Domestic Relations Division, and a Disabled Adults Division. Approximately 100 older IPs die each year. About 40 percent of OPG IPs were living in the community, with 25 percent having been exploited prior to service by OPG. Of those, an agent under a power of attorney exploited 90 percent. Mr. Murphy reported that he had lost only one exploitation case in 25 years.

To qualify for the program, disabled adult IPs must have an estate of over $25,000, although no one could explain why this designation separated the OSG and the OPG. The OPG in Cook Country is an attorney-run program with an annual budget of approximately 16 million dollars. The office assesses hourly fees for its work, which are collected from the IPs' estates.

Mr. Murphy is highly regarded for his excellent staff of attorneys, whom he recruits from law schools all over the country. Slightly less than 80 percent of his staff attorneys are women. Office staff members include employees fluent in American Sign Language, Polish, and Spanish. The Office boasted approximately 17 percent minority attorney hires, the highest in any office in the state. Two hallmarks of Mr. Murphy's success are his ability to leverage funds and to focus media attention on guardianship. By his own admission, he regards his work as a vocation, with his special contribution being advocacy.

The features of OPG include a unit that hires independent contractors and agencies to assist with IP needs. The Office receives numerous referrals from elder abuse services. Staff meetings are held on each case. Assessments, care plans, and time logs are kept for each IP, all of whom are visited monthly and consulted with regarding their own decision making. Contact sheets are completed each time an IP is visited. Efforts are made to place IPs of various racial and ethnic groups in facilities with a special emphasis on that population. Murphy described appropriate placement as representing 95 percent of IP success. IPs with mental illnesses are an increasing part of the OPG caseload and a function of the mental health system. Annual reports and yearly accountings are filed for each IP, and an annual report is also filed for the entire OPG office.

The office petitions for guardianship. Murphy did not regard this as a problem, stressing that this system works well. He suggested that there is a "philosophy to make the system more complex" in order to maximize dollars for all of the entities involved. In his view, the system is best kept simple so that it poses the least possible expense to IPs.

An exceptional feature of the office is the pooled trust, which allows IPs' public benefits to be maximized. This payback trust allows the supplementation of dollars for IPs as needed. Mr. Murphy characterized the trust as a form of Medicaid planning.

By his own admission, perhaps the greatest threat to the OPG in Cook County was the loss of Patrick Murphy himself. In late October 2004, a successor had not been named. Since then, Robert Harris, who worked with Mr. Murphy for 13 years, was named to the position. As a judge, Mr. Murphy hoped to begin the nation's first guardianship court.

Judges and Court Administrators

Composition. Probate judges in Cook County represented individuals with no fewer than 10 years on the bench and some with more than 28 years (the Presiding Judge of the Probate Division). Cook County does not have a specific probate court, but it does include a probate division. According to the judges, at least two OPG attorneys were in their courts on behalf of clients. They saw the OSG less frequently but stated that those cases were also handled with commitment and sensitivity. On any given day, the judges reported that 25 percent of their cases emanated from the public guardian, as opposed to the 75 percent of cases dealing with private guardianship matters. The judges did not regard the public guardians' ability to petition as guardians as problematic and estimated that the public guardians' appointments originated from the overwhelming majority of their own petitions. Judges are required by statute to file a written finding to appoint a petitioner as guardian. Each judge reported personally reading guardians' annual reports. A computer system flags the reports due to the courts. Guardianship cases are randomly assigned to the judges in the probate division.

Cases. Most guardianships arise in court due to changes in an individual's lifestyle, with a high percentage arising because of the need for nursing home placement. Once a public guardian is appointed, it is not necessary to return to the court to authorize a change in nursing home placement. The Health Care Surrogate Act removed the need for many emergency hearings for a guardian. The Act covers all emergency medical issues, including end-of-life decision making, and equips statutorily identified surrogates with legal authorization to consent to or forego medical decisions for persons considered incapacitated. One result of the Act is that guardianship petitions have declined.

In most cases, a GAL is appointed to each case, though the requirement for a GAL can be waived if the appointment is deemed unnecessary. The judges stressed the importance of having a good GAL who performs his or her job thoroughly. For example, a good GAL should investigate the least restrictive alternatives possible for the alleged incapacitated person. The GAL offers a finding in writing if a less restrictive alternative is unavailable.

Although the judges noted their wish to have limited guardianships where possible, they estimated that the highest percentage of limited guardianships granted

would not exceed 20 percent. Fewer limited guardianships than plenary guardianships were contested. Limited orders usually concerned driving and voting
privileges. According to one judge, more limited guardianships are presented for
elderly people, with the scope of the guardianship growing with an individual's
needs. This judge uses a technique by which he vests limited guardianships with
full powers, although the guardian must seek the specific authority to use them.
The guardian is given a sliding power to employ as an IP's situation worsens, subject to the judge's specifications. This particular judge reported using this strategy
successfully for over eight years.

The judges reported that the monitoring of public and private guardianship
cases is the same, and they did not hold the opinion that public guardians were
any better or worse than private guardians. They did acknowledge that problems
arise when guardians are inexperienced with filing reports. The judges are educated on guardianship in general at judicial educational sessions, but there are
few, if any, distinctions made regarding public and private guardians. The judges
emphasized that there was one guardianship statute. They did not believe that
there should be separate laws for each.

Complaints. When there are complaints against guardians, judges act on them.
The judges are not allowed to participate in efforts to help secure funds for the
public guardianship programs. They maintained that lack of funds is not a defense
for inadequate service being provided to the IPs.

Appraisal. The judges said that Patrick Murphy "has an ability to hire great
people." They regarded OPG employees as consistent and well-trained attorneys.
In spite of the many attorneys and staff members, the judges emphasized that
OPG needs more staff members. They believed that the OSG also needed more
staff and funding and that securing additional funding was far more difficult for
OSG because it could not use the IP's assets to offset costs for IP needs as the
OPG could.

Adult Protective Services

Composition. APS officials, known as elder abuse specialists (EAS), work with
the Illinois Department on Aging. Participants brought a wide range of experience
with them, from relatively new employees to highly seasoned ones. The EAS
provide the bulk of referrals to both the OPG and OSG. They reported seeking
guardianship in approximately 45 percent of cases. The Illinois Department on
Aging earmarked funds out of General Revenue funds to pay attorneys to petition
in some guardianship cases. The Department could also pay for guardians *ad
litem*. EAS stressed the importance of training for GALs, an important link in
establishing the guardianship correctly.

Guardianship cases arose from various situations, including financial exploitation, the inability of a caregiver to provide adequate care, and self-neglect. Once

a public guardian is appointed, the EAS rarely follows up, usually because the risk for the client drops to an acceptable level. The EAS remains involved in situations in which the family tries to sabotage the public guardian. The EAS conduct screening prior to a guardianship, using a standardized assessment instrument that includes a risk-assessment component.

Coordination with other entities. EAS have undergone cross training with OSG and OPG. Both OPG and OSG appeared to have slow responses to EAS referrals. Specialists stressed the importance of maintaining a paper trail on the need of the at-risk individual. They emphasized that there is a gap in services for individuals who need public guardians, but could be maintained in the community. They emphasized that nursing home placement was typically automatic for OSG IPs.

Appraisal. Although the Cook County OPG generally received strong endorsements, such was not the case for other counties in Illinois, where the OPG was not necessarily responsive to the elder abuse referrals. At least one participant cited problems working with OSG, stating that it was difficult to get OSG to take a case, with some workers being more helpful than others. This participant stressed that a consistent set of standards regarding when cases are accepted by OSG would be very helpful, as case acceptance seemed ill-defined and capricious. There was a propensity for high-risk cases to languish, though less often with OPG, because there did not appear to be a time frame for action.

Strength, weaknesses, opportunities, threats. A reported strength of the public guardianship programs, specifically OPG, was that IPs are kept in the community if possible. One drawback of the guardianship programs, specifically OSG, was that IPs are not seen enough and little contact is made with the EAS once OSG takes a case. Still, EAS reports using the public guardianship programs as a tool for the provision of protective services.

Aging and Disability Advocates

Composition. Participants included representatives from the Department on Aging, Equip for Equality, Inc. (the designated Protection and Advocacy provider in Illinois), and the Illinois Protection and Advocacy Group, a nonprofit guardianship agency, as well as a member of the Illinois Guardianship Association.

Appraisal. Participants reported unevenness in the systems. They indicated that in some counties, the local OPG does not even know the IPs it is serving and that OSG frequently provided this information to OPG. In some instances, county public guardian (OPG) administrators outside of Cook County appeared to understand the financial side of guardianship, but were strikingly ignorant regarding the personal aspects. Due to insufficient funding and staffing, OSG was not seeing its IPs frequently enough. Participants stressed that the guardianship system was set up as a money system and that the courts emphasize the money trail versus the maintenance of the individual, noting that the annual personal statement on the IP is optional. Some participants acknowledged that some courts had not reviewed IPs' records in over 20 years.

The participants indicated that OSG does not generally petition for removal when individuals may no longer need a guardian. They noted that for removal, an IP must work though Equip for Equality. Although the OSG could perform this function, it does not regularly do so due to a lack of funds.

OPG and OSG were apparently exempt under statute from having to consult the court about moving an IP. The ability to move IPs as needed, but without notification, made keeping track of IPs extremely difficult. Participants reported that in one instance, OSG pulled IPs from a poorly run facility, but did not make efforts to petition for other people living there who may also have needed a guardian. One place where guardians are needed, but inadequately provided, is in nursing homes. Though nursing homes can seek guardians, most do not unless residents are discharged to a hospital. In rare instances, a public health agency or a long-term care ombudsman may petition. Area agencies on aging sometimes pay for the drafting of guardianship petitions by legal services, naming the nursing home administrator as the petitioner. In many of these instances, OSG becomes the guardian.

Both OPG and OSG are also exempted from some reporting requirements, which are described by the statute. Though it may free up the offices to perform other tasks, participants regarded this exemption negatively. The two systems were viewed as divergent and lacking in uniformity, despite statutory requirements.

Participants reported that the Department on Aging had received funds for a pilot project to assist older parents caring for children with developmental disabilities. They noted that this is a growing group of people in need of guardianship services. Participants remarked that financial problems often drew them into the system, which is also true for older people. Exploitation by unchecked powers of attorney was seen as increasing in frequency.

Participants did not regard the ability of the public guardian to petition as problematic. A striking comment was that "No one rocks the boat if everyone gets a piece of the action." Few limited guardianships were awarded—according to this group, only about 1 percent of all cases. Representative payees are used in conjunction with guardianships by OSG.

Strengths, weaknesses, opportunities, threats. The reported strengths of the public guardianship program (OSG) are its excellent leadership and compassionate and dedicated staff. Nearly all OSG staffers are Registered Guardians with the Center for Guardianship Certification (CGC). Participants noted that both OSG and OPG maintain good relationships with the judges, who apparently respect the actions of the staff.

The performance of local OPG offices outside of Cook County was regarded as highly uneven across the state. Problems included high caseloads and the warehousing of IPs in facilities, both of which were attributed to inadequate funding. One problem mentioned was that some public guardians developed relationships with nursing home administrators to encourage IP placement at a certain facility.

Participants stressed that the lack of interest by OSG in filing pleadings to restore capacity was surprising, given that doing so would result in lower caseloads and would provide freedoms to IPs. Participants said that the main reason for not doing so was a lack of funds. Another problem with restoration is the lack of baseline assessment at the time of appointment and the need for continuous assessment from that point forward. Participants also described a lack of reporting by the public guardianship staff, which contributed to a lack of involvement in IPs' cases by physicians and attorneys. One participant described the inadequate completion of forms as "rather scandalous."

In a misuse of power and a misunderstanding of the Mental Health Code, OPG and OSG placed IPs in a locked facility without going through the courts. This may be because the public guardianship programs did not interpret the regulations as being applicable to them, even though such actions are prohibited by statute. Participants perceived an unwillingness on the part of the public guardianship programs to go though mental health court and stressed that the programs continue to place IPs in this manner because they are rarely, if ever, held accountable. OSG and other public guardians maintain that such placements were routinely authorized by probate courts applying adult guardianship statutes and case law, but the practice was rejected when challenged by Equip for Equality in a mental health cause of action. OSG believes the dispute illustrates the bifurcated nature of addressing issues related to incapacity (Probate Act) and mental illness (Mental Health and Developmental Disabilities Act.) After being challenged by Equip for Equality, OSG now complies with the law.

Another problem, cited with OSG in particular, was the lack of integration of persons with disabilities into the community. Participants noted a propensity by OSG to warehouse IPs in one large facility that did not necessarily meet the needs of IPs. An *Olmstead* challenge to OSG was pending. More than one participant spoke of open efforts to place mentally ill persons sent from a psychiatric hospital in a specific facility. IPs were apparently given few options in placement decisions. Part of the problem was the relationship of the psychiatrist to the Institution for Mental Disease (a designation applied by the Illinois Department of Public Health for facilities that specialize in the treatment of persons with mental illnesses). When recommending placement, psychiatrists not only suggested the level of care required, but also specified the facility.

Participants believed that public education on OSG represented a true opportunity. They stressed that the public was much more familiar with OPG, and, in particular, with the actions of OPG in Cook County. The resignation of Patrick Murphy was regarded as the ultimate threat to the OPG.

Attorneys

Composition. Attorneys who participated in the site visit focus group worked with both the OSG and the OPG and specialized in GAL activities, as well as in estate planning.

Cases. For the county program, particularly Cook County, OPG acts as petitioner, which is not true of OSG. Downstate, hospitals have attorneys on retainer who act as petitioners in the event that a hospitalized patient needs a guardian. In addition, the Center for Prevention of Abuse (in effect, APS) may act as petitioner. Attorneys perceived that OSG's statewide policy is that they do not petition. Some attorneys serve in several roles (e.g., GAL), representing petitioners filing for guardianship, independent petitioners on behalf of persons in need of guardianship, and respondents opposing guardianship. Attorneys indicated that though the OSG is the guardian of last resort, and therefore cannot refuse any guardianship case, it, in fact, often finds ways to do so.

One legal group, The Center for Disability and Elder Law, is contacted to serve as petitioning attorney when a nursing home realizes that a patient who has been in the facility for "five, ten, fifteen years, and has never had a visitor, and then for some reason, the nursing home gets nervous and realizes that they shouldn't be making . . . at least . . . end-of-life decisions for those people," despite the fact that the nursing home has been making medical decisions for these residents for their entire stay. Clients are also isolated elders, or socially isolated persons with disabilities who are exploited by third parties and are referred by clergy, police, or social workers. Other sources of clients include hospitals, nursing homes, and local elder abuse agencies.

In some cases, a GAL is appointed. One attorney insisted that in every case involving OPG in Cook County, a GAL is appointed. Cases involving OSG in the Chicago area often do not involve a GAL. Participants noted that GALs are only mandated to read the prospective incapacitated person his or her rights and to solicit his or her opinion about being adjudicated as an IP.

Appraisal. Participants perceived that guardianship oversight was spotty. In one case, a guardian had been dead for two years, and the court never requested a report. Another case had been open for 10 years, but a report had never been filed. It is important to note that the attorneys did not see evidence of any difference between private and public guardianship cases: in all cases, reporting was deficient. This appears to be changing due to recently implemented computerized monitoring. Annual reports to the court are more likely in cases where there is an estate, and in the Cook County program, the asset report includes information on the status of the IP. Downstate, attorneys representing private guardians are fairly good about reporting. If there are limited assets, the court may require less frequent reporting (i.e., once every two to three years, rather than annually).

Attorneys were equivocal regarding the unmet need for guardians. Some pointed out that people who are mentally ill are not well served by guardianship. Others just as adamantly indicated that the unmet need is huge. The difference (not surprisingly) appears to rest on whether or not the individual has assets. They also pointed out that to the best of their knowledge, there is no study of unmet need in Illinois.

Strengths, weaknesses, opportunities, threats. Participants observed that Cook County OPG has good attorneys and can step in with services very quickly. OPG has robust internal resources and links with external networks. Cook County OPG is at the forefront nationally: it advances the quality of life of the IPs while identifying and maintaining resources. OPG tries to keep people in the community.

Participants perceived that the OSG uses a cookie-cutter approach. They stressed that OSG serves IPs without assets and with very limited resources and prohibitively high caseloads. Thus, OSG cannot focus on the needs of individual IPs as extensively as the OPG.

Outside of Cook County, they perceived that OPG is concerned about making money. If a client is under the guardianship of the OPG and resources are depleted, the IP may be appointed to the OSG.

Summary and Comments

Illinois has two systems of public guardianship operating in the same state: (1) The Office of State Guardian (OSG) is an independent state office that has statewide coverage and serves indigent IPs with estates of $25,000 or less; and (2) The other system, OPG, operates at the county level and serves IPs with estates of $25,000 or more. Inquiries by several focus groups and individual interviews about the distinction regarding dollar amounts yielded no information about why the numbers are set the way they are or whether the amounts should be reconsidered.

The OSG did not exist when Schmidt and his colleagues studied public guardianship. The OSG serves approximately 5,500 IPs. The Office maintained that guardians of person and property had a 77:1 ratio, whereas the guardians of the property had only a 31:1 ratio. The Office can petition for itself, although it rarely does so. OSG may also serve as the representative payee for its own IPs, but only if it also serves as the guardian of both person and property. OSG compensates for its high caseload numbers by providing extensive staff training, including having nearly all staff tested as Registered Guardians with CGC. Cross training with other entities was notable. Staff members came from a wide variety of disciplines, predominately social work and law. Visits to IPs were made once every three months or less.

The Cook County OPG was included in the Schmidt study 25 years ago. At that time, director Patrick Murphy had just arrived to a staff of three and a cloud of criminal activity perpetrated by his predecessor, who had been removed from office. The current investigators again interviewed Mr. Murphy, along with two other staff members. Ironically, he was preparing to leave his position after 25 years to assume a judgeship. OPG serves both younger people and older adults, with children predominating in the caseload. OPG petitions for itself, and Mr. Murphy did not regard that ability as a conflict of interest, but rather, as increasing expediency and efficiency so that the estates of IPs are not meted out to interested parties. Murphy has expanded his office staff to more than 300 people, who are generally attorneys, and gained both national and international attention, sometimes through aggressive and high-profile litigation.

Focus group participants emphasized that OSG serves far too many IPs with far too few resources and complained that some areas do not accept IPs unless they will be living in institutions. They stressed that IPs were not given enough personal attention because of inadequate staffing and funding, and that account-ability suffered. They indicated that OSG was not as responsive to requests for assistance as they thought would be appropriate. They said that at times, IPs were inappropriately placed by both OSG and OPG in a locked facility without court approval because they knew they would not be held accountable, even though such actions require court approval.

Overall, participants had fewer comments about the Cook County OPG, al-though one individual who wrote in after the interviews raised some issues over delays in handling an end-of-life case. The main concern was what would happen after Patrick Murphy left the office. Even Murphy expressed concern, although he had been grooming successors, one of whom, Robert Harris, succeeded him in the spring of 2005. Less clear but of clear concern was how county OPG pro-grams served the rest of the state. Based on comments from focus group partici-pants, OPG in other counties is highly uneven and has problems similar to those of OSG, specifically inadequate staffing and funding.

THE LOS ANGELES COUNTY, CALIFORNIA, PUBLIC GUARDIAN

In November 2005, the *Los Angeles Times* published a four-part series on guardianship, with the final part of the report focusing specifically on public guardianship. The article, "For Most Vulnerable, a Promise Abandoned," stressed that the Los Angeles County Public Guardian (LAPG) had been stripped of its funding for more than a decade, and, because of such an overwhelming and chronic lack of funds, turned many needy citizens away from the state guardian of last resort. The article cited a rejection rate higher than four out of five older adults and alleged that, since 1998, at least 660 older adults had died waiting for the public guardian office to determine if it could help them. In 2002 alone, more than 330 people were reported as being on the LAPG's waiting list. For younger vulnerable adults, the agency accepted approximately 16 percent of over 4,000 requests from 1998–2003.

To stem crushing inadequacies in funding, the LAPG attempted to reduce its fiscal hemorrhaging by using such tactics as: keeping the difference between the interest rate it received on clients' cases and the lower, state-authorized rate; charging over $70 an hour for work, collecting fees from qualified Medi-Cal IPs (which results in more visits to the IP than non-Medi-Cal IPs); and making fiscal arrangements with private hospitals to prioritize their patients for investigation and acceptance into the public guardian program.

Statutory Authorization

The LAPG program is established statutorily under California Government Code §§27430 through 27436; California Probate Code §§2920 through 2944, and California Welfare and Institutions Code §5354.5. (Under California law, the term "conservatorship" means the guardianship of the person and/or property of an adult, whereas the term "guardianship" refers to minors. However, this book uses the more generic term "guardianship" for court appointments concerning adults.)

Recent Litigation

Although the LAPG was not the subject of recent litigation, neighboring counties were, including suits against the public guardian in San Joaquin, Riverside (Orange), and Amador counties.

Organization and History

In California, public guardianship programs are located in county government, as authorized by the California government code. Public guardians are county-appointed positions. Each county may name a public guardian. The public guardian serves two target populations: older or dependent persons and persons of all ages with mental illness who are determined "gravely disabled" by a court. The public guardian typically serves the older or dependent adult population, while the public conservator usually serves the mentally ill population, including minors.

Each county has a distinct program that has evolved as a result of the organizational design of the public guardian office and local court rules. Each county also interprets the areas of statutory code differently. No state office of the public guardian exists in California. Most county public guardians are members of the State Association of Public Administrators/Public Guardians/Public Conservators and participate in regional meetings and bi-annual training conferences. Regional meetings are designed to provide trainings and problem-solving forums.

Typically, the public guardian/conservator is housed in one office. However, some counties divide the related functions between two offices. The office of the public guardian is either an independent office or is combined with other county functions. For example, a common organizational function combines the public guardian with the public administrator. The public administrator handles decedent estates when no family members are available or willing to come forward. In other counties, the public guardian is combined with the office on aging, social services, or mental health.

Public guardianship was authorized in Los Angeles County in 1945. The LAPG was separated from the public administrator's office in 1987, and placed under the jurisdiction of the Los Angeles County Department of Mental Health. The public administrator's office was placed under the jurisdiction of the county treasurer and tax collector. When the public guardian office was divided, all of the estate support functions were placed with the treasurer and tax collector, and the public guardian was required to contract for estate services with the treasurer and tax collector.

In this study of the LAPG (conducted during fall 2004 and winter 2005, followed by a site visit in January 2005), the primary contact was Mr. Christopher Fierro, the Deputy Director of the Office of the Public Guardian, who has direct oversight of the LAPG. Mr. Fierro, who began his work at the agency in 1975 as an entry-level caseworker, provides planning, direction, and control over the functions of the office. He provides direct supervision for two division chiefs and a mental health coordinator. Each division chief has supervising deputy public guardians who, in turn, provide direct supervision for deputy public guardians. Mr. Fierro attempts to have a ratio of one supervisor for every five deputy public guardians.

Probate Conservatorships

The LAPG receives referrals from community members, agencies, and hospitals asking the public guardian to investigate the appropriateness of an individual for guardianship. The public guardian may conduct an investigation to determine if the AIP qualifies for a conservatorship pursuant to California Probate Code §1800 et seq. The LAPG is the guardian of last resort. If the public guardian determines that a case is appropriate for intervention, the public guardian files a petition for appointment (the county attorney draws up the petition on behalf of the public guardian). A superior court investigator reviews each petition to determine if the proposed conservatee agrees with or opposes the conservatorship. Fifteen days' notice is required if the petition is mailed, and 10 are required if it is delivered via personal service.

If there is no objection, the public guardian is appointed. If the AIP objects to the guardianship or the court investigator so recommends, the court appoints an attorney for the client who will (a) consent to the appointment, (b) set the matter for a court trial, or (c) set the matter for a jury trial. The standard of proof is clear and convincing evidence. The client has a right to a jury trial.

Lanterman-Petris-Short Conservatorships

Lanterman-Petris-Short (LPS) conservatorships are part of the LAPG's responsibility and are reserved for clients who require involuntary psychiatric treatment. Under an LPS conservatorship, a client is typically involuntarily hospitalized (some are in jail) for three days, based upon a request for evaluation by a mental health professional or police officer. Such an evaluation is referred to as a 5150 evaluation after the applicable welfare and institutions code section. A client is involuntarily hospitalized for three days for the following conditions: (a) danger to self, (b) danger to others, or (c) gravely disabled, meaning that as a result of a mental disorder, a person is unable to provide for his or her own food, clothing, or shelter. In this case, the client is also not willing or able to accept treatment voluntarily and is unable to accept assistance from third parties. Within the three days, physicians must evaluate the client. Should a treating physician determine that the client is either a danger to herself, a danger to others, or gravely disabled, an additional 14 days of hospitalization is possible. During the 14-day period, the client may file a writ of habeas corpus requesting release from an acute psychiatric hospital.

The 14-day period is regarded as a certification period. If the treating physician determines that the client remains gravely disabled, the doctor may complete a declaration requesting LPS conservatorship, including the appointment of a temporary conservator. This application is sent to the public guardian. If the doctor's declaration is legally sufficient and the county mental health director approves the hospital as a designated LPS facility, then the public guardian will advise legal counsel to petition for LPS temporary conservatorship. Should a judge rule that the petition is sufficient, the public guardian is appointed as the temporary conservator. At the same time, a petition for general conservatorship is filed. During the 30 days of temporary guardianship, the public guardian conducts an intensive court investigation to determine if the AIP is still gravely disabled. If so, a recommendation for permanent LPS conservatorship is made, and the court investigator recommends the appointment of a family member, friend, or the public guardian. Approximately 60 percent of the cases result in the appointment of the public guardian.

An attorney, usually a public defender, represents the AIP at the hearing. The AIP may consent to the appointment or oppose it. If the AIP consents, a conservator is appointed. If he or she is in opposition, the AIP has the right to a court hearing or jury trial. The standard of proof is beyond a reasonable doubt.

LPS conservatorships are for one year only and are subject to re-evaluation by two physicians, who may recommend the extension of the conservatorship for another year. Clients have a right to a re-hearing on the status of the conservatorship once every six months, as well as a right to a placement hearing every six months.

The Application of 1981 Criteria

Adequate Funding and Staffing

The LPS program is funded by state mental health realignment funds, conservatorship fees, and targeted case management (TCM) funds provided through the Medi-Cal program. Conservatorship fees and TCM fund the probate program. Funds for LPS and probate conservatorship programs are awarded on an encounter basis, meaning that the encounter costs are based on cost records. Targeted case management is generally restricted to persons living in board and care facilities (some exceptions include clients in hospitals who are within 30 days of discharge). Services include assessment, service plan development, linkages and consulting, accessing services, periodic review of cases, and crisis assistance planning.

Unlike LPS funding, probate conservatorship services are provided by contract. These contracts are held between the public guardian and (a) the Hospital Association of Southern California, (b) selected county hospitals vis-à-vis the LA County health department, and (c) APS. Unlike in many other counties in California, the LAPG does not receive any funds from the county general fund.

The annual budget for the office is $9.9 million, including salaries, benefits, attorney costs, supplies, and other administrative costs. Mr. Fierro said that it would take an additional $20 million in funds to ensure adequate public guardian program support. For a 1:20 ratio of full-time equivalent paid professional staff to IPs, an additional $50 million for the budget was required.

For FY 2003–2004, the program spent $1,113 to complete a probate investigation and $1,384 for each LPS investigation. The office spent $1,897 per annum to maintain a probate conservatorship and $1,433 to maintain an LPS conservatorship. The office tracked no cost savings to clients.

The program had 90 full-time equivalent (FTE) professional staff on its payroll, including support staff. On average, a FTE paid professional staff member spent 16 hours working each case. The 16 hours does not include the amount of time contributed by support or contract staff. More than 16 hours is required during the first year of establishing the guardianship. A professional staff member is required to hold a bachelor's degree, and for FTE staff making binding decisions for IPs, there is a two-year experience requirement. A minimum of 16 hours is estimated for deputy staff to work on the case of an individual IP, with that figure exclusive of support of contract staff. The program no longer directly utilizes volunteers due to liability issues.

Collection of fees for services. The program has the authority to collect a fee or charge the incapacitated person for services. Each year, the office of the LAPG conducts a cost study in order to determine the cost of service. Based on the cost study, fees are determined and approved by the Los Angeles County Office of the Auditor Controller.

Three major losses have affected the program in the past 10 years, all of which were due to county budget reductions. First, the public guardian's medical consultation team was disbanded. This team included one psychiatrist, a part-time physician, and two public health geriatric nurses to provide consultation and oversight when there were requests for surgery, unusual medical treatments or procedures, issuances of "no codes," and the removal of life support. Second, mental health department professionals, who provided assistance in placing clients living outside acute hospitals and long-term psychiatric care facilities into board and care facilities, were no longer available. The program was centralized and designed to assist the public guardian division. When the mental health department director de-centralized the office and services, the services were discontinued. Finally, TCM funding was reduced to exclude clients residing in skilled nursing facilities (SNFs). The Centers for Medicaid and Medicare Services recently requested that the state's Department of Health Services amend the state plan, jeopardizing all TCM revenue. Other priorities of the public health department have contributed to budget reductions for the LAPG.

Structure and Function

Conflict of interest—ability to petition. The program petitioned for legal incapacity 2,300 times in FY 2003. The program petitioned for itself as guardian 1,500 times in FY 2003.

Incapacitated Persons

The program was serving 3,400 IPs in March of 2004, and, for that year, it accepted 700 new IPs into the program. In FY 2003, based on a one-month analysis, the majority of IPs served came through referrals from a mental health facility (2,400 IPs), followed by hospitals (372), nursing homes (240), and APS (84). An interesting feature of the referrals is that contracts are held between the public guardian and (1) the Hospital Association of Southern California, (2) selected county hospitals through the county health department, and (3) APS. The contracts are designed to address cases that were not handled by the office or not handled quickly. The purpose of the arrangement was to expedite probate investigations and to have a dedicated staff member available to address cases referred by these sources.

For FY 2003, the program served as guardian for person and property for 4,200 people, serving 50 IPs solely as guardian of the person and 50 IPs solely as guardian of the property. In California, limited guardianship refers to clients who are developmentally disabled and served by regional centers. Of the population of IPs served, there were 2,322 men and 1,978 women, and of that breakdown, the program served 86 minors, 2,709 persons age 18–64, and 1,505 persons over 65. Of this group, approximately 2/3 (or 2,236) were white and 1,032 were black or African American. Other populations served included 344 Asians or Pacific Islanders and 43 Native Americans.

The program predominately serves IPs with mental illnesses (3,200), as well as 746 dual diagnosed people with substance abuse, 337 persons with Alzheimer's disease (AD), and 35 people with developmental disabilities. The vast majority (3,354) had annual incomes of $2,000 or less, and for FY 2003, 210 IPs died. The primary living setting of the IPs was nursing homes (1,720), followed by board and care homes (1,132), mental health facilities (674), those living at home (86), in group homes (43), and in jail (43). In FY 2003, 820 IPs were restored to legal capacity, and 650 had a family member appointed as conservator instead of the public guardian. The *Los Angeles Times* reported a guardian to IP ratio of 1:84 (average caseloads per deputy).

Adequacy of Criteria and Procedures

For each public guardianship IP, the following records are maintained:

1. Functional assessment (updated quarterly)
2. Care plan (updated quarterly)
3. Computerized time logs
4. Advance directives (only if the IP executed one prior to the guardianship)
5. Periodic report to the court
   a. Mental health conservatorships (annually)
   b. Probate conservatorships (at initial appointment, 14 months after the establishment of the conservatorship, and biannually thereafter)

6. Program review of wards' legal incapacity (quarterly)
7. Review of appropriateness of public guardian to serve in that capacity (quarterly)
8. Documentation regarding how and why decisions are made on behalf of each IP

Various reports are used to monitor different aspects of the program: (a) the internal control certification program, in which an assistant division chief reviews a percentage of each deputy's caseload each month, (b) an audit tool to evaluate each case, and (c) departmental risk management meetings.

The *Los Angeles Times* stated that the "agency has been consistently late in filing court reports showing how it handled IPs' money, often missing deadline by a year or more. As of August 2005, reports were overdue in 192 cases."

The office has a policy for DNR (do not resuscitate) and the withdrawal of life support.

Decision-making. Typically, a best-interests standard is used in decision making. The program was in the process of collecting additional information for staff members to use a substituted judgment standard (what the individual would have done if competent) when possible and appropriate. Court authorization is required to sell a conservatee's personal residence and stocks that are not traded over a recognized stock market.

Variations in LPS and probate conservatorships. In LPS cases, the court must authorize any surgery or medical treatment for which the conservatee lacks the capacity to authorize. In probate cases, if the conservator does not have exclusive medical authority to consent on behalf of the conservatee, the conservator must petition for authority to petition for surgery or other medical treatment where the client lacks the capacity to consent. For persons with a dementia diagnosis, California law gives the public guardian the power to place IPs in a locked facility and to consent to the administration of appropriate medications.

Outside Assessments of the Office

The local unmet need for public guardian services was deemed huge. Because the agency could not meet the need, most of the people who were interviewed admitted that the program was highly criticized by many agencies. One commentator stated, "I think the county abandoned the public guardian a long, long time ago in terms of probate in particular." Most acknowledged that the root of the negative view was due to the program's gross underfunding. Another commentator suggested that higher salaries were needed for the public guardians, and the same individual believed that Los Angeles County had a disproportionate number of persons needing public guardianship.

Outside commentators believed that the office sets case limits per month, which limited the number of AIPs that were either investigated or accepted. Many commentators considered the acceptance of AIPs into the program to be capricious, with one person in particular highlighting the need for the program to assess people in a systematic way, using standard protocols for accepting them. Tensions with several agencies were notable. As an example, APS was often confused regarding the nexus of the missions of the agencies: for APS to protect the safety of the client, and for the public guardian to protect the rights of the client.

One of the features of the office that was deemed cost-effective was the interdisciplinary team, which had been abandoned due to fiscal constraints. The interdisciplinary team was wired into available services, which expedited assistance to needy IPs.

Some commentators suggested separation of the LAPG from county mental health so that the agency could better advocate for itself, although at least one commentator viewed guardianship as house arrest. Conversely, one participant in the interviews suggested that guardianship could facilitate people seeking treatment compared to an involuntary commitment system.

Notable Features of the Office

The specter of the looming *Los Angeles Times* exposé created uncertainty for the office and its administration. Once the *Los Angeles Times* story was published, changes to California law that addressed all types of guardianship resulted. A major change to the office of the public guardian was that the county board of supervisors approved an additional 32 new positions for the probate conservatorship program, representing an increase of over 100 percent.

The LAPG has computerized records dating back to 1984. This allows an important before and after picture of IPs over time and presents the wherewithal to assess guardianship outcomes.

Concluding Assessment

Strengths

1. Committed and experienced staff.
2. 24/7 accessibility to service.
3. An internal computerized system that is utilized as a client database, for banking and/or accounting, and case documentation, specifically the Los Angeles Public Administrator/Public Guardian Information System (LAPIS).

Weaknesses

1. Severely inadequate budget.
2. Inordinately high caseloads.
3. Large numbers of retiring staff.
4. At the time of the site visit, an audit commissioned by the board of supervisors was underway. The audit reportedly[3] found that funds were so chronically short that the LAPG took up to six months to consider cases and turned down 84 percent of referrals. Staff supervise 75 to 90 cases apiece, twice as many as comparable agencies. Unlike most counties in California, Los Angeles County had allocated no funds to probate con-

servatorships since the early 1990s. The auditors recommended adding three employees, two to manage cases and one to investigate potential cases, at a cost of $201,021.

5. At the time of the site visit, Mr. Fierro was waiting for the release of press coverage on guardianship by the *Los Angeles Times*. As mentioned earlier, a four-part series on guardianship, with one part devoted exclusively to public guardianship, was released in fall 2005.

Opportunities

1. To bolster income, as well as to increase efficiencies to the IPs, the program was exploring the idea of serving as a representative payee for clients.
2. The program was also exploring serving an oversight function for private conservators.
3. The program stood to ingratiate itself in the public eye by conducting public education regarding surrogate decision making. The program could also potentially reduce the number of guardianships through educational efforts.

Threats

1. The chronically underfunded budget serves as a constant threat to the program's viability and integrity.
2. The privatization of this public function is another threat to the program.
3. Public scandals from programs in Amador and in San Joaquin tainted other public guardian programs in surrounding counties, including the LAPG.

An Assessment of Then and Now

When researchers studied the LAPG in late 1979, the agency had one of the largest offices in the state. In 2005, the LAPG did, in fact, have the heaviest caseload in the state. There were approximately 100 staff members in 1979, and 90 FTE paid professional staff in 2005. Caseloads were 105 per staff in 1979, and a reported 84 per deputy in 2005. The office was reported to have a history of unrest, and so it again appeared in 2005.

One recent improvement was that a LAPG career employee, Mr. Fierro, was running the office. This was not true in 1979, when a former journalist was running the office. Mr. Fierro reportedly had experience in all phases of the office over a long period of time (20+ years). He was a relatively new employee when the first study was conducted and remembered the original research.

As in 1979, the office was severely underfunded and understaffed, and in order to meet this lack of funding, the office had developed creative measures to prioritize clients. Although the reasons for this creativity can be understood, it is disconcerting to find an office employing measures that incentivize the investigation and acceptance of one class or cohort of IPs versus another. Indeed, the comment of one of the individuals interviewed was striking: "I think the county abandoned the public guardian a long, long time ago in terms of probate in particular."

Impressively, the office was able to provide statistics regarding the program, but it is surprising that more in-depth studies of the program are neither encouraged nor conducted.[4]

Some concerns remain regarding the following features of the LAPG:

1. The office can petition for its own IPs, which creates the potential for self-aggrandizement.
2. The mechanisms that allow the office to inappropriately prioritize investigation and the acceptance of clients and take fees for services are insupportable.
3. The collection of client fees for public guardian services creates conflicts of interests, including incentivizing both over- and underpetitioning.
4. Clients are not visited in a timely fashion, and reporting lags deadlines in a number of cases.
5. Staff-to-client ratios were too high in 1979, and have not declined appreciably in over 20 years.
6. There are inherent systemic differences in the LPS conservatorships and probate conservatorships that result in inequities for older IPs. As it stands, this arrangement appears ageist.
7. Computerized records, which present a wealth of potential evaluative information, are not being effectively utilized.
8. Although there are internal audits of the program and media press coverage, audits by persons knowledgeable in the area of public guardianship have not been conducted.
9. The agency should accumulate information on its cost savings for the county.
10. The 2005 county allocation of funding for more public guardian staff is endorsed. Qualified staff should be adequately recruited, trained, supported, and retained. The agency stands to lose a vast amount of institutional knowledge through retirements within the next five years.
11. The greatest concern is the significant underfunding of the LAPG and the unwillingness of the county board of supervisors to make it a funding priority. Such a lack of funding places scores of vulnerable California citizens at great risk for criminal victimization, institutionalization, and early death.

The Delaware Office of the Public Guardian

The Delaware Office of the Public Guardian (DOPG) was visited in September 2005. Robin Williams-Bruner, M.S.W., R.G., was appointed public guardian in 1993, after previously serving as deputy public guardian since 1990. Ms. Williams-Bruner was anticipating retiring from her position in 2006, and she did so. All of the interviewees characterized her tenure as Delaware's public guardian as excellent. Many people were concerned about her possible successor after her visible and unwavering dedication to the office. Of the many individuals interviewed in Delaware, it was significant that a state representative from the legislature was among the persons interested and available for interview about public guardianship in the state, something that did not occur in any other state that was visited.

Statutory Authorization

The office was established statutorily in 1974 due to the plight of elderly persons and other adults subject to abuse, neglect, or exploitation, and the loss of their ability to manage their personal or financial affairs. Statutory provision for the office is found under Delaware Code §§6-3991 through 3997. The program is operated statewide, with no regional or local public guardianship programs. By statute, the DOPG is mandated to provide public guardianship, trusteeship, and personal representation of decedents' estates to all citizens in the state who qualify. In practice, however, the DOPG rarely serves as a trustee or personal representative, absent an initial appointment as guardian.

Recent Litigation

None reported.

Fee-for-Service Guardianship Programs

In addition to the public guardian, and for persons with the ability to pay, Delaware has four fee-for-service guardianship programs. A former Delaware public guardian runs one of the four, the first established. The people interviewed said that there were more complaints about the fee-for-service programs than the DOPG. Commentators reported that there is little oversight of the fee-for-service agencies. There was some disagreement regarding which fee-for-service program is best equipped to handle specific problems with the guardianship (e.g., social work issues, medical issues). At least one commentator said that there are cases contracted to the fee programs for which the public guardian is more appropriate.

Another commentator acknowledged that the fee-for-service guardianship programs have grown up *ad hoc* and are not supervised to the extent that the

DOPG is. Fee-for-service guardianship programs are required to provide a report to the court once a year versus the biannual report requirement for the DOPG. The DOPG is also required to have an overall bond, whereas the fee-for-service guardians must have individual bonds.

One of the fee agencies mysteriously left the state, and the court had to divide up its IPs among the other agencies and the DOPG. According to Ms. Williams-Bruner, "It is my understanding that this fee-for-service agency was bought by Life Solutions, Inc. . . . Also in 2003, another fee-for-service agency, Adult Guardianship Services, Inc., went out of business, and all of their cases were transferred to DOPG—about 26 cases." One interviewee said, "I don't know what the status today is of private agency guardianship appointments in the state of Delaware, but they have certainly incurred some disfavor fairly recently in the courts." Some respondents stated that they would make sure, prior to petition, that the DOPG would obtain the guardianship over a fee-for-service agency.

Organization and History

Delaware's Office of the Public Guardian is a state agency under the Delaware judiciary. The agency is considered a non-judicial social service agency of the Delaware courts. The public guardian is generally regarded as being the same as any other guardian under Delaware law. The public guardian, appointed by the chancellor of the Court of Chancery, serves at the chancellor's pleasure and is considered the administrative head of the DOPG. At the time of the site visit, the staff consisted of the public guardian, deputy public guardian, three full-time senior social worker/case managers, a part-time senior social worker/case manager (vacant), an administrative officer, and a financial case manager. Referrals are received from all of the APS agencies, state and private long-term care facilities, hospitals, the courts, and private individuals. The DOPG is the guardian of last resort.

The agency is housed under the judicial branch of Delaware's government. Adult guardianship matters are heard in the Court of Chancery. This location is favorable in view of the potential conflict that could exist if the agency were housed with other social service agencies, such as the Department of Health and Social Services. However, given that the agency is small with a very specific mission, the DOPG is reportedly not always well understood by the court's administration and cannot adequately compete with the larger courts or agencies when vying for funding and administrative support. The agency's relationship with the Court of Chancery itself can present areas of conflict when the office is the petitioner to the court or is asked to serve as a neutral guardian in a contested matter. The courts have considered other alternatives for the location of the agency, including one suggestion to move it to the executive branch of government under the governor.

The Miller Trust

In its fiduciary role, the office administers "Miller Trusts," which are trusts used to qualify a Medicaid applicant with income that exceeds the Medicaid eligibility limit for long-term care assistance. Such a trust can be named as the recipient of the individual's income from a pension plan, Social Security, or other source. The office reported that it uses this type of income-only trust for the purpose of depositing an IP's income. The only part of the IP's income deposited into the trust is the monthly income that goes over the Medicaid income limit. Income paid into the trust monthly is paid out monthly for the purposes of the IP only, and cannot accrue in the account, as two months of income overage cannot remain in the trust. The funds are used for patient payments in a facility, including for personal needs allotments.

Guardian *Ad Litem*

In Delaware a GAL is appointed in every guardianship case and represents and/or advocates for the indigent person, and also serves as the eyes and ears of the court (i.e., the best interest standard). The court appoints a GAL from an established panel of attorneys. The court can appoint an attorney as a fact finder only, but, in practice, this rarely happens. The dual function of the GAL role in Delaware was reportedly creating confusion among state bar members. Commentators echoed the confusion and said changes or amendments to the role are under consideration. Though awareness of the problem exists, the state bar has not taken much action on it. None of the commentators knew of any instances in which the GAL became the guardian after serving as the GAL. This differed from the other states that were visited.

The Application of 1981 Criteria

Adequate Funding and Staffing

The agency receives 100 percent of its budget through state of Delaware appropriations. The budget for FY 2006 (July 1, 2005, through June 30, 2006) totaled $458,570. The following are the specific budget allocations:

Personnel	$427,500
Travel	$3,000
Contractual	$16,000
Supplies	$3,200
Special Need	$3,000
Special Need	$5,870 (rolls over year to year)

At the time of the 2004 survey, the budget was deemed inadequate. To make it adequate, approximately $160,000 in state funds was required to fund four additional paid FTE professionals. This amount was necessary to bring the FTE paid-professional-staff-to-IP ratio to 1:20. On average, caseloads reflected a ratio of approximately 55 IPs per staff member. According to one staff member, "In order to visit everybody every month, it can't happen at 1 to 65 [sic; staff to IP ratio experienced by this staff member]. So you're pretty much on an as-needed basis, and you make the best of the quarterly meetings you do have, or the annual meetings."

Another member of the DOPG stressed that the job of the public guardian (i.e., case manager) is completely different from that of any other state agency employee. "Our job title and state classification is the same as an individual doing financial eligibility for food stamps. And our job responsibilities [include] making . . . end-of-life decisions. I think the level of decisions that we make have far more reaching consequences and in 37 and 1/2 hours, with public assistance or eligibility or whatever, you do your job during that period of time. Our job extends well beyond that time. We're responsible 24 hours a day pretty much for our folks."

A bachelor's degree is required for a FTE paid professional staff member who makes binding decisions for IPs, as well as experience with providing social service case management. In 2004, the program employed seven FTE paid professional staff. The DOPG does not have the staff to devote to the development of a cadre of volunteers by overseeing recruitment, training, and monitoring. Ms. Williams-Bruner, the public guardian, regarded the development of a volunteer pool as an area that the state of Delaware could utilize to expand guardianship services while simultaneously retaining the quality of its service to the larger number of persons in need.

Collection of fees for services. The DOPG has the authority to collect an administrative fee approved by the court, but, in practice, it rarely does so. Fees are determined by an administrative fee schedule and have not been reviewed or revised for many years. Any funds that the office receives are returned to the general fund for the state of Delaware.

Structure and Function

Conflict of interest—ability to petition. The public guardian may petition for the appointment of the agency as guardian, who is recognized by the court as a *pro se* litigant in this case. If the petitioner for the appointment of the public guardian is a state agency, then the attorney general's office files the petition. If no other alternatives to the appointment of the state agency as guardian exist, then the case is assigned to the DOPG. The court requires that the office consent to act as guardian in those cases in which the DOPG is not the petitioner, as well as for those cases in which the office is the proposed guardian. The court generally notifies the office in advance of the appointment, if it has not been previously involved in the case. Generally, if the court requests that DOPG take a case, the office assumes the case. However, there are occasions when the office has suggested alternatives to its own appointment.

The public guardian can represent the office in petitioning for appointment as guardian and in matters involving the public guardian that come before the court. However, the Department of Justice assigns a deputy attorney general (DAG) to serve as counsel to the DOPG. The assignment for the DAG is part time, and the assigned DAG serves as counsel for several other state agencies and represents the state in other matters, including civil commitment hearings. In FY 2003, the office petitioned for the adjudication of legal incapacity 77 times and petitioned for the appointment of itself as guardian 77 times.

The present public guardian is not an attorney. She represents her agency and presents the petitions herself. The present public guardian requests counsel in the attorney general's office to represent her in difficult or contested matters. Although a DAG was appointed for that purpose in the past, the public guardian currently represents herself. In the latter years of her tenure as public guardian, she rarely represented herself in complicated, contested guardianship cases, but would routinely ask the DAG to enter her appearance on behalf of the DOPG.

Pertinent to this problem, one commentator suggested dividing the roles of the public guardian. It was suggested that a court investigator, as an arm of the court, but not the DOPG, should make a determination about the condition of the IP. The same person remarked that due to the DOPG's location in the court, if the public guardian did have a breach of its fiduciary duty (which had never occurred), then the court would be investigating and adjudicating itself.

Incapacitated Persons

For FY 2003, the office served 174 IPs. Of that number, 154 were women. The office served as guardian of the person only for 161 people, as guardian of the property only for 2 people, and as both guardian of the person and guardian of the property for 89 people. There were no limited guardianships reported. During that time period, two people were restored to legal capacity, and five were transferred to a private guardian. In FY 2003, 47 IPs died.

Referrals to the office in FY 2003 came from a variety of sources, with an equal number (21 each) emanating from the Court of Chancery and nursing homes (8 from private homes and 13 from state facilities). Other sources included hospitals (18 referrals) and APS (14 referrals).

The DOPG serves persons of all ages with mental retardation and developmental disabilities, the older adult population, and persons with mental illnesses. The social workers and/or case managers who act as guardian case managers are assigned based on their areas of knowledge, experience, and expertise. For instance, a case manager who came to the office with over 15 years of experience working with the Division of Developmental Disabilities Service (DDDS, formerly DMR) is almost exclusively assigned those persons with mental retardation and developmental disabilities diagnoses.

The staff standard for visiting IPs is monthly, but the DOPG is unable to comply due to large client-to-staff ratios. Thus, visits are conducted on an as-needed basis. Staff members attend quarterly care plan meetings for nursing home residents, which creates the opportunity for quarterly visits.

Considerations of cultural diversity are a part of the evaluation of need for service, decisions on behalf of the persons for whom the office is asked to serve, and interactions with family members and others who are also working with the IPs. Sensitivity to the IP's cultural perspective is reportedly paramount in office interactions and decision-making. The staff is encouraged to participate in cultural diversity training and in decision making. In case reviews and discussions, case managers are required to take a cultural perspective in analyzing a decision, a care plan, and/or a behavior, or an interaction with a family member or close friend.

Two IPs served by the DOPG were interviewed. Both were men working at a sheltered workshop, with working hours extending from 8:30 a.m.–3:00 p.m. At the time of the interview, one of the men was working a press machine. The IPs said that they both came to the attention of the public guardian through social services, but that they did not know how. Both were happy with the services they received and remarked that they were treated well. One IP said, ". . . you know, 'cause the public guardian is really doing a big favor [to us]. They really are."

The second IP emphasized this: "We could wind up as, I could wind up in the streets."

One of the men said that he and his male guardian get along very well and that if there are any problems, the IP is able to contact the guardian. The IP believed that his guardian knows him well. The IP was able to contact his guardian by cell phone when he needed to do so.

Both men reported that their health was good, although one man reported having elephantiasis and having to wear supportive stockings. One man said he had a girlfriend and enjoyed spending time with her on weekends. The other man was a devoted baseball fan and enjoyed watching games on television.

According to office staff, the new IPs are increasingly younger people in their forties and fifties, as well as children under the age of 18. A third of the caseload is comprised of people receiving services from DDDS. More frequently, IPs are people with drug addictions, HIV/AIDs, and histories of alcohol abuse. Oftentimes, the IPs are not receiving the benefits that they are entitled to and require, such as housing, programming, and other services. The public guardians are forced to work quickly to form linkages with various agencies in order to procure services to meet client needs.

Unmet need. To its credit, the DOPG participated in a study of need (2004) that was conducted by a graduate student seeking an M.S.W. and employed by the office. The study identified an increasing need for guardianship services and the changing profiles of the people in need of guardianship services (e.g., young adults aging out of children's homes). Many of the people interviewed stated that there is an unmet need for public guardian services, and this need is growing. This appeared to be substantiated by the office's periodic imposition of a moratorium, which will be discussed later. One interviewee suggested that many older adults are moving to Delaware because of its beach, absence of sales tax, and negligible property tax. This same person also stressed that there were many Delawareans, who, when they finally surfaced, would need referrals to the DOPG: "I think there's lots of them out there just waiting to be found." Another population, an increasingly younger and Hispanic group, particularly in downstate Delaware, was also regarded as requiring public guardianship services.

Adequacy of Criteria and Procedures

The records kept for each IP included the following:

1. Advance directives (if executed).
2. Reports to the courts (every six months on each guardianship—a review and request for continuance).
3. Periodic program review of the IP's legal incapacity, as part of the six-month report.
4. Periodic review of the appropriateness of the DOPG to serve as guardian, as part of the six-month report.
5. Documentation of the rationale for the decisions made on behalf of each IP.

Case management software was purchased to conduct functional assessments and care plans, as well as to implement time logs or timekeeping records. Regular staff meetings are not held due to the workload. According to Ms. Williams-Bruner, the DOPG abandoned the use of the software when it could not obtain approval from the tech support unit of the judiciary to install it for use. Additionally, the public guardian had no access to the software company to receive technical assistance and updates as needed.

Decision making. As a first standard, the office uses substituted judgment decision making. However, in cases in which the office is unable to determine or has no knowledge of the IP's prior wishes, it relies heavily on the best interest standard. If an IP is able to discuss a decision, the staff arranges for the discussion, sometimes with treatment team staff or family or both. The DOPG returns to the court regarding decisions on selling real estate, DNR orders, and adverse medical treatment. Moreover, the DOPG returns to court for direction, instructions, and clarification in any case where the level of its authority to make a decision is unclear. The DOPG must grapple with an increasing number of procedures that require informed consent, but the law does not cover the many medical procedures that people presently receive, and the public guardians are not as well versed in medical training as needed for authorization. The DOPG can contract out with a fee service (e.g., for the completion of Medicaid applications). In practice, this is rarely done. The office is more likely to arrange for a fee-for-service agency to assume a successor guardianship to handle property issues when the estate of the IP supports this service.

During the referral process, in seeking an alternative to DOPG services, for notification, and to determine the pertinent level of interest or involvement, the office attempts to obtain as much information as possible regarding family and friends. The office promotes family involvement even after appointment, maintains correspondence with family members, and encourages visitation and contact, as well as attendance at care planning meetings. At times, family inclusion meets with considerable resistance in some long-term care facilities, when staff members refuse to engage a family member because the resident is a "ward of the public guardian."

When it is deemed necessary to place an IP in a facility (the location of most IPs), the decision is made based on the IP's level of care needs and the available community and family supports. There is no review process. Many IPs were already placed in a long-term care facility by APS prior to the appointment of the DOPG. The office reviews these cases in order to determine that the placement is the least restrictive one possible and to explore other viable alternatives. However, gaps in the availability of competent, affordable, and reliable home and community services, combined with the limited staffing of the office needed to broker, monitor, and maintain needed services, makes the deinstitutionalization of nursing home IPs difficult, if not impossible.[5]

Most IPs receiving services through DDDS are not institutionalized. Instead, the DOPG advocates for the IPs' discharge to an appropriate residential placement in the community. The DOPG is not legally authorized to consent to voluntary mental health services in an institution. Delaware law requires involuntary commitment of the IP to mental health services under a separate statute.

Internal Issues for the Program

The office reported working with such entities as the long-term care system, the courts, Social Security, the Department of the Attorney General, the mental health community, the hospitals, DDDS, and APS.

Relationship with APS. APS staff members thought that annually, approximately 30 percent of their cases, typically abuse or neglect cases, were resolved by guardianship, and of that percentage, most are referred to the public guardian. If APS petitions for guardianship, it is done through the deputy attorney general. If the public guardian cannot accept a case or a case is inappropriate, Ms. Williams-Bruner may refer the case to one of the four fee-for-service guardianship programs in Delaware. APS cannot refer a case to a private agency. If the public guardian is appointed as interim guardian, APS keeps the case until a permanent guardianship is established and works hand in hand with DOPG staff on case management and decision making. The public guardian and APS also provide cross training annually.

The APS staff, as well as others interviewed, noted that due to limited resources, the DOPG had issued a moratorium on the cases they could accept. The APS staff said that it was in effect for approximately a year. (Ms. Williams-Bruner later stated that that it was actually instituted in May 2005, and the office continued to take cases, specifically emergencies and court cases.) APS staffers indicated that the office had also issued a moratorium nearly two years earlier. (According to Ms. Williams-Bruner, she was not aware of any official moratorium in 2003. At that time, DOPG was taking adult guardianship services cases and so was likely looking closely at all of these cases to determine alternatives to DOPG services). The APS staff members explained that the public guardian would accept cases on an emergency and interim basis (30 days only). When asked what APS does with people who need public guardianship services while a moratorium is in effect, one person declared, "We have to be very creative. At times, it could be just a situation where we have to do a protective placement until we can get all the players identified and come up with other individuals who may be appropriate and willing to petition."

The APS staff members considered their relationship with the DOPG to be a positive one, but that some staff members became frustrated when their request for a guardianship was turned down, feeling "like they have to beg." Staff members acknowledged that their frustration sometimes occurred because there was an available family member who was not explored fully.

Another complaint mentioned was that the DOPG had allowed perpetrators of the IP's neglect to return to a home or had allowed an unsupervised visit with a perpetrator. However, Ms. Williams-Bruner stated:

> The DOPG would not knowingly permit contact between an IP and some-one charged with or found guilty of abusing an IP. In the majority of the APS cases, no charges were ever filed. The court often required or requested that the guardian facilitate reunification with the IP's family. The APS staff may be blaming the DOPG for allowing an IP to return to the home of a perpetrator when they did so after the court denied the appointment of the DOPG. Therefore, this paved the way for the IP to return to the care of the family. I recall clearly supervising visits between an IP and her daughter, who stood accused of abuse and did so several times at the request of APS staff because they were unable to do so.

Outside Assessments of the Office

Of the guardianship cases that flow through the courts, commentators estimated that at least 25 percent are public guardianship cases. Of that 25 percent, 15 percent begin as interim guardianships. Interviewees noted that the program helps lay people who are considering serving as private guardians. No difference was reported in IP restoration to competency between public and private guardians. No problems were reported with timeliness or the thoroughness of completing reports, either.

If the court appoints the DOPG, then the DOPG must take the appointment in all cases, but the nexus of the court and the office is helpful in that the courts are appraised of the resource limitations and their effect on the quality of the public guardianship services provided.

Despite information about the helpfulness of the office and the small size of the state, many of the people interviewed perceived that the office is largely misunderstood by many state agencies, who believe that the DOPG possesses "mystical powers" to fix problems no one else is able to fix. One individual said, "Robin and her staff are certainly to be commended for their closet full of magic wands, but I don't really think they have them."

Commentators stressed that accountability for the DOPG is greater than that of a private guardian because the public guardian is a state agency representing a private person. Even though the private person may not have appropriate family members or friends, it is important to account for the state's decisions on his or her behalf, as well as to deflect any criticism of the office that might arise from disgruntled family members. Another reason for greater accountability is that it will bring the court up to date on the guardianship so that issues or concerns are not missed. One person confessed, "It's a rule of money that the more assets the individual has, then the [greater] challenge there is [to the guardianship]."[6]

The DOPG was regarded as a vital linkage for persons in nursing homes who required guardianship services. The DOPG's work was extolled by persons associated with the hospitals. In particular, Ms. Williams-Bruner was much appreciated and beloved: "Robin . . . has been our longest-standing public guardian and will be extremely hard to ever have to replace." The office was well regarded across the state.

All of the persons interviewed remarked upon the professionalism and dedication of the staff, saying that they are involved at the very personal level of the individual. One interviewee said, "They become advocates for these people, and actually, in this particular case, they became, at least in this disabled person's eyes, her friend."

Another person had this to say: "When there is nobody else, the public guardian automatically steps in, especially when people are indigent. They're lifesavers. You know, without them, these people would have nothing; most people would have nothing."

Commentators said that several attorneys and others would go to bat for the office in an instant if given the opportunity. Yet, universally, for all of the interviewees, the office simply did not have enough funding or staffing. The comment by this individual was enlightening and poignant: "I feel that historically, the DOPG has been crippled somewhat by their staffing constraints. I think now they have seven and a half full-time equivalents, maybe. I think that's what they have today. And they've got approximately 240, maybe 250 IPs. That, I think, is doable. I think when they had three people in the office covering the state of Delaware, which wasn't that long ago, that they really could not perform the function [of the guardian]. I've never heard a complaint about the public guardianship process except from the public guardian, who will tell me, she said, 'I don't know how we can keep doing this without, without adequate staffing.'"

Notable Features of the Office

The DOPG has a public guardian with many years of experience and exceptional institutional knowledge. She is not an attorney, but she represents the office in court nonetheless.

The DOPG is the only court model program that was visited.
The DOPG is located in a small state, which facilitates greater networking than what offices in larger states could achieve.

Concluding Assessments

Strengths

1. The pubic guardian shares knowledge with all of the people with whom she works.
2. The DOPG has highly experienced and dedicated staff members that are personally involved with the IPs and are their true advocates.
3. The office has greater independence for serving IPs and higher visibility in the Court of Chancery than it would if it were in a Social Services department.
4. The Center for Guardianship Certification certifies four of the seven DOPG staff.[7]

Weaknesses

1. The office needs an individual with a medical background on its staff.
2. Funding is highly inadequate, while service requests are steadily increasing.
3. The office needs legal representation in the form of at least a part-time deputy attorney general.

4. Caseloads are far too high.
5. The office lacks an effective and efficient data management system.

Opportunities

1. The office should cross train with the medical community.
2. The office could focus advocacy efforts on people with mental health needs.
3. The office should partner with organizations and entities in the state in order to increase its visibility and clout.
4. The office should provide better public education about itself.
5. The office should have the ability to authorize voluntary mental health care.

Threats

1. The chronic underfunding and understaffing of the office.
2. The influx of older adults into Delaware and the growth of younger adults needing services.
3. The increasingly complex needs of all IPs.
4. Litigation, if the DOPG breaches its fiduciary role.

An Assessment of Then and Now

The previous study visited the office in 1979, and researchers for this study visited the office 26 years later. At the time of the first site visit, there were no protective services in the state. The office budget was nearly $400,000 less than it was in 2005. The DOPG was not headed by an attorney during the earlier visit and was not headed by one 26 years later. There were 42 IPs served by the office in 1979, and 174 in 2005. The percentage of annual referrals from hospitals is remarkably similar across the years (23% versus 18%). Staffing shortages remain in place over the years and are reflected in the office's inability to accept clients. A hand review of client files was possible in 1979 because the number of IPs was low. The data system in 2005, however, could not generate quantitative information about where IPs resided.

These recommendations for the Delaware Office of the Public Guardian are offered:

1. When the DOPG collects fees from IPs, the fees should be returned to the office for utilization, rather than being funneled to the general funds of the state.
2. The office should explore cross training with the medical community.
3. The office should employ a staff member with a strong medical background.

4. The state of Delaware should move to quickly resolve the dual and sometimes conflicted role of the GAL, as the function of attorneys serving in this capacity is compromised and does a disservice to clients.

5. The DOPG needs an accessible and easily understandable data system for the management of client needs. The data that are entered and retrievable from the system should include, at a minimum, the information requested by the survey conducted for this study.

6. The head of the office should be an attorney.

7. There is a clear and unmet need in the community, especially since the office has had a moratorium on new cases for over a year and has had to institute moratoria in the past.

8. The office should marshal its support from the State Bar to leverage more funds for its chronic problems with understaffing and underfunding.

9. The DOPG should educate the professional and lay community about its function. Linkages could be explored with a law school or a school of social work.

10. The formation of a multidisciplinary team could help with accessing services for IPs.

11. The implementation of smooth relationships with APS. Cross-training sessions appear to be an excellent opportunity to achieve this goal.

12. Hospitals petition for a large percentage of DOPG cases, something that is much rarer in the other states visited. This phenomenon is a longstanding one. While hospitals petition for emergency guardians, many cases eventually become permanent ones, as summarized by one of the interviewees: "I think there should be a concern on the part of the public guardian's office that they're taking on patients at the request of the hospital for some sort of emergency and then they have them for the rest of their lives. And, I mean, that's a drain on resources."

13. The office has an exceptional reputation, and its dedicated staff members were highly praised by every person interviewed.

14. Departure of the head of the office was imminent. The office may suffer in quality due to the departure of such a well-regarded and strong leader. At the very least, if Ms. Williams-Bruner is willing to continue her role with the office, she could be retained as a consultant to the new public guardian.

THE MARYLAND ADULT PUBLIC GUARDIANSHIP PROGRAM

Introduction

The Maryland Adult Public Guardianship Program (APGP) was established in 1977 and is a bifurcated system. For all persons deemed incapable of managing their affairs, a guardian of the property, generally an attorney, is appointed. For incapacitated adults age 18 to 64, guardianship of the person is provided by the Maryland Department of Human Resources (DHR/APS), which then follows them as they age. For incapacitated adults age 65 and over, guardianship of the person is provided by the Maryland Department of Aging (MDoA).

The office directors of the 24 local departments of social services (LDSS) are the named guardian of the person for incapacitated adults aged 18–64 as a last resort, when no other person is available to serve as guardian. The adult services administrators within LDSS keep the statewide program specialist for APS and the Adult Public Guardianship Program apprised of changes or issues surrounding these IPs.

The director of the local area agency on aging is the court-appointed guardian for persons over the age of 65, but in most cases, a guardianship case manager provides the services. According to the state long-term care (LTC) ombudsman, there are instances where the local ombudsmen are also the guardianship program managers. She pointed out that in these cases, the IP may complain to the ombudsman, who is also the IP's guardian. She recognized that this clearly constitutes a conflict of interest.

Despite this clear delineation between the providers of services, which is dependent upon age, there are counties where public guardianship for both the younger cohort and the older cohort are handled in the same office (e.g., Montgomery County). Professionals from this county considered this an advantage. One participant said that the general public views the public guardianship system as an "unfortunate necessity," but that it is also a significant protection.

Statutory Authorization

Maryland has two statutory schemes for public guardianship: one for elders and another for younger incapacitated adults. Both provide for guardianship of the person only. For adults under 65, the director of the LDSS may serve as guardian; and for adults 65 years old or older, the secretary of aging or the director of the area agency on aging may serve. These officials may delegate guardianship responsibilities to staffers whose names and positions are registered with the court.[8] The legislative intent is that the provisions for the appointment of public officials as guardians of the person are used sparingly, with the utmost caution, and only if an alternative does not exist.[9]

Maryland law also established a system of public guardianship review boards. Each county must have one review board, but two or more counties may agree to establish a single multi-county review board. Each review board consists of 11 members appointed by the county commissioners (in Baltimore City, they are appointed by the mayor with the advice of the city council, and in any county with a county executive, by the county executive with advice of the county council); or if the board is for more than one county, appointments are made jointly by the appropriate officials. The members include a professional from a local department of social services, two physicians, including one psychiatrist from a local health department, a representative of a local commission on aging, a representative of a local nonprofit social service organization, a lawyer, two lay individuals, a public health nurse, a professional in the field of disabilities, and a person with a physical disability. Members serve for a term of three years.

The board must review each public guardianship case at least once every six months. Once a year, the review is an in-person review, alternating with a file review (except for the first year, when the review is in-person both times). The review is based on a report submitted by the public guardianship agency concerning the placement and health status of the IP, the guardian's plan for preserving and maintaining the future well being of the IP, the need for the continuation or cessation of the guardianship, any plans for altering the powers of the guardian, and the most recent dates of visits by the guardian. The review board must recommend the continuation, modification, or termination of the guardianship to the court. The individual under guardianship must attend each in-person review board hearing (unless waived by his/her attorney) and have representation by a lawyer of his or her choice or one appointed by the court.[10]

Recent Litigation

There is no recent litigation involving the public guardian in Maryland.

Recent Legislation

In the 2007 Maryland General Assembly session, H.B. 672 concerning certificates of competency to be filed with a petition for guardianship. While the previous requirement was for two physicians or one physician and a psychologist to make the certification, the new law allowed certification by one physician and one licensed certified social worker-clinical, effective October 1, 2007. The bill authorizes that a petition for the guardianship of a disabled person should include signed and verified certificates of competency by a specified licensed physician and a specified licensed certified social worker-clinical (LCSW-C). LCSW-Cs were added to the law that allows a licensed physician and licensed psychologist to authorize certificates of competency for disabled individuals' guardianship petitions. House Bill 672 was effective October 1, 2007.

Organization and History

Age 18–64. The statewide program specialist for the APS and APGP in Maryland has held this position since 2000. She has 13 years of experience in APS, with 8 of those as a direct services case manager. The program is administered through the 24 jurisdictions of LDSS. The LDSS office directors are the named guardians of the IPs. The LDSS adult services supervisors oversee case management staffers who provide services to the IPs.

The statewide program specialist was unable to provide cost-per-IP information, but expressed interest in knowing how to calculate this information.[11] The APGP includes a performance measure system that "randomly selects APS cases under the guardianship project code for annual review and Council of Accreditation[12] compliance standards."

Court approval is required to change the abode of the IP (but court approval is not required within certain residence change categories, such as from nursing home to nursing home or group home to group home), to consent to medical treatment that involves significant risk to the IP's life, and to withhold or withdraw life-sustaining procedures. The majority of petitions for those aged 18–64 are filed by APS, but in recent years, Maryland has seen an increase in health facilities (hospitals) filing petitions for guardianship. If an IP below the age of 65 is appointed a guardian within the APGP, they remain IPs of the APGP regardless of their age.

Age 65+. The statewide guardianship program manager was in the position for 10 months at the time of the interview. She holds a master's degree in aging studies, has more than 15 years of experience in the field of disabilities, and had served on the Adult Protective Guardianship Review Board for 4 years. Either the state secretary of aging or the director of the local area agency on aging (AAA) serves as the guardian of the person for adults age 65 and over. The director of the AAA is the named guardian, and local guardianship managers manage the duties of guardianship. When the state secretary of aging is the named guardian, the statewide guardianship manager handles those cases.

The statewide guardianship manager oversees the distribution of state grants to each of the local AAAs. Oversight of local and/or regional programs consists of annual monitoring visits for file review and an "interview session with lead guardianship managers on their accomplishments and challenges with the program." One county area agency on aging (Calvert) has never served as public guardian, so the statewide manager serves as guardian to IPs in this county. APS and hospitals are usually the petitioning parties.

Adequate Funding and Staffing

The annual budget for FY 2003 for APS programs (LDSS), which includes the public guardianship functions, was $4,638,788, broken down as follows:

Local Funding	$127,042
State Funding	$786,327
Social Services Block Grants (Title XX)	$3,030,062

Title IV-E	$519,509
MD Medical	
Assistance Program	$175,848

The statewide program specialist was unable to provide cost-per-IP information, but specified that in FY 2003, they had 494 IPs.

The annual budget for FY 2005 and 2006 for MDoA (age 65+) was $642,692, reflecting a 14 percent decrease from the budgeted amount in 2003. In FY 2003, the budgeted amount was $739,272, and for 2004, it was $644,424. These funds are for the MDoA and include public guardianship funding, although it is not broken out separately. The statewide public guardianship program manager stated that some of the budget reductions "were taken in the guardianship program." According to the statewide public guardianship program manager, Medicaid funds are not directly used for guardianship services. The 65-and-over public guardian program in Maryland had 772 IPs at the time of the interviews (December 2005). They do not track the cost per IP, but they are interested in having the wherewithal to do so.

Collection of Fees for Services

In the few cases where the IP has the resources, fees are collected for services rendered. This would require LDSS and/or MDoA to deal with attorneys who stonewall. This is the exception rather than the rule.

Structure and Function

The MDoA sponsors statewide training sessions on a quarterly basis. The statewide guardianship manager (65+) and statewide program specialist for APS and APGP meet quarterly with local managers and conduct annual monitoring visits in each jurisdiction. NGA standards are not used, but some of the local guardianship managers are NGA certified and do adhere to the NGA standards.

The MDoA guardianship program (IPs aged 65+) contracts with a physician, who provides consultation on IPs' medical and end-of-life issues. Some local programs seek court and physician assistance with formulating advance directives in consultation with IPs.

Court permission is required for change of abode (unless the change is within the same category of abode), for medical procedures involving substantial risk to an IP's life, and for the withholding or withdrawal of life-sustaining procedures.

Many guardianship cases are routed to the fast-track system, which does not involve a jury. One judge with extensive tenure indicated that in a given day, the fast-track system might adjudicate 25 cases, of which 7 to 10 are guardianship cases, and 15 percent of these are public guardianship cases. The petitioner is generally either a health care facility (e.g., hospital) or a person believing that an individual is incompetent to make decisions for himself or herself, and prefers to place the individual in a nursing home. There is a pool of attorneys willing to undertake AIP representation. The Department of Human Resources administers contracts for legal services to indigent adults in need of a guardian and to represent indigent adults at review board hearings. The court often appoints these contractors to represent the AIP because payment is guaranteed. Their role includes interviewing the AIP, getting a sense of the case, and exploring less restrictive alternatives to guardianship, and they represent the AIP during the court proceedings. According to one judge, the judge is conceptually appointed as guardian of the AIP, and she or he may then delegate to a representative, the guardian, who is then responsible for implementing the wishes of the court regarding the AIP. Often, the AIP is not present at the guardianship proceeding, and this is of concern to some judges.

Conflict of Interest—Ability to Petition

The majority of guardianship petitions reportedly originate in hospitals. This occurs when a patient has reached the reimbursement limit of the Diagnostic Related Group (DRG) for which they were admitted. The discharge social worker will attempt to determine the feasibility of a release home, but often finds that the patient does not recall the reason for hospitalization. The social worker will then contact a physician who may determine that the patient is no longer competent. At this point, the relevant APS program is notified of the hospital's intent to file a petition for guardianship. The age of the patient determines whether LDSS or MDoA is appointed guardian of the person. Hospitals have attorneys on retainer to serve as petitioners.

Incapacitated Persons

The statewide program specialist for APS and APGP was unable to provide a diagnostic profile of IPs. A Guardianship Characteristics Report is completed quarterly by LDSS. At the time of the interview, the quarterly results for October–December 2005 were not due until January 31, 2006.

Under Maryland law, a child in foster care is not emancipated until he or she reaches 21 years of age. Thus, there is a gap into which those who are aging out of the foster care system fall—the years between 18 and 21. Upon reaching 18, those who have had a guardian as children are not covered by child services but remain ineligible for adult guardianship services. A state disability professional found this of significant concern.

The majority of the IPs age 65 and over are in nursing or assisted living facilities. Those in facilities are visited at least once each quarter. Those IPs residing in the community are visited at least monthly, and sometimes more often.

Upon the death of an IP age 65 and over, the guardianship staff arranges for burial services and facilitates the payment of funerals through the guardian of the property and/or any available family members. The bodies of those IPs without the means to cover burial expenses are donated to the state anatomy board or local DSS funds are accessed.

Questions regarding practices and procedures that are culturally and ethnically sensitive yielded the following response: "This is not addressed in the policy and procedure [sic] of the guardianship handbook."

Two individuals (IPs of Baltimore City MDoA) were interviewed, both of whom have benefited as IPs of the public guardian. One of the IPs was a man whose son was originally appointed guardian. Within two weeks of being appointed guardian, the son had moved his father to a nursing home. Eighteen months later, due to his failure to submit annual mandatory reports to the court, a judge appointed a public guardian to serve. Both of the IPs interviewed have experienced improved health, including fewer admissions to psychiatric hospitals, with one enrolled in a medical adult day care program, and the other regularly attending a local senior center. Both are currently residents in assisted living facilities.

In one jurisdiction, a surprising proportion was placed in facilities after their adjudication as IPs. Five to six caseworkers handle a caseload of 250 to 300 IPs. In some cases, the visitation of IPs was delegated to paraprofessionals.

Baltimore County makes an effort to ensure that pre-death burial arrangements are put in place because, as one participant said, "Once that person [IP] dies, we have no authority." The participant also said that working with attorneys as guardians of the property has fewer pitfalls than working with family members who are named guardians of the property.

The Adequacy of Criteria and Procedures

The LDSS, in its role as APS, petitions for guardianship, even in cases involving persons over the age of 65. The LDSS is represented in court by the county attorney's office or by the LDSS-appointed agency attorney, who is paid for with LDSS budgeted funds or the county attorney's office.

The courts require that the guardian submit an annual report on each IP. The Adult Public Guardianship Review Board reviews each case semi-annually and at least monthly in larger jurisdictions, such as Baltimore City and Prince George's County. The board's recommendations are submitted to the court.

Maryland Public Guardianship Review Board

The local Adult Public Guardianship Review Board, an entity established by statute (Maryland Code Annotated §§14-401 through 14-404), reviews each case twice a year. The board does not review temporary guardianship cases, even though some of the cases termed temporary are open for an extended period.

At each board meeting, several cases are presented. The board members discuss each case in turn, and make recommendations to the court for the continuation, modification, or termination of the guardianship. Members sometimes make suggestions for resources or contacts, or comment on the guardian's options for care and placement. It is unclear to what extent the court considers these recommendations in its review.

The review hearings are informal and recorded; evidentiary rules do not apply. The hearings vary in length depending on the issues. The guardian (guardian's representative/agency case manager) files a report with the board giving the background of the case, diagnosis, current status and living arrangements, medications, any changes since the last hearing, prognosis, the protective services planned, and a recommendation about the continuation or modification of the guardianship. The court-appointed attorney (frequently an attorney awarded a contract under the Maryland Legal Services Program's legal representation contract program, i.e., the Maryland Legal Aid Bureau) appears and represents the individual. The attorney remains on the case after appointment for this purpose. The case manager appears as the guardian's representative. The IP attends, if possible. In the review board hearing attended during the site visit, six cases were considered, but no incapacitated individuals were able to attend. Of the six cases, four concerned individuals in nursing homes or group homes, and two concerned a couple living at home. In all six cases, the recommendation was to continue the guardianship. Review board members may conduct hearings at nursing home facilities in order to observe the IP in his or her current living setting.

Previously, there was a council of review boards, and a 1987 handbook described the role and function of the boards. However, at the time of the site visit, the handbook had not been updated since December 1998.

Variations in DHR and MDoA Guardianships

There are instances where the guardianship program manager in MDoA is also the long-term care (LTC) ombudsman, creating, at the very least, the appearance of a conflict of interest. In their interviews, people who serve as ombudsmen and as guardians cited concerns about the actual conflict of interest that may exist.

One county (Montgomery) has not separated DHR and MDoA. In fact, this county has a large DHHS program that includes the services of the public guardian for all ages.

Outside Assessments of the Office

A number of participants, including attorneys, judges, APS workers, and others, expressed serious concerns about the guardian of the property. A guardian of the property was interviewed who described his role as "all aspects except guardianship of the person. . . . I don't like that role because it's 24/7. And you actually have to eyeball the person. If you make a mistake, you cannot correct it."

Some attorneys reportedly not only serve as guardians of the property, but also serve as the attorney for hospitals and nursing homes who are filing petitions for guardianship. This dual role may set up a conflict of interest.

Notable Features of the Office

The LDSS office director serves at the pleasure of the governor, and is the court-appointed guardian of the person for IPs aged 18–64.

One of the participants mentioned that MDoA was appointed guardian of the person for an individual who is a multi-millionaire. This participant said, "There is no private guardianship in Maryland; it's either family or it's us." He also indicated that this happens quite frequently.

Concluding Assessments

Strengths

1. The office is generally thought to do a creditable job protecting vulnerable adults who can no longer make wise choices.
2. Personnel and their dedication to the job they perform.
3. Specific judges who are well versed in public guardianship issues.
4. The DHR has a training budget that includes training for APS staff members and staffers involved in guardianship cases through a contract with the University of Maryland's School of Social Work.

Weaknesses

1. Lack of coordination and communication between service provision agencies and public guardian.
2. Workload overload and lack of time.
3. In some cases, the LTC ombudsman also serves as the guardianship manager (thus serving as both advocate and guardian).
4. Limited or no use of temporary or limited guardianships to address specific issues.
5. Unmet need in nursing homes (residents are increasingly incapacitated, and unable to make decisions, but no public guardian is appointed).
6. The continuing priority assigned to child welfare cases versus adult cases.
7. Lack of attorneys within MDoA to provide services during court hearings to determine capacity. The Maryland DHR has contracted attorneys that represent indigent adults and children under CINA (Children in Need of Assistance) cases through the Maryland Legal Services Program

(MLSP). These contracted attorneys are listed through the court system and are monitored yearly by MLSP staff. The Maryland DHR assistant attorney general's attorneys do represent the LDSS, staff, and court-appointed IPs in complex guardianship cases, as needed.

8. Lack of inter-county communication.
9. Budgetary constraints.
10. The public guardian is situated within a state human services agency. The program is administered under the APS program through the 24 local departments of social services.
11. Unwieldy court reporting mechanisms.
12. Guardians of the property (attorneys) are not in adequate contact with guardians of the person.
13. Elder law attorneys need more education regarding public guardianship.
14. Unevenness in service across the state makes it difficult to get a clear sense of the statewide public guardianship program.
15. Lack of recognition of the burgeoning developmentally disabled adult (DDA) population that is aging and increasingly making demands on the MDoA program.
16. No uniform statewide data collection forms, including IP characteristics, diagnoses, living arrangements, and the like. However, the DHR has a statewide data collection system in place to record the various guardianship characteristics listed above for each LDSS. In addition, data are monitored under the statewide Client Information System for Adult Services programs.

Opportunities

1. Public education.
2. The availability of cross training, dual roles, and clear communication.
3. The office's role as representative payee. A Maryland reviewer states that as of November 2005, DHR no longer provides statewide monitoring of the former representative payee program,. This program service area is only offered within certain local jurisdictions. The DHR's assistant attorney general's office will continue to provide legal advice and consultation to representative payee program advisory boards, upon request.
4. Training of family members about the role and responsibility of guardianship.
5. Technical assistance to family members who agree to serve as guardians, particularly with regard to court-mandated reporting procedures.
6. A volunteer program that would provide a pool of college students who could serve as friendly visitors, or act as public guardian ombudsmen.
7. Finding ways to use Medicaid funding for public guardianship costs.

8. Using Social Services/social work interns to assist in provision of services to older IPs.
9. Encouraging judges to specialize in public guardianship cases.

Threats

1. Budgetary constraints.
2. Persons in LTC facilities have no one monitoring major decisions (e.g., Medicare Part D, and which program to select).
3. Hospital and nursing home interpretations of Health Insurance Portability and Accountability Act (HIPAA) requirements make the public guardian's job difficult.
4. Physical location results in cross-jurisdictional issues. Maryland is in close proximity to Washington, D.C., and public guardians have encountered difficulty getting Maryland court orders recognized in hospitals in the District of Columbia.
5. The expected doubling of need in the MDoA program due to the aging of Baby Boomers.

An Assessment of Then and Now

In 1979, it was not unusual for the guardian of the person (public guardian) to be assigned as guardian of the property. This has changed, and, at this time, the guardian of the property in the state of Maryland is usually an attorney. Due to its location within DHR, the APGP is a conflict of interest model. The public guardianship role of the MDoA may still be perceived as minimizing the extent of conflict of interest in that services are provided by DHR. However, of significant concern are those instances where the LTC ombudsman is serving a dual role: that of LTC ombudsman and the guardianship program manager. The latter is, in effect, the provider of services, thus setting up a significant conflict of interest. An IP residing in an LTC facility, who might normally seek redress through the LTC ombudsman, is then in an untenable situation.

These recommendations are offered for the Maryland Adult Public Guardianship Program:

1. Coordination and communication between provision agencies and the public guardian needs to be strengthened.
2. Caseloads are far too high, and this needs to be effectively addressed.
3. Attorneys serving as guardians of the property, but also serving as attorney for the hospitals and nursing homes in which the IPs live, are filing petitions for guardianship. This dual role is a conflict of interest, and the practice should be discouraged.

4. Funding should be provided for training, particularly in the community.

5. In some cases, the LTC ombudsman also serves as the guardianship manager (thus serving as both advocate and guardian). This conflict of interest should be avoided.

6. The utilization of temporary or limited guardianships to address specific issues should be encouraged.

7. There is unmet need in nursing homes (residents are increasingly incapacitated, and unable to make decisions, but no public guardian is appointed). This problem should be addressed.

8. Adult cases should receive the same priority as child welfare cases.

9. The lack of attorneys within MDoA to provide services during court hearings held to determine capacity should be ameliorated. The DHR has contracted attorneys that represent indigent adults and children under CINA cases through MLSP. These contracted attorneys are listed through the court system and are monitored yearly by MLSP staff. The DHR assistant attorney general's attorneys do represent the LDSS, staff, and court-appointed IPs in complex guardianship cases, as necessary.

10. Budgetary constraints should be addressed.

11. The public guardian is situated within a social service provision agency; this conflict of interest should be avoided.

12. Court reporting mechanisms should be streamlined.

13. Mechanisms should be in place so that guardians of the property (attorneys) are in adequate contact with, and supporting, the guardians of the person.

14. Elder law attorneys need additional education on public guardianship.

15. The office should prepare for the burgeoning developmentally disabled adult population that is now aging.

16. The office should facilitate easily retrievable and accessible uniform statewide data collection on IP characteristics, diagnoses, and living arrangements.

THE MARICOPA COUNTY, ARIZONA, OFFICE OF THE PUBLIC FIDUCIARY

The Maricopa County Office of the Public Fiduciary in Phoenix, Arizona, was visited in January of 2006. Richard T. Vanderheiden, J.D., served as the head of the Office of the Public Fiduciary since 1991. The term used in Arizona to refer to a public guardian and public administrator is the public fiduciary. The office has enjoyed a stable administration with many staff members who have served for long periods of time, some since the inception of the public fiduciary in 1975. However, as explained in greater detail below, although the office had amassed 624 years of fiduciary experience via 33 Maricopa County Public Fiduciary (MCPF) associates, with 27 percent having worked there for over 20 years, 64 percent of these associates were planning to retire by 2010.

Statutory Authorization

An Office of the Public Fiduciary is located in all counties in Arizona. The office was established statutorily in 1975, and is authorized by Arizona law (Arizona Revised Statutes §§14-5601 through 14-5606). Per statute, the public fiduciary is appointed by the county board of supervisors and authorized to hire staff to carry out the duties of the office.

In 1995, in response to perceptions of widespread abuses within the guardianship system, the Arizona Supreme Court enacted administrative rules requiring the certification of all public and private fiduciaries deriving payment for services. Contemporaneous with the enactment of these certification requirements was the establishment of the Fiduciary Certification Program, which is under the auspices of the Arizona Supreme Court's Administrative Offices of the Court. The Fiduciary Certification Program provides education, certification, and discipline for public and private fiduciaries in Arizona. A state organization of fiduciaries, both public and private, is able to meet and discuss subjects of mutual interest.

In the offices of the public fiduciary, the certification of both the public fiduciary and his or her staff members is required. Staff members are certified individually, and the office is also certified as an entity.

Litigation

Though it is an older lawsuit, *Arnold v. Sarn* (1985) was a major class action against the state of Arizona and Maricopa County that is still ongoing today. The county was originally named as the defendant, and Sarn was, at the time, director of the Department of Health Services. The case addressed the performance of service providers for the seriously mentally ill, with whom the public fiduciary was involved due to its guardianship service for IPs under court-ordered treatment. Charles Arnold, the plaintiff and then-head of the Office of the Public Fiduciary, believed that his fiduciary responsibility exceeded his employment responsibility, and so he filed a class action lawsuit and was fired the next day. He was reinstated by the court because of its finding that a guardian cannot be fired. The county can fire an employee, but only the court can remove a guardian.

Organization and History

The public fiduciary office in Maricopa County is not housed with any other department. It operates as an independent county office with its own budget within Maricopa County government. Pursuant to state statute, a priority list of those persons eligible for appointment as guardian and/or conservator for persons has been established. When no one else is qualified or otherwise able to serve, the court appoints the Maricopa County Public Fiduciary (MCPF). The MCPF also administers decedent estates and is responsible for the county's indigent burial program.

Mental Health Powers

If a person in the state of Arizona is a guardian and is also granted mental health powers through Title 14, then the guardian is authorized to sign an IP into a level-one secured mental health facility (inpatient authority) without going through the civil commitment process. Without that authority, a guardian must seek court approval for civil commitment through Arizona's Title 36 regarding civil commitment.

Title 14 mental health powers are renewed annually. Mental health powers are obtained through a lengthy court process (approximately 45–60 days), during which the proposed IP has a hearing with notice and court-ordered representation. In comparison, the Title 36 civil commitment process is more compressed (approximately seven days). During that time period, the person is given notice and an attorney, but in nearly every case, that person is also confined to a hospital. In fact, the Maricopa County Mental Health Court is physically located in the hospital.

In some cases, a guardian may want both Title 36 civil commitment authority and Title 14 mental health powers. Such power moves the IP up a level of priority for a bed at a state hospital. Thus, if there is Court Ordered Treatment (COT), there is both court ordered treatment and the authority of a guardianship with mental health powers. Sometimes, having the mental health powers along with the guardianship creates tension between the public fiduciary and the county's regional behavioral health agency (RBHA). The tension occurs when the RBHA's treatment team's determination of what is best for the IP and the public fiduciary's best interest determination diverge. When the differences are unresolved, the two go to court to determine whose decision will prevail. One commentator perceived that "Our population of seriously mentally ill is enormous relative to many other states. [I]t's also a battle of funding, and it becomes a tug of war sometimes between a treatment provider or coordinator and the guardian, with or without the mental health powers."

The Application of 1981 Criteria

Adequate Funding and Staffing

The requirements for a full-time equivalent (FTE) paid professional staff member, who makes binding decisions for IPs, have a bachelor's degree, and three years' experience. With 36 FTE staff, the MCPF office contains guardian administrators, estate administrators, estate analysts, division managers, and in-house legal coordinator. There are 18 certified fiduciaries in the office; they are mandated to have 20 hours of fiduciary education every 2 years. A guardian administrator staffs each case and is expected to become knowledgeable about the IP's unique condition and needs. Periodically, staff members are also provided with in-service training, often using outside speakers. There has been no increase in staff in the past 15 years. The MCPF reported that because they are a state-mandated and county-funded organization, there are no threats to their funding, but alternatively, because the MCPF is an appointed county office (as opposed to elected), securing adequate funding is difficult.

The average caseload was approximately 65 IPs per guardian administrator. In FY 2003, the cumulative total of IPs served by the public fiduciary was 550, with approximately 100 IPs accepted into the program for that year. For approximately half of these persons, the public fiduciary served as guardian of the person only. For around 20 cases, the program had limited authority over the person and for about 15, limited guardian of the property. The majority of the program's referrals came from probate court.

On average, a FTE paid professional staff member spent 25 hours per year working on the case of a single IP. The program provides services other than public guardianship, including serving as conservator, representative payee, and personal representative of decedents' estates. Half of the clients of the public fiduciary were persons with mental illnesses and incomes under $20,000. Most were non-Hispanic. During FY 2003, about 20 IPs were restored to partial or full legal capacity.

The MCPF anticipates significant staff attrition in the near future. One of the strategic goals of the program was to develop a Succession Management Plan. Information from a succession survey completed in April 2005 revealed that although the office had amassed 624 years of fiduciary experience among 33 MCPF associates (and of that group, 401 years of fiduciary experience directly with the MCPF office), 64 percent planned to retire in five years' time, and 30 percent were currently eligible for full state retirement benefits. The MCPF estimated that as few as six current associates, or 10 percent of the current workforce, could remain in 2010. In 2009, information confirmed that 15 percent of the staff had retired since the interviews in April 2005.

To implement the management plan, staff members were asked to determine the core competencies and behavior traits they regarded as crucial to serve as a guardian or estate administrator. The top three categories were knowledge (tax laws, investment management, banking); skills (negotiation, drafting legal documents, investment skills); and behavioral traits (forward thinking, compassion, perseverance).

Collection of fees for services. The MCPF has court-approved authority to collect fees that amount to $850,000 per annum. The fees cover guardianship, conservatorship, and probate services. Collected fees are deposited directly with the Maricopa County treasurer.

Structure and Function

Conflict of interest—ability to petition. The MCPF petitions for legal incapacity, as well as for the appointment of itself as guardian. In FY 2003, the public fiduciary reported petitioning for the adjudication of legal incapacity 105 times and petitioning for appointment of itself as guardian 105 times. The county attorney's office represents the office in appointment hearings, although the public fiduciary prepares or coordinates 90 percent of the legal pleadings.

When queried on the problem of apparent conflict of interest, most of the people interviewed did not see one. However, one commentator remarked that a real conflict occurs when the court orders that the public fiduciary must file the petition and the public fiduciary feels there is no need for a guardian and/or conservator. For example, the court has a court investigator who investigates the need for a guardian and identifies a guardian to the court. The public fiduciary can, in such instances, file a report saying they object, but if an individual needs a guardian, and there is no one else, the public fiduciary is, by statute, the guardian of last resort and will be appointed as guardian.

The public fiduciary office stated that even if ordered by the court to petition, if the office determines at the evidentiary hearing that a demonstrated need for a guardian does not exist, they argue against their own petition. The interviewee noted: "It is a continual education process to keep the court, attorneys, and social services agencies informed about alternatives to guardianship."

Incapacitated Persons

In March 2004, the MCPF reported serving 575 IPs. Approximately 100 new IPs were accepted into the program in the previous fiscal year. The annual budget for the program was $1.8 million. The estimated cost per year per IP was $1,850. The public fiduciary suggested that the program might end up costing the county, as the public fiduciary is likely to advocate for the appropriate services, which may be more expensive than the generally minimal services the IPs receive prior to appointment. IP referrals to the program came predominantly through the probate court, private attorneys, mental health facilities, nursing homes, or family. For most of its cases, the program served as the guardian of the person only, the guardian of the property only, and of both the person and property in equal numbers. The program served as limited guardian of the person and limited guardian of the property in fewer than 20. While the program did not provide the gender breakdown of its IPs, the majority of its incapacitated population consisted of individuals with mental illnesses, low incomes (less than $20,000), and who were non-Hispanic. In FY 2003, 12 people were restored to legal capacity, 8 were restored to partial legal capacity, and 15 were transferred to a private guardian. All IPs are visited quarterly or more often if necessary. Approximately 80 percent of the IPs are impoverished, although approximately 60 percent of the conservatorship clients had real property as their most significant asset.

Only one IP, a male who lived at an assisted living facility, was interviewed. The IP was 46 years old at the time of interview, and received Social Security disability and Veterans' benefits. He was diagnosed as bipolar, manic, and schizoaffective. Before living in the assisted living facility, where he had resided for the past five years, he resided in a state hospital. Before the state hospital, he was in jail for six months for three or four felony convictions related to damaging property. He has been under the care of the public fiduciary since he was 18. The public fiduciary had mental health powers along with the guardianship.

The IP smoked, and his health was not good, which was attributable to his smoking. He took his own medications with staff supervision. He enjoyed reading the newspaper, especially the sports news. He enjoyed going to the library. He reported that he liked his guardian and that she makes sure he receives his monthly checks (e.g., cable, incidentals, groceries). He stated that he needed his guardian. He believed that she knew him well, that she made good decisions for him, and that, without her, he would be in a state institution or in jail.

Adequacy of Criteria and Procedures

The records kept for each IP included the following:

1. Functional assessment, updated quarterly.
2. Care plans, updated quarterly.
3. Time logs for each IP.
4. Values histories (one of the rare instances).
5. Advance directives.
6. Periodic reports to the courts and the annual reports of guardians to the court.
7. Documentation of the rationale for why and how decisions are made on behalf of each IP.

Documentation is reviewed on an ongoing basis, and decisions are discussed and reviewed with a guardian administration manager. Statistics are kept on the filing timelines of required reports; these requirements are part of the strategic plan for the department. Managers at monthly fiduciary committee meetings conduct an annual review of cases. The office uses the Computrust computer system for accounting purposes and case management. The office had their internal information technology (IT) person create an online accounting review process.

Several different staff members audit cases. One person enters the assets into the computer, several people do the accounting, and an accounting review sheet is sent to the guardian administrator and estate administrator approximately three months before the accounting is due for filing with the court.

Decision making. The office uses a substituted judgment standard when such information is available, and a best interest standard if it is not. The office has a formal policy related to do-not-resuscitate (DNR) and end-of-life decisions. The office is able to authorize the removal of support systems (e.g., breathing machines, medications), as well as the withholding of nutrition and hydration. If the IP made advance directives when competent, the public fiduciary follows the guidelines and requirements of that document.

Internal Issues for the Program

The office reported that they do not have a formal relationship established with other entities. However, they regularly network with APS, Veteran's Services, the attorney general, and the Alternatives to Guardianship Program.

The Alternatives to Guardianship Program, a program unique to the area, meets once a month and includes members from APS, the public fiduciary, Veterans' Administration's (VA) fiduciary, detectives working with the geriatric population, attorneys for the VA, social services for the VA, the attorney general's office, the LTC ombudsman, and an attorney from APS. The group has worked together for seven years. They triage cases and work on systems issues. The group produced a surrogate identification worksheet that they were trying to get into hospitals, nursing homes, and assisted living facilities that identify the health care surrogate for those who did not have a power of attorney. The worksheet helps identify people who can make decisions, thus ensuring that persons receive the care they need as quickly and efficiently as possible. The head of that group thought that there was little unmet need for guardians, but that the investigation for someone to serve was often not as thorough as necessary.

Relationship with APS. One of the persons interviewed thought all that was needed to make the public fiduciary take a case was to locate a petitioner, often the attorney general. This person believed that APS would seek guardianship for self-neglect. The person stated that the wait period for the public fiduciary is too long: six months or longer. One interviewee believed the office needs more than one investigator and more than one person making decisions about acceptance. "My experience with the public fiduciary was they will probably end up being placed, and that is a sad commentary." The interviewee suggested that it was easier for the public fiduciary to take care of someone in a facility than to care for him or her in his or her own home. Another suggestion was to formalize the relationship with APS through memoranda of understanding, particularly related to referrals and timeframes.

Outside Assessments of the Office

Most persons interviewed outside the office felt that once the public fiduciary was involved, they did a good job. Many expressed the belief that the county board of supervisors should hire more people for the office. Some commentators suggested reconfiguring the office as an independent office outside the county or establishing a statewide system. Some commentators stated that a conflict of interest existed within the county fiduciary system since the county was also providing human and mental health services to the IPs, as well as guardianship services. Several interviewees remarked that they would like to see the office take more cases, but they also understood that funding for the office was a problem.

Notable Features of the Office

An unprecedented wealth of institutional knowledge resides in the people who have worked with the MCPF office.

The mental health powers afforded to the public fiduciary may stem the numbers of persons who become involuntarily civilly committed and help secure priorities in the mental health system in the county. The mental health powers may keep IPs out of the penal system.

The office assists the probate court in investigating cases.

Having an attorney as head of the office is crucial to the efficient and expeditious resolution of legal problems and issues.

The public fiduciary provides information for private guardians and the fiduciary profession at www.maricopa.gov/pubfid/default.asp.

Concluding Assessments

Strengths

1. Highly experienced and dedicated staff.
2. Public fiduciaries are certified by the state.
3. Low staff turnover.
4. The mental health powers afforded to the public fiduciary may reduce the number of people who become involuntarily civilly committed and help secure priorities in the mental health system in the county. The mental health powers may keep IPs out of the penal system.

Weaknesses

1. Funding is inadequate.
2. The court does not adequately understand the role of the public fiduciary as last resort only, and the limits on the number of clients it can adequately take on.
3. The public fiduciary does not have similar systems across the state, creating an uneven system. The site visits were conducted only in the two most populous areas. Respondents reported fewer resources in rural counties.
4. The public fiduciary was often directed to petition for cases, as opposed to writing a report regarding whether it was appropriate to serve.

Opportunities

1. Strengthening the relationship with APS.
2. Educating the service community on what the public fiduciary can and cannot do.
3. Developing a public relations plan.

Threats

1. The apparent underfunding of the office.
2. Over-regulation of the program by the administrative offices of the courts.
3. The probate court's unnecessary dumping of cases onto the public fiduciary.
4. Increased caseloads and case complexity.
5. Lack of awareness by many commentators from the various service sectors regarding the rising and unmet need of persons requiring the services of the public fiduciary.

An Assessment of Then and Now

The 1970s research team decided to study the public fiduciary in Maricopa County because it understood that a well-developed program existed there. At that time, as today, the office was headed by an attorney and funded by county funds and funds generated by IPs' estates. The same is still true today.

What differs is that programs and staff are licensed (certified). The MCPF office regards this difference as positive because it results in increased cumulative knowledge in the office. The major referral source had also shifted from the county health department to the probate court. Relationships with APS were present, but referrals from APS were far fewer in number than other sources. The total caseload of the office had not changed appreciably in over 25 years, although the type of IPs and their problems had. Some office problems were similar across time, and some agencies and commentators thought the office was slow to respond to some referrals.

Although a citizen board was recommended to help with agency policy over 25 years ago, this was not mentioned at the site visit, with the exception of one external interviewee. A group of people were questioning the administrative location of the office, saying that it should be an independent state-funded office, not in a conflict-of-interest situation in a county that provided both guardianship and other services for the IPs.

These are the final observations regarding the Maricopa County Office of the Public Fiduciary:

1. The office can petition for its own IPs, which creates the potential for self-aggrandizement.
2. The office does have computerized information and the office has created an informational Web site. However, some basic data appeared too difficult to produce. The office should develop the capacity to collect and retrieve more data for each IP. This should occur for both the Maricopa program and on a statewide basis.
3. The unmet need for guardians is not well understood. The office should educate various service sectors and the state bar regarding the unmet and rising need for public guardians.
4. The level of professionalism in this office was impressive. As the office staffers pointed out, the potential for huge staff turnover due to retirement poses a clear threat to the office's functionality. The office is to be applauded for developing a succession management plan.
5. One strength of the office is that the director is an attorney.
6. Having an investigator for the Office of the Public Fiduciary helps the office screen cases and provides for early intervention when IPs are adjudicated.
7. Staff-to-client ratios remain too high.
8. The office, despite its many positive features, is underfunded and is subject to pressures to accept clients that it cannot adequately serve. Staff-to-IP ratios (1:20) should be added to the public guardianship statute.
9. More states should adopt mental health powers in tandem with the authority granted to public guardians, in order, among other things, to make mental health care more like health care.

THE PIMA COUNTY, ARIZONA, OFFICE OF THE PUBLIC FIDUCIARY

The Pima County Office of the Public Fiduciary in Tucson, Arizona, was visited in February 2006. Anita Royal, M.S.W., J.D., has served as the head of the Office of the Public Fiduciary (the term used for public guardian in Arizona) since 1991. Like Maricopa County, the Pima office has enjoyed a stable administration with many staff members who have served for long periods of time, some since the inception of the office in 1975. Ms. Royal is fortunate to follow highly prominent elder law attorneys who preceded her in office. One of them, Alan Bogutz, served as the second head of the Pima County Office of the Public Fiduciary and was interviewed in 1979 for Schmidt's first study. Fortunately, Mr. Bogutz was available for another interview in 2006. Since the inception of the office, a licensed attorney has held the position of Pima County Public Fiduciary (PCPF).

Statutory Authorization

Like Maricopa County, the office was established statutorily in 1975 under Arizona Code Revised Statutes §14-5601. By statute, the public fiduciary is mandated to provide court-ordered guardianship, conservatorship, and probate services to county residents. Each county must ensure funding of the Office of the Public Fiduciary. The staff and the office are certified by the Fiduciary Certification Program, which operates through the Arizona Supreme Court's Administrative Offices of the Court.

Recent Litigation

None reported.

Organization and History

The Pima County Public Fiduciary (PCPF) is one of 26 departments under the Pima County Board of Supervisors. The PCPF is appointed by the board of supervisors and serves at its will. The PCPF provides comprehensive, full-service fiduciary services to residents of Pima County who are in need and qualify for these services. Specifically, the office investigates community referrals; petitions for court appointment (where appropriate); case manages IPs using substituted judgment or best interest standards; ensures that the IPs receive all of the entitlements and benefits for which they are qualified; inventories, manages, stores, disposes of, and accounts for all personal and real property; manages all financial assets of its clients, as well as its decedents' estates; administers an indigent burial program; coordinates funeral arrangements for IPs; and probates estates. In discharging its statutory duties, the PCPF is guided by the Arizona Fiduciary Certification Program standards of the CGC, its own internal procedures, and prudent practices. The director, Ms. Royal, is hired by the Pima County Board of Supervisors. Ms. Royal provides supervision and oversight of the office and maintains primary responsibility for departmental risk management.

The Application of 1981 Criteria

Adequate Funding and Staffing

The PCPF receives a general fund allocation from the Pima County Board of Supervisors on an annual basis. The general fund allocation is supplemented by fee revenue generation by the PCPF ($430,000 in FY 2003). For FY 2004, the PCPF received a general fund allocation of approximately $1.435 million. The office does not receive funds from private, state, or federal sources. The state auditor general audits the PCPF office annually. The county does a quasi-financial audit, conducting internal audits of cash and accounts.

The requirements for a FTE paid professional staff member who makes binding decisions for IPs include a bachelor's degree and two years of experience. There were 37 FTE paid professional staff during FY 2003–04, 24 of whom provided professional service delivery. The requested caseload information was not compiled due to staff involvement in other essential tasks and because the computer program used by the PCPF could not generate such information accurately or easily. It was confirmed much later that caseloads are between 60 and 65 IPs per case manager.

Ms. Royal indicated that she managed a fairly independent staff and that it was essential that persons in positions such as hers learn how to manage professionals. She reported she possesses some independence and autonomy in managing clients and their assets, but is accountable at all times to both the Pima County Administrator and the board of supervisors for all of the funds under her control, including general funds allocations. She reported, like other similarly situated governmental managers, she does not possess the absolute authority to hire, compensate, promote, and/or terminate subordinate employees because she is subject to Pima County Human Resources policies and procedures.

Ms. Royal was emphatic that the demands of the office had changed and that it was very important to have legal expertise in the office. "Years ago, I would have said that a social worker could have this job. I think because it has changed so over the course of the last decade, you almost have to have a lawyer." She reportedly was the only licensed attorney in the public fiduciary system in Arizona.

Between the time of the site visit and this writing, another licensed practicing attorney was hired as the Pima County Public Fiduciary.

One staff member reported carrying a caseload of 70 clients, which he reported was down from 120 when the office had also provided representative payee services. Staff members carry mixed caseloads, but Ms. Royal was considering switching to a specialized approach. She remarked, "I found it very intellectually dishonest for me to ask case managers to make medical decisions. Even though they have the support and input from the medical community, I still find that to be dishonest . . . I believe that there are people who appreciate populations better than others and work well with that population. Do I think they should predominately have that population? Probably not."

Ms. Royal stated that the office maintains a pooled checking account from which IPs' monthly bills are paid. Excess funds are placed in interest-bearing tools. For short-term investments, the office utilizes money market accounts and CDs; for long-term investments, it retains the services of at least two brokerage firms to invest and monitor clients' funds. The interest accrued on short- and long-term investments is credited to each IP's account; none of this interest is forfeited or used by the PCPF. While these client funds are maintained in a pooled account, the office manages individual accounts for each client at no cost to his or her estate. The pooled checking account accrues earned interest credits, which offset the monthly bank charges that typically would be assessed for each client's account. Earned interest credits are utilized for the monthly maintenance fees for office accounting and asset management software products.

Collection of fees for services. The court has granted the PCPF the authority to collect a fee, and in FY 2003, these fees generated $430,000 in revenue.

Structure and Function

Conflict of interest—ability to petition. The PCPF petitions for legal incapacity and the appointment of itself as guardian. In-house attorneys handle court appearances. Only in extraordinary cases does Ms. Royal testify in court or handle litigation.

Some commentators discussed a conflict between a limited mental health guardian and agencies. While any guardian has a duty to pursue the rehabilitation of an IP, the guardian is placed in the position of watchfulness such that once the public fiduciary gets the IP through the mental health process, the IP is checked on, and if he or she moves out of placement or stops taking medication, then he or she is put back in the mental health system and under closer supervision. Thus, the guardian serves in two conflicting roles, with the "carrot" of advocating and promoting the freedoms of the IP, but also with the "stick" of severely restricting those freedoms if the IP does not comply. The court is a gate-keeper, but not necessarily a supervisor of the guardian's actions. However, when these conflicts occur, the PCPF routinely petitions the probate court for guidance on how to proceed. Moreover, in some cases, court-appointed counsel remains involved in the case and provides advocacy for the IPs.

Pursuant to applicable Arizona statutes governing the priority of appointment, public fiduciaries are deemed "entities of last resort." As such, when investigating community referrals, the PCPF is mandated to locate qualified persons with statutory priority to serve in a fiduciary capacity before seeking its own appointment. Due to a statutory mandate, the PCPF must also investigate all reasonable "least restrictive alternatives" to the appointment of a fiduciary. Absent a person or entity with priority or a less restrictive alternative plan, the PCPF does petition for its appointment in appropriate cases. Regarding the conflict of interest issue, one judge said:

What I have done is appoint the PCPF as limited mental health [guardian], a limited guardian for persons with medical consent and which doesn't take on placement issues. So I am saying this: typically, the public fiduciary is not out there trying to get business; they are out there, their funding just doesn't [allow aggrandizement]. I don't see a conflict of interest there.

Incapacitated Persons

Ms. Royal said that the program, which utilizes an accounting and case management software system known as Computrust, stores the data gathered upon intake, including the referral source, demographics, and type of guardianship or conservatorship. However, she indicated that information retrieval is cumbersome and, at times, inaccurate. Ms. Royal estimated that 90 percent of the persons who received guardianship services were indigent. Seven persons served by the program died during FY 2003. Typical guardianship clients included elderly persons with dementia, who lacked familial involvement or support, and men with mental illness in their late thirties to mid-forties who had problems with substance abuse. The office also provided fiduciary services to developmentally disabled adults.

Three of the IPs served by the PCPF were interviewed. The first was a female who was 36 years old and had had the public fiduciary as guardian since she was 18. She needed help staying on her medications and admitted that she made the "wrong" decisions sometimes. Her bad decisions included setting fires and damaging vehicles, which resulted in arrests and jail time, then time in a state hospital. The woman said she was taking a variety of medications. She said that she felt good about her health. She stated that she had two case managers and a guardian. She said that the public fiduciary, who was with her for 10 years, was "there when she needed them." However, she also said that she would rather not have a guardian at all and that sometimes her telephone calls were not returned.

The second IP interviewed was a male. He was an older gentleman who said that he was pleased with his guardian, whom he said was with him a long time. He said that his guardian was "very competent and very helpful and very pleasant to work with." He reportedly served time in the Air Force, but was forced to leave because he was color-blind. He said that he enjoyed reading during the day, especially history.

The third IP was a 73-year-old male. He had experienced problems with alcohol, drugs, and exploitation. He had also experienced health problems. He did not think that conservatorship was good for him because his spending was restricted, but he also acknowledged that he was not going hungry. At one point in his life, he had been a government employee.

According to Ms. Royal and the case manager, IPs are far more dangerous than they were years ago. Some IPs carry weapons and are aggressive. Some younger clients are violent. IPs are more frequently using illicit drugs, such as crack cocaine and methamphetamines. The individuals preying on the IPs are also more dangerous than 20 years ago. Persons more openly exploit older adults and are criminals themselves, sometimes exploiting the older adult for money or drugs. The office seeks law enforcement assistance when warranted to protect its clients and their estates against dangerous and unscrupulous elements.

Ms. Royal said:

> Also, what is dangerous is when we take people's rights away and citizenship away because we are getting more and more callous about the needs of the vulnerable population that we serve. I think that this population is in danger. But, see, you really have to look at what we are doing to these people. We take their personage away. We take all their legal rights away from them. We take their sense of being citizens away from them. We control whether they drive or vote. The talk and walk and the pain that I see is that people are not particularly incapacitated in all facets of their lives. They are functionally incapacitated in areas of their lives, and what we do is we may turn them into what I call legal zombies. Once they become legal zombies, what happens is they have no value to society and they become these people other people prey on and exploit, and that to me is the biggest thing that is a threat.

Adequacy of Criteria and Procedures

The records kept for each IP included the following:

1. Functional assessments, updated quarterly.
2. Care plans.
3. Time logs or recordkeeping logs for each IP.
4. Values histories (one of the rare instances).
5. Advance directives (if executed).
6. Annual reports to the courts.
7. Periodic program reviews of the IP, both of which are informally ongoing as part of the annual report.
8. Documentation of the rationale for why and how decisions are made on behalf of each IP.

Staff meetings are held on a quarterly basis or as needed. They consist of information provided by a representative from each office unit involved with a case. Each case is reviewed quarterly and as needed. Case managers can only approve personal-needs monies of $65 to $75. The release of greater sums requires Ms. Royal's approval. All accounts require two signators.

Decision making. The office uses a substituted judgment standard when such information is available, and a best interest standard otherwise. The office has authority to approve DNRs (do not resuscitate orders). Ms. Royal is typically the individual who makes end-of-life decisions, although she indicated that the office will frequently go to court and ask for instruction in areas that seem troublesome or where there is a competing interest.

Internal Issues for the Program

The office reported working with such entities as the long-term care system, DDD (Division of Developmental Disabilities), the courts, Social Security, Access (Medicaid), the mental health community, Community Partners of Southern Arizona, Jewish Family Services, Catholic Charities, Victims of Crime Advocacy, and the office of the attorney general. The PCPF reported trying to use every available resource.

Relationship with APS. APS staff members perceived that a healthy relationship exists with the PCPF and said they share information and refer cases to each other. An estimated 10 percent of APS cases end up with the public fiduciary annually. Occasionally, APS petitions for guardianship by using the office of the attorney general as a last resort. APS reported that very few persons who were already in placement were accepted by the public fiduciary. Interns of the public fiduciary shadow APS staff when they begin. The APS cases close once the public fiduciary is appointed. APS staff members commended the especially fine work of the public fiduciary investigators and said they maintain an excellent relationship. They remarked that they become frustrated when cases are not accepted, which is frequent, and they believe denial is due to the need for fee generation. Said one interviewee, ". . . if the person doesn't have resources, that often will not be a person they [public fiduciary] will accept." One question posed frequently of the investigators was, " What is there to conserve?"

APS reports that a couple of times a year, the public fiduciary freezes case acceptance when the office reaches to the point where need outstrips available staff and resources. That situation is communicated to APS staff.

Outside Assessments of the Office

As in the other states, stakeholders from many professions outside the office of the PCPF were interviewed and asked to comment on its performance. Most of the people interviewed felt that once the public fiduciary became involved, it did a good job, especially given the lack of resources available to PCPF. The professionalism of the PCPF staff was regarded as one of its outstanding features.

Many commentators believed resources for the office were limited in relation to the population it served and that the county had an unmet need that was exploding. Some of the interviewees said the public fiduciary did not want to do much outreach because that would increase client numbers.

Interview with Mr. Bogutz, Prior Office Director

Allan Bogutz, the second head of the office of the PCPF, was interviewed during the first study over 25 years ago. Good fortune provided the opportunity to interview him again in 2006. His "long view" of the office afforded an important commentary on changes that have taken place over time. Mr. Bogutz believes that two strengths of the office are its committed staff and careful oversight by the courts.

He stressed that over time, the program had become increasingly institutionalized. With each new public fiduciary, there was an "enthusiasm of creation." Mr. Bogutz suggested term limits for the PCPF, perhaps similar to the management rule in the Peace Corps, in which volunteers, as well as key staff, are limited to a tenure of five years, a figure he characterized as an "inspired number." "In that five years, people figure you spend the first year getting the lay of the land and getting an assessment of what is going on. In the second year, you start to develop a plan, the third and fourth you implement and refine that plan, the fifth you sit back, enjoy, and maybe do a little tweaking. The sixth year, you start to coast." He supported that notion by saying that in Canada, the public trustee has a six-year limited term, with one possible reappointment. He emphasized that it is consistent with civil service also, but is perhaps not a political reality.

Mr. Bogutz addressed the fee-generating ability of the program, stressing that he would not eliminate it. He said he believed there was no reason that the government should provide free services to people who could afford to pay for them. He thought the program was not established as a program for indigent people, but was a program for those who did not have anyone else willing and qualified to serve as guardian. He suggested greater aggressiveness by the court in weeding out the fee-generating cases in which a private attorney is willing to serve and the maintenance of a referral file of those professionals willing to take such cases. He emphasized that the fee feature should not be used as a measure of the office's success.

Mr. Bogutz said that the public fiduciary stands in the unique position of a public advocate. He stated that IPs face a number of systemic issues, including eligibility complications for Medicaid benefits or quality of care in nursing homes. He analogized the public fiduciary to legal reform units in legal aid offices in the U.S. during the 1970s, and said that the public fiduciary was the ideal entity to take on such work for this group of people. He used the example of the public trustee in British Columbia, who recently settled an action for women with developmental disabilities who were sterilized in the 1970s and received damage settlements for them, as well as changing the policy so that it would not happen again. He emphasized that a private practitioner would not bring such cases, but a guardian with several hundred IPs would bring such cases, and that a public official in such a position should look for these issues.

Finally, he suggested that every public fiduciary office in every jurisdiction should generate an annual report that sets forth: the number of cases; the types of cases; the activities in which the office is engaged in terms of making the IP's situation better; how the office is involved in advocacy, litigation, legislation, and local rulemaking; caseload characteristics and statistics; the fees generated; and the adequacy of fiscal support. He remarked that such information should be sent to the presiding judge, the chief justice of the Supreme Court, the county board of supervisors, and the state bar association. "If you had to really account for what you are doing, and you had to put out what the achievements were, what the failures were, you will [sic] be a whole lot more attentive during the course of the year as to what it is you are doing." He went further to suggest requiring this information through the courts as part of the court's rulemaking authority.

Mr. Bogutz spoke about the unmet need for guardians, saying:

> But what is happening as the Boomers turn 60 at the rate of 7,000 a day? [We are] completely unprepared in all levels for that. The Baby Boomers will be geographically distant from their families. . . . They are, as much as they look like they are driving BMWs, they are owned by the bank. The average retirement plan is less than $10,000 in value for the Boomers. Eighty-five percent of women over sixty, according to AARP, have to work until they are 74. And so what is public guardianship across the county going to be doing to meet that need other than standing back and saying, "We will put you on a waiting list?"

He stressed that with society becoming more and more geographically isolated, the public fiduciary needs to fill a greater and greater role.

Notable Features of the Office

The public fiduciary has a wealth of institutional knowledge in terms of the people who have worked with the office for many years.

The role of the court investigator is especially strong in Pima County. One court investigator recently served as President of the NGA. The PCPF has had a practicing attorney as the head of the office since its inception.

Concluding Assessments

Strengths

1. Highly experienced and dedicated staff.
2. Public fiduciaries are certified by the state.

3. Low staff turnover in a 15-year period.
4. Use of a nurse in the office for medical case management.

Weaknesses

1. Funding is inadequate, while requests for services are steadily increasing.
2. As mentioned in the commentary about Maricopa County, the public fiduciary does not have similar systems across the state, which reduces uniformity for the offices, but allows them to tailor to local needs. Site visits were conducted only in the two most populous areas. Respondents reported that there are generally fewer resources for rural counties.
3. Staff-to-IP ratios are too high.
4. Interest from the pooled trust was used to purchase office equipment. (Ms. Royal reports: "Earned interest credits accrue to pay for accounting and case management software, which defrays the cost to each estate. Moreover, due to this arrangement, clients are not subjected to regularly [sic] monthly banking service fees. It should be noted that the amount of interest that would accrue to each individual account is *de minimus* and thus, is not construed as an unlawful taking of client property. Finally, since most checking accounts do not accrue interest, overall this arrangement has proven to be extremely cost effective and in the collective best interest of our client population.")[13]
5. The office lacks an efficient and effective data and asset management system.

Opportunities

1. The continued development of a medical case management model.
2. The expansion of the office to include guardians of minors, but only with adequate staffing and funding. (Ms. Royal notes that such an expansion is not currently statutorily authorized.)
3. The continued use of limited guardianships.
4. The maintenance of national, state, and local collaborations and partnerships ensure adequate knowledge bases, inspire innovation, and enhance staff development.
5. Secure voting rights for IPs who are able to vote.
6. Creative approaches to running the office.

Threats

1. Underfunding of the office.
2. Phenomenal growth of older adults in the Pima County area.
3. The fragmentation of the mental health and social service systems.

4. The aging of the public fiduciary workforce.
5. Litigation.

An Assessment of Then and Now

Like Maricopa County, the 1970s research team studied the office of the public fiduciary in Pima County due to its reputation as a well-run program with a visionary leader. Since its inception, the office has been headed by an attorney and funded by both county funds and funds generated by the estates of IPs.

The inclusion of a court investigator and the overall maturation of the office have increased its efficiency and service, but the caseloads are too high, especially when cases are increasingly complex and more dangerous.

These final observations are made regarding the Pima County Office of the Public Fiduciary:

1. The collection of a fee for service has become a marker for the effectiveness of the office. Discontinuing the county's requirement of fee generation for the office is recommended. The office is in a position to petition for the adjudication of incapacity and the appointment of itself in more fee-generating cases than indigent cases. (Ms. Royal states that she totally disagrees "since only clients who can afford to pay are required to do so subject to court approval.")
2. The PCPF should not use a pooled trust for any purpose other than the direct benefit of the individual IP. The use of the interest from the IPs' accounts for purchasing office computers is not appropriate; such needs should be included in budget requests to the county. (However, see Ms. Royal's previous explanation in #4 under Weaknesses).
3. The office can petition for its own IPs, creating the potential for self-aggrandizement.
4. The office was unable to produce information on the number of IPs it services, and no comparison is possible to the number of IPs (353) in 1979. The office should prioritize installing a system of easily retrievable data on each IP and on the program in general. (Ms. Royal says: "This information is readily available, but we were in the midst of a conversion and bank change at the time, so it was not a priority to expend precious staff time to retrieve this information. It should be further noted that monthly reports are generated, which provide an abundance of essential statistical data.")
5. Related to observation #4 above, the office should, at a minimum, provide an annual report that sets forth the number of cases, types of cases, activities in which the office is engaged in terms of making the IPs situation better, activities of the office related to advocacy, litigation, legislation, local rulemaking, caseload characteristics and statistics, the fees

generated, and the adequacy of fiscal support. This information should be sent to the presiding judge, the chief justice of the Supreme Court, the county board of supervisors, and the state bar association.

6. The office should further explore its potential for advocacy.

7. The unmet need appears real, especially given that interviewees reported that the office had instituted a freeze twice in one year. (Ms Royal reported that "when resources are overextended and staff are swamped," a freeze on new cases is permitted as a preventative measure and "its duration is typically for only one week at a time.") The explosion of the population of older adults in Pima County and the need for IP guardians is not well understood. The office should educate the various service sectors and the state bar regarding the rising and unmet need for public guardians.

8. The level of professionalism in this office is impressive. Current staff members are active at national levels, a circumstance that infuses the office with knowledge of best practices.

9. The long history of excellent PCPF heads is impressive. All have left the office and continued distinguished careers as elder law attorneys. More use should be made of their collective wisdom to improve the offices of the public guardian at both state and national levels.

10. The departure of some long-time office personnel appears to be imminent. The office should develop a succession management staffing plan similar to that of the Maricopa County Public Fiduciary.

11. The PCPF needs more funding to meet its current unmet need, as evidenced by having to freeze case acceptances twice a year and the burgeoning population of older adults.

THE SAN BERNARDINO COUNTY, CALIFORNIA, PUBLIC GUARDIAN

The San Bernardino County Office of the Public Guardian (SBPG) was undergoing administrative changes during the site visit in March 2006. As a result of political realignment in the county, the office was moved in January 2005 from its previous location within the coroner's office. The board of supervisors placed the public administrator, the treasurer, and the coroner in the same office. The SBPG was moved to the Department of Aging and Adult Services (DAAS). At the time of the site visit, the director of that program was also responsible for the area agency on aging (AAA) adult programs, including in-home supportive services and APS. The public guardian office was physically moving to a different office in Redlands, which would increase travel times for all of the deputy public guardians.

The upper-level administrator was Jane Adams, the deputy director of the Department of Aging and Disability Services. Ms. Adams had transferred from a position in the traditional assistance department six months earlier. She brought 20 years of experience working in San Bernardino County, and holds a master's degree in business administration.

Ms. Adams explained that the recent structural change was prompted by a need for greater administrative efficiency. Interviews revealed that before the administrative change, the office experienced a budget shortfall of $300,000. The office had apparently anticipated receiving an amount of targeted case management funds that was not forthcoming from the federal government. These funds were not necessarily deemed appropriate for the functions of public guardians. The office had counted on these as hard monies, but this calculation proved fiscally unwise. At the time of the site visit, the SBPG was undergoing a study to improve office efficiencies, with the issue of targeted case management (TCM) funding representing an area of particular scrutiny. The office is determined not to expend any further efforts pursuing that funding stream. Instead, the office will pursue Medical Administrative Assistance funding.

Statutory Authorization

The SBPG, like the LAPG, is established statutorily under California Government Code §274340.

Recent Litigation

Although the SBPG was not the subject of recent litigation, the neighboring county of Riverside in the 1990s had a scandal involving a private conservator who was taking money from conservatees. Also involved were the conservator's attorney (both were serving prison sentences) and a judge, who was reportedly funneling cases to her. As a result of the case, all conservators were required to provide more detailed accounting records than had been required previously.

Organization and History

Prior to the site visit, a survey requesting basic information concerning the office was sent. Unfortunately, very little information was provided, and so the picture of the administrative organization of the office is sketchy. The office was under the direction of a first-line supervisor, who was leading the office while a second-level manager was out of the office on extended medical leave. The lack of detail about the structure and functioning of the office continued during the site visit. Detailed information about the budget under which the office operated or the number of IPs served was not provided. Ms. Adams indicated that there were 27 staff persons in the office, including resource management, clerks, and deputies. She said that the office served approximately 500 IPs.

A San Bernardino County court investigator, who holds a law degree and has 26 years of experience with the position, investigates new cases. The investigator visits the proposed IP under Probate Code §1826 and attempts to obtain medical information on the person's condition. The court investigator serves as the eyes and ears of the court and, upon investigation, submits a report to the judge, generally five days prior to a hearing. The court investigator both investigates complaints about conservators that may arise, and monitors existing conservatorship cases. The court investigator regarded approximately half the complaints concerning guardianship cases as bogus. Many of these cases involved relatives who had been denied conservator appointments.

Lanterman-Petris-Short Conservatorships

The LPS conservatorships, discussed in detail in the LAPG site visit, were by far the most common cases served by SBPG.

The San Bernardino Department of Behavioral Health (DBH), referred to by Ms. Adams as the "customer of the SBPG," provides the office with $1.3 million for services such as assuming control of the IP's property, caring for the person, providing services to support treatment and/or placement, establishing treatment plans (which are supported by DBH) and care assessments, and serving as the liaison to state, county, and private agencies. This arrangement was specified in a memorandum of understanding (MOU) between the Public Guardian/Conservator Program and the Department of Behavioral Health.

Some of the DBH conservatorships are authorized dementia powers (discussed below), and some are probate conservatorships, but all are LPS conservatorships. The Department of Behavioral Health prefers public guardianship over private guardianship for the persons it serves, due to problems regarding placement. A representative from the Department indicated that with a public guardian, there is no conflict of interest regarding placement, emotional attachment to the client, or money management. The public guardian manages the finances and allows DBH to make placement decisions, as outlined in the MOU.

Probate Conservatorships

Probate conservatorships comprised a lower number of the IPs served by the office and are explained in detail in the description for the LAPG.

One streamlining measure that the DBH was considering was to "drop 50 or so probate conservatorships [of persons] who are old and no longer mentally ill or demented." Some of the DBH staff thought there were persons on the public guardian rolls who did not need their attention. The belief was that the condition of those persons was stable, that nothing clinical was appropriate for them, and that the public guardian rolls were inflated by the care of such individuals. The DBH concluded that there was no real need for services and that there were other cases that warranted the attention of the public guardian rather than the older persons.

DBH reportedly did not serve such persons. Dementia is not an allowable diagnosis under MediCal/Medicaid, and so DBH was unable to treat. "Drop," as understood from the interview, meant a drop from the public guardian rolls, but what would happen to them (e.g., restoration of capacity or the location of a family successor) was not clearly explained.

Dementia Powers

Dementia powers came into existence in the 1990s as a mechanism to avoid the LPS conservatorship. A public authority initiates the LPS conservatorships. Practitioners and the courts recognized that some categories of individuals needed 1) the administration of psychotropic medications, and/or 2) to be placed in a secured-perimeter facility. Until the establishment of dementia powers, if an individual needed either, an LPS conservatorship was required. Reportedly, restrictions on LPS conservatorships make them difficult to administer and re-quire much time and public resources. The law was amended to allow probate conservators to have those powers if they were warranted medically and to add an additional layer of protection for advocacy. Thus, when petitioners request "dementia powers," it is mandatory for the court to appoint an attorney for the proposed IP. The petitioning attorney does not typically continue on the case after the conservatorship hearing.

The Application of 1981 Criteria

Adequate Funding and Staffing

The requirements for full-time equivalent professional staff are the comple-tion of department training and four years of experience, an associate's degree plus two years of experience and the completion of training, or a bachelor's de-gree and the completion of department training. The office contains deputies, supervising deputies, and senior deputies. Deputies have a caseload and manage the affairs of the client, or perform professional and technical work. Junior depu-ties work with senior deputies in order to understand the nuances of the job. The average LPS-conservatorship caseload was 55 to 70 IPs per staff member. The probate conservatorship ratio was 55:1. One interviewee indicated, "Somebody does a good job of weeding out a lot of cases we shouldn't be getting." Although the public guardian's overall numbers were down compared to past years, public guardian staffers thought their clients were more severely mentally ill and were quite often criminals. Included in the mix are persons with alcohol or drug prob-lems. Persons in the criminal justice system noted that court appearances were problematic: the public guardian did not have caged cars and did not transport.

On the probate side of the house, the SBPG quite often has IPs who are abused either physically or fiscally by family members. The family members, in turn, became abusive to the public guardians. Often, the IPs still wanted contact with the family members, but the family members continued to abuse them. Also in probate are clients with developmental disabilities who are put under probate conservatorships because their care-giving mothers are reportedly abusing them. Probate conservatorships increasingly involve special-needs trusts and successor trusteeships.

Staff members thought the office needed more clerical staff. At one time, there was one clerk per deputy. Now, there is one for every two deputies. There are not enough placement options in the county. Most IPs live in board and care facilities, but the public guardian staff felt that many clients needed a level of care with higher supervision. Public guardian staffers considered state reimbursement for clients to be far too low, and fewer facilities were in business. No clients of the SBPG were living in their own homes. If clients are not in facilities, the SBPG reportedly does not take them.

Collection of fees for services. Like the LAPG, the program has the authority to collect a fee or charge the IP for services. The court approves a fee schedule with the amount predicated on the size of the IP's estate.

Structure and Function

Conflict of interest—ability to petition. Similar to the LAPG, the SBPG petitions for legal incapacity and the appointment of itself as guardian. Unlike the LAPG, no data were provided on how often that occurred, nor were there exact figures regarding the IPs served. The exact size of the staff beyond Ms. Adams' estimates was unavailable. Staff members came from a variety of backgrounds and educational levels. Several persons had been with the office for over 20 years. There was an investigator for the public guardian on the staff who determined, based on the referral coming into the office, whether or not an individual met the criteria for a probate conservatorship. This individual also identified assets and whether there were any alternatives to the service of the public guardian or conservatorship. Persons with mental health problems were referred to DBH for LPS conservatorship assessments.

Regarding the possible conflict of interest of location in a service-providing agency, public guardian staff members indicated that the law lays out how they perform their role and who is appropriate for conservatorship. They thought that if they were not under DAAS, another service-providing agency would provide placement, such as the DBH, that would also create conflicts of interest.

Incapacitated Persons

Beyond Ms. Adams' estimate that the office served around 500 IPs, no further data were provided. The LPS conservatorships, which tended to concern more male IPs, were a greater part of the SBPG caseload than probate conservatorships, which tended to concern more female IPs.

The IPs at this site were unavailable for interviews, unlike at other interview sites. The county attorney advised the SBPG that the job of the public guardian was to advocate and protect individual IPs. The country attorney was wary of individuals studying conservatorship and looking to interview IPs in particular. An example cited was the *Los Angeles Times* article that was, according to him, distorted and did not give the full picture of the problem. His concern was that distortion would happen again. Even after speaking with him personally, his answer remained the same, and so there were no interviews with any IPs in San Bernardino.

The Adequacy of Criteria and Procedures

Although the information received did not indicate what records were kept for each IP, at a minimum, the following was reported for each public guardianship client:

1. The public guardian relied upon the care plans of nursing homes and DBH.
2. There is an internal audit of cases every three months, and there is an internal audit of all cases received every six months. It was explained that there were two types of ongoing audits. The first is an internal audit of cases that the program has had for over a year. The second is an initial audit of those cases they have had for three to six months. The auditor comptroller also audits the office. The auditor comptroller audits the fiscal side of the program and the program is occasionally audited by the grand jury. The Social Security office has also audited the office.
3. The relationship with the courts was regarded as nonadversarial. The public defender contracts with a private attorney to represent the AIPs, and there is a tacit agreement between county counsel, the public guardian, and the private attorney's office that the case goes to a jury if the potential conservatee is objecting.

Decision making. When the office receives a potential probate conservatorship, medical consent is requested in the petition. This was a recent change in procedure intended to streamline the amount of time and resources spent going to court. The LPS conservatorships require that the program go to court for any medically invasive procedure. All deputies have the same authority to make decisions. During his or her first year, a new deputy has all decisions authorized by a more senior deputy.

Internal Issues for the Program

Relationships with APS. The program apparently has a rocky relationship with APS. APS perceived that the SBPG is not responsive when APS refers a case to them. The SBPG program was slow to respond to requests. The public guardian program thought that there were conservators available for people in their own homes and that a private conservator was often found for many of the individuals APS referred.

Relationships with DBH. The DBH and the public guardian had issues in need of resolution. The DBH thought that the public guardian should manage the day-to-day assessments of the clients. The public guardian office thought that the DBH did not make appropriate placement decisions for the clients. The SBPG had its own policy stipulating that conservatees be placed only in licensed facilities, thus eliminating room-and-board placements and community-care licensing. San Bernardino County public guardian clients were placed only in licensed board and care facilities reviewed and approved by the SBPG. The DBH is acutely aware of a shortage of beds and feels that room and board beds are already licensed and appropriate for some SBPG clients.

Outside Assessments of the Office

Outside commentators thought that the office needed more funding and more staff members. The office, due to the fiscal shortfall, did not visit clients as much as necessary and was not as responsive to other care community partners in the county. If the office had more funding for more staff, it could assume more guardianships. Despite the difficult conditions created by underfunding, the longevity of the deputies in the office was regarded as a plus.

Notable Features of the Office

The SBPG will accept clients living in their own home, though outside commentators reported that it was not currently doing so.

The SBPG office was in transition and was unable to provide information about its size or the IPs being served.

Concluding Assessments

Strengths

1. Dedicated and experienced staff.
2. Warmth of the staff for the persons served.

Weaknesses

1. Caseloads are too high.
2. Increased inconvenience due to moving the office.

3. At the time of the site visit, there was a new administrator who was relatively unfamiliar with the functions of the public guardian.
4. Tenuous relationship with the DBH.

Opportunities

1. Strengthening the relationship with APS.
2. Strengthening the relationship with DBH.
3. Changing oversight of the administration of the office from the office of the Coroner to that of the Department of Aging and Adult Services.

Threats

1. The apparent underfunding of the office.
2. The complexity of the LPS conservatorships.
3. The loss of the MOU with DBH.
4. Administrative changes were made too quickly and without staff buy-in.

An Assessment of Then and Now

When researchers studied the SBPG in late 1979, an individual with a social work background, whose assistant had a business administration background, staffed the office. Today, an individual with an M.B.A. oversees the office. Caseloads ranged from 110 to 165 per staff member in the 1970s, and were apparently cut in half by 2006. It appears that the office was skeptical about maintaining IPs in their homes at the time of the first study, and that skepticism appears institutionalized in 2006, as no IPs were maintained in their homes. Unlike in the 1970s, the majority of the IPs were male since LPS conservatorships dominate SBPG caseloads.

In the late 1970s, the unmet need for guardianship was reportedly substantial. However, the same sentiment was not encountered during the 2006 visit. The office had taken steps, largely through the program's public guardian investigator, to stem the tide of appointments. Acceptance criteria were apparently put in place in the interim. The office did not appear to be under as great a crush of work as it did at the time of the initial site visit.

In the 1970s, one conflict of interest was that the public guardian office was administratively placed under the domain of the coroner, and while that arrangement was altered, a conflict of interest remained in the form of the office's placement under the Department of Aging and Adult Services. While a conflict theoretically exists, a severe problem was not caused practically, unless it was manifested with the Department of Behavioral Health. Because the SBPG had the DBH as its customer, it appeared to have little leverage when its staff believed that decisions for clients were made inappropriately or improperly.

An attitude in SBPG that DBH is its customer seems inconsistent with a guardian's fiduciary responsibility to its client, the IP. This suggests the continued relevance of Alexander and Lewin's caution against guardianship primarily serving third-party interests, rather than the IP's interests,[14] as well as Erving Goffman's identification of the "true clients" of mental hospitals.[15]

Concerns were raised regarding the following features of the SBPG:

1. The office can petition for its own IPs, which creates the potential for self-aggrandizement.
2. The relationship of the SBPG with the DBH is a source of concern. The MOU may not permit the SBPG to advocate fully for clients due to the established service arrangement. The concerns over the office's arrangement with the DBH were raised because a conflict of interest exists that may stifle the advocacy function of the public guardian when the DBH is involved.
3. While staff-to-client ratios have reportedly been cut in half since 1979, they are still far too high.
4. There is a danger that LPS conservatorships, due to their complexity, receive far more attention than the more stable probate conservatorships.
5. Surprisingly, the office did not produce answers to relatively simple questions about clients and staff in the office. There was an inability to determine if the office maintained computerized records. To fail to maintain them and ensure that they are easily accessible in 2006 seems anachronistic.
6. There were two levels of internal program audits and those audits performed by the county, but audits by persons knowledgeable in the area of public guardianship were apparently not conducted.
7. The agency should accumulate information on its cost savings for the county.
8. The greatest concern for this office is its administrative change from its placement under the umbrella of the coroner's office to that of the Department of Aging and Adult Services.

NOTES

Portions of this chapter are based on Teaster, Pamela, Erica Wood, Susan Lawrence, and Winsor Schmidt. "Wards of the State: A National Study of Public Guardianship." *Stetson Law Review* 37, no. 1 (2007): 193–241. Courtesy of the *Stetson Law Review*.

1. This very issue was hotly debated in the Terri Shiavo case, which was under a worldwide lens as the Florida site visit was being written up.
2. Schmidt et al., "A Descriptive Analysis of Professional and Volunteer Programs."
3. Robin Fields, "Adult Caretaker Program Overworked, Underfunded: Report Finds That the County Office That Serves As Conservator for Incapacitated Clients Is Beset by Problems," *Los Angeles Times* (May 12, 2005).

4. See, e.g., Sandra Reynolds and Kathleen Wilber, "Protecting Persons with Severe Cognitive and Mental Disorders: An Analysis of Public Conservatorship in Los Angeles County," *Aging and Mental Health* 1, no. 1 (1997): 87–97.

5. Cf. Lachs et al., "Adult Protective Service Use and Nursing Home Placement," 737–738 ("The relative contribution of elder protective referral [including "pursuit of guardianship] to [nursing home placement] is enormous ["4-to 5-fold risk conferred by elder mistreatment and neglect"] and far exceeds the variance explained by such variables as dementia, functional disability, and poor social networks").

6. This resonates with the interview of an Arizona psychiatrist for a county general hospital in the 1981 study, who made the following observation:

There is a question of pursuing a tradition of having a family member serve as guardian of an elderly parent or of using a private guardian for that purpose. Neither may be appropriate, in this instance, because, he suggested, "*for every $100,000 in a given estate a lawyer shows up, for every $25,000 a family member shows up.*" [If there is no money, then no one shows up.] Government, therefore, should be involved in guardianship because the private system is not trustworthy. For example, family members can take steps to ensure that the ward never leaves the state hospital and so could private attorneys. By contrast, a public guardian has no financial or other bias, so the physical location of the ward is not an issue. [Emphasis added.]

Schmidt et al., *Public Guardianship and the Elderly*, 109.

7. "The Center For Guardianship Certification was created in 1994 as an allied foundation of the National Guardianship Association (NGA) to enhance the quality of guardianship services through national certification." See http://www.guardianshipcert. org/.

8. Maryland Code Annotated §13-707(a)(10); §14-203(b); and §14-307(b).

9. Maryland Code Annotated §14-102(b).

10. Maryland Code Annotated §§14-401 through 404.

11. Schmidt et al., "A Descriptive Analysis of Professional and Volunteer Programs for the Delivery of Guardianship Services"; Teaster et al., "Staff Service and Volunteer Staff Service Models for Public Guardianship and 'Alternatives' Services: Who Is Served and With What Outcomes?"; Teaster, et al., *The Florida Public Guardian Programs*; Teaster and Roberto, *Virginia Public Guardian and Conservator Programs: Summary of the First Year Evaluation;* Teaster and Roberto, *Virginia Public Guardian and Conservator Programs: Evaluation of Program Status and Outcomes.*

12. The Council of Accreditation is a New York-based "international, independent, not-for-profit, child- and family-service and behavioral healthcare accrediting organization," http://www.coastandards.org/about.php.

13. Cf. Washington Certified Professional Guardian Board Standard of Practice 406.10:

A guardian shall not commingle the funds of an incapacitated person with funds of the guardian or the funds of staff. A guardian may consolidate client accounts, using appropriate accounting software and procedures, including pro-rata assignment of interest earned and fees paid and accurate individual accounting for each client's funds, provided the guardian has received specific authority from the court to do so. Each payment from a consolidated account shall be from funds held in the account on behalf of the individual for whom the payment is made.

See: http://www.courts.wa.gov/committee/?fa=committee.child&child_id=30& committee_id=117.

14. Alexander and Lewin, *The Aged and the Need for Surrogate Management*, 136.

15. Erving Goffman, *Asylums: Essays on the Social Situation of Mental Patients and Other Inmates* Garden City: NY Anchor Books, 1961, 384:

In citing the limitations of the service model [I do not] mean to claim that I can suggest some better way of handling persons called mental patients. Mental hospitals are not found in society because supervisors, psychiatrists, and attendants want jobs; mental hospitals are found because there is a market for them. If all the mental hospitals were emptied and closed today, tomorrow relatives, police, and judges would raise clamor for new ones; and these true clients of the mental hospital would demand an institution to satisfy their needs.

Chapter 4

CONCLUSIONS AND RECOMMENDATIONS

Chip is a 58-year-old man with Down syndrome. Social services intervened and placed him in an institution when he was six, when they determined his mother was unable to care for him. In the 1970s, Chip moved into a group home in the community, and was appointed a public guardian. Chip learned how to navigate the public transportation system and for many years, was able to hold a job at the local grocery store. Five years ago, he began to show early signs of Alzheimer's disease (AD). As his AD progressed, his behavior became more problematic and unpredictable. Twice, Chip has been found wandering downtown very late at night by the local police department. The group home is no longer an appropriate and safe placement for Chip, but nor is a nursing home a good option, although it is likely that he will be placed in one.

This chapter presents conclusions and provides both recommendations for the future and the hallmarks of an effective, efficient, and economical public guardianship program. This chapter is of particular interest to persons interested in advocacy and public policy, and will guide the next 25 years of both public and private guardianship.

The conclusions and recommendations in this chapter arise from: (1) the findings of the 2004 national survey, and (2) site visits in Florida, Illinois, Los Angeles, California, Delaware, Maryland, Maricopa County, Arizona, Pima County, Arizona, and San Bernardino, California.

The conclusions and recommendations follow the key areas set out in the conclusions of the 1981 study, thus enabling a direct comparison over time. A departure from the 1981 study is that the 2007 study includes more empirical information because more is available. Nonetheless, some of the conclusions are less empirical than others and should be regarded as preliminary findings for future, more in-depth scrutiny.

A key task of the study was to identify states with public guardianship statutes and programs of any kind. Fifty jurisdictions were discovered (49 states plus the District of Columbia) with either explicit or implicit forms of public guardianship or guardianship of last resort. As in the 1981 study, some explicit statutes proved to offer little in the way of programs, while some of the implicit programs were highly evolved.

Also consistent with Schmidt's study was the considerable variation in public guardianship programs, both interstate and intrastate. Collapsing the states into the organizing models (i.e., court, independent state office, social service providing agency, and county) is challenging because the variations in law and practice do not always fall neatly into categories. Although the social service agency model was the predominant model in 1981, its application has jumped considerably, from 19 states to 32 states in 2007. As Schmidt highlighted in his earlier work, the heterogeneity of public guardianship programs is emphasized as the conclusions and recommendations below are delineated.

CONCLUSIONS

Overarching Observations

1. Public guardianship programs serve a wide variety of individuals.
The overwhelming majority of the state statutes provide for services to incapacitated individuals who are determined to need guardians under the adult guardianship law, but who have no person or private entity qualified and willing to serve. However, four state schemes limit services to elderly people, four focus exclusively on individuals with specific mental disabilities, three specifically reference minors, and some target services to APS clients. Responses to the survey conducted in 2004 reveal that there is a relatively even distribution of male and female clients. Minority populations constitute 30 percent (Illinois—Office of State Guardian) to 33 percent (California—Los Angeles) of those IPs in some programs and a surprisingly slight proportion of the total population of IPs in others, such as in Kentucky (which is likely a factor of state demographics). As expected, most of the individuals under public guardianship are indigent. The majority are placed in an institution of some kind, usually a nursing home or state hospital. Although more options for habilitation exist now than 25 ago, if the IPs are poor, then often the only available living arrangement is a nursing home as a result of federal and state funding restrictions, especially those issued by Medicaid.

2. Public guardianship programs serve younger individuals and individuals with more complex needs than those served 25 years ago.
The 2004 survey found that individuals age 65 or over constitute between 37 percent and 57 percent of a state's public guardianship clients, while those age 18–64 comprise between 43 percent and 62 percent of the total. Younger clients include a range and increasing number of individuals with mental illnesses, mental retardation, developmental disabilities, head injuries, and substance abuse issues, reflective of the general population. Some clients, both younger and older, have a history of involvement in the criminal justice system.

In addition, many older clients have a dual diagnosis of dementia and severe mental illness. Many individuals with mental retardation or developmental disabilities are aging. For example, interview respondents in Kentucky report, "The typical clients, older women in nursing homes, are now only half of the caseload," and "Clients are younger and have many more drug and alcohol problems. Public guardianship used to be regarded as a custodial program, but no longer." These complex cases involving people with challenging behavioral problems are much more labor-intensive than the previous population set.

A public guardian in Arizona stated similar concerns. IPs have become far more dangerous than in past years, as some are aggressive, carry weapons, and are frequently using illicit drugs, such as crack cocaine and methamphetamines. In addition, persons preying on incapacitated people are more dangerous than they were 25 years ago. People more openly exploit older adults and may be criminals themselves, sometimes taking advantage of elders for money or drugs.

3. In states with institutionalization data, the majority of individuals under public guardianship are in facilities. In the survey, 15 programs (14 states) report that their proportion of institutionalized clients ranged from 37 percent to 97 percent. Eleven of 15 programs providing this information indicated that between 60 percent and 97 percent of their clients lived in institutional settings. Twelve jurisdictions indicated that between 60 percent and 100 percent lived in institutional settings. Interviewees in some states noted that very few individuals are in the community by the time they are referred to the public guardianship office, that nursing home placement often is automatic after appointment, and that IPs generally have little say in this placement decision. Other states and programs described making greater efforts than in the past to locate appropriate community placements.

The U.S. Supreme Court's 1999 *Olmstead*[1] decision provided a strong mandate for an evaluation of the high proportion of public guardianship clients who are institutionalized. *Olmstead* served as a charge to public guardianship programs to assess their institutionalized clients for possible transfer to community settings and to vigorously promote home- and community-based placements when possible, a challenging goal when both public guardianship staffing and community-based care resources are at a premium. Nonetheless, "unjustified isolation . . . is properly regarded as discrimination based on disability."[2]

Program Characteristics

4. Public guardianship programs may be categorized into four distinct models. In 1977, Regan and Springer outlined four public guardianship models: (1) a court model, (2) an independent state office model, (3) a division of a social service agency model, and (4) a county model. Borrowing from Regan and Springer, the 1981 Schmidt study used these same four models, but recognized that many exceptions and variations existed and that, in some states, public guardianship did not fit neatly into this taxonomy.

The 2004 national survey conducted in Phase I of the current project used a variation on the classification, and in reviewing the state responses, found that the original Regan and Springer taxonomy remained appropriate. Note that the social service agency model includes both state and local entities. Thus, some county-level programs are, in fact, located in social service agencies and are therefore described in the social service agency model, rather than in the county model.

At first blush, the social service agency model might seem the most logical placement for public guardianship, given that its staffers are knowledgeable about services and have networks in place to secure services. However, this model presents a serious conflict of interest in that the guardian cannot objectively evaluate and monitor the services provided, nor can the guardian zealously advocate for IPs' interests, including by lodging complaints about the services provided. The filing of an administrative action or a lawsuit may be stymied or prevented entirely.

The 2007 study found that 5 states and 6 programs use the court model, 4 states use the independent state office model, an overwhelming 32 states place public guardianship in a division of a social service agency (either state or local), and 11 states use a county model. (Illinois and Wisconsin use two different models.)

5. All states except one have some form of public guardianship. In 1981, the Schmidt study found that 34 states had public guardianship provisions. The 2007 study found that all of the states except Nebraska have some form of public guardianship. In most cases, there is statutory authority for these programs (see Appendix B), but some states have developed programs or expended funds for public guardianship without explicit public guardianship statutes.

It is critical to note that while a state may nominally designate an official to serve, or provide some limited dollars for guardianship of last resort, vast areas of many states are unserved or underserved, and the unmet need is compelling (see #13 below).

6. A clear majority of the states uses a social services model for public guardianship. A striking finding in this study was the rise in the number of states (32) falling under this model. This compares with 19 states in 1981.

The social service agency model might seem the most logical placement for public guardianship because staff members are knowledgeable about services and have networks in place to secure services. However, this model presents a serious conflict of interest, as described above in section 4.

Interview and focus group respondents were repeatedly asked if they regarded such a placement as a problem, and most did. As emphasized earlier, the advocacy needs of the IP are severely compromised when the program serves as both guardian and service provider. The ability to zealously advocate for the IP's needs and to objectively assess services is gravely diminished, and the ability to sue the agency if necessary is effectively nonexistent. As a result, the person's physical and mental outcomes may be adversely affected.

7. Some of the governmental entities providing public guardianship services do not perceive that they are doing so. The question of "What is public guardianship?" goes to the heart of this study, and the answer is far more difficult to discern than anticipated. The study's definition of public guardianship is broad and based on government agency and government funding. It includes some administrative arrangements that are not explicitly labeled as "public guardianship" under the corresponding state laws. For example, a social service agency is designated to serve if no private guardian is available, or APS is appointed in certain situations. The definition also includes some instances in which state or local governments pay for private entities to serve as guardians of last resort. For instance, a state may fund private non-profit organizations, attorneys, or private individuals to serve. A number of states with such implicit or de facto systems maintain that they do not have public guardianship. This perception may undermine the visibility and accountability of these fiduciary functions, which occur under public or governmental aegis.

8. A number of states contract out for guardianship services. Schmidt's study did not examine this phenomenon, but today, 11 states contract out for public guardianship services. Arguably, this "contracting out" approach allows states to experiment with various models of public guardianship service provision tailored to the needs of a particular region. However, this practice is not without peril and presents a service effectiveness and efficiency conundrum. Public administration literature indicates that contracting out for services is appropriate when the government services in question are discrete (e.g., repairing potholes). However, when the services are highly complex, as with public guardianship, it is best that they are provided by a governmental entity. Under the "privatization premise",[3] contracting of this nature may pose a substantial threat to the provision of public guardianship services due to attenuated and unclear lines of authority (accountability).

Guardianship of Person and Property: The Functions of the Public Guardianship Program

9. Many public guardianship programs serve as both guardian of the person and the property, but some serve more limited roles. A high number of clients receive guardian of the person services only. The vast majority of state statutes provide for public guardianship programs to serve as both guardian of the person and property, but two specify powers over property only and one is limited to personal matters only (Appendix A). Although the statutory emphasis in the earlier Schmidt study was on money management, which reduces the importance of guardianship of the person, the current statutes provide more broadly for a range of guardianship services.

In practice, programs more frequently function as guardian of the person than as guardian of the property. In the 2004 national survey, 32 programs reported serving as guardian of the person, and 27 reported serving as guardian of the property. The number of individuals receiving guardian of the person services was significantly higher. In the social services model, which includes a majority of the states, the total reported number of IPs receiving guardian of the person services was 6,080; the number receiving guardian of property services was only 282; and the number receiving both guardian of the person and guardian of the property services was 3,866.

10. Public guardianship programs vary in the extent of the community education and outreach they perform. In 2004, 30 of 34 respondents indicated that they educated the community about public guardianship. They balance the function of education with provision of guardianship services to IPs. Nineteen programs provided technical assistance to private guardians, and four monitored private guardians. Not all programs are conducting this important education function, however. If client caseloads are far too high and projected to increase further, education serves as a possible mechanism for reducing caseloads, with suitable individuals recruited to serve as guardians. Raising public awareness of the function (or existence) of public guardianship could be an effective tool in raising funding levels. It bears mentioning, though, that the "woodwork effect" may occur along with public awareness (i.e., more general information about the programs may increase the number of clients the programs are asked to serve).

11. Petitioning is a problematic role for public guardianship programs. The 1981 study observed that public guardianship programs that petition for their own appointment are subject to clear conflicts of interest. On one hand, they may have an incentive to self-aggrandize by petitioning in cases where there may be another alternative. On the other hand, programs may decline to petition when they have an overload of cases, or when the case presents difficult behavior problems that would require a great deal of staff time. They may have an incentive to cherry pick the more stable cases. However, if the public guardianship program may not or does not petition, frequently, there is a backlog of cases in which at-risk individuals in need are simply not served, or in which preventable emergencies are not avoided.

In the 2004 national survey, some 25 responses (14 from service-providing agencies, 7 from county programs, 2 from court programs, and 2 from independent public guardianship programs) indicated that the public guardianship program petitions the court to serve as guardian for IPs. Some interview and focus group participants regarded this as a conflict and reported that the public guardianship program sought ways around it.

Some saw petitioning as a barrier to guardianship because of the filing fees and court fees paid by the petitioner. Others pointed out that the public guardianship program is stuck between a rock and a hard place: petitioning is a conflict, yet not petitioning means those in need may languish without attention. Still others found petitioning to be an appropriate role for public guardianship programs to play in light of the overwhelming need and noted the necessity for appropriate checks. Said an Arizona respondent:

> There are, more times than not, the petitioner and the individual nominating themselves to be the guardian. I don't see the conflict in that relationship. I believe the due process, the appointment of an attorney for the ward or protected person, as well as a probate court with general knowledge of the circumstance coming from the court investigator and other sources, I believe the process is such that the conflict, if there is a conflict, is eliminated in the sense of concern.[4]

12. Court costs and filing fees are a significant barrier to utilization of public guardianship services. People interviewed in several states indicated that court costs and filing fees often present an insurmountable obstacle to filing petitions for court appointment of the public guardian. In some areas, filing fees are waived if the respondent is indigent, but other areas have no such indigency waivers for the payment of fees that can easily run up to several hundred dollars. Nursing homes, assisted living facilities, and hospitals all may have an interest in filing a petition, but frequently, they do not step forward to provide payment. One state where nursing homes and hospitals are the most frequent petitioners for public guardianship is Delaware.

Funding and Staffing of Programs

13. States have significant unmet needs for public guardianship and other surrogate decision-making services, but they frequently cannot quantify the unmet need. A striking majority of survey respondents could not estimate the unmet need for public guardianship in the state. Only 16 of 53 jurisdictions were able to provide this critically important information. In Washington, a bar association task force made a projection of unmet need (4,500 Washington residents), as cited in the background report for the state's 2007 legislation.[5] Many interview and focus group respondents commented that the need was vast, but few estimates exist. Some respondents specifically cited a high and growing unmet need among people with mental illnesses, as well as among institutionalized adults.

The unmet need for public guardianship represents the moral imperative for seeking additional program funding and is the seminal reason that public guardianship exists. A number of states have conducted unmet need surveys (i.e., Florida, Virginia, and Utah). Not only should each state establish its unmet need numbers (with an unduplicated count), but, in addition, such an estimate should be calculated on a periodic, rather than one-time, basis. For example, Virginia conducted an updated unmet needs study from 2006–2007.[6]

14. Staff size and caseloads in public guardianship programs show enormous variability. In the 2004 survey, staff size varied from 1 individual in a single program to 90 individuals in one county alone. Caseloads also varied widely, with a low of 2 in Florida (a program in its infancy) to a high of 173 per staff person (New Mexico). The average ratio of staff to incapacitated individuals was 1:36. The total number of IPs per program ranged from 2 (the new program in Florida) to a high of 5,383 (Illinois Office of State Guardian). The median number that any program served was 216. Though most numbers are still significantly too high, in most cases, these numbers represent a decrease from those in Schmidt's study, with ratios cut in half in some instances. The reported time spent with individual clients ranged from 1 hour biannually to over 20 hours per week.

15. The educational requirements for staffers at public guardianship programs vary. In the 2004 survey, the educational requirements for program staffers varied considerably, with some requiring a high school diploma (two programs) and others requiring an advanced or terminal degree, such as a J.D. or Ph.D. Many persons from diverse fields are public guardians, but most tend to be from social work backgrounds or are attorneys. The certification of guardians, including public guardians, is now required or available in some states (i.e., Alaska, Arizona, California, Florida, Nevada, Oregon, Texas, and Washington). In addition, the CGC conducts an examination that certifies both "registered guardians" and "master guardians." The CGC has developed a Code of Ethics and Standards of Practice, portions of which many programs now use.[7]

16. Public guardianship programs are frequently understaffed and underfunded. Virtually all states reported that lack of funding and staffing is both their greatest weakness and their greatest threat. The study identified ratios as high as 1:50, 1:80, and even 1:173. Caseloads are increasing, yet program budgets are not rising commensurately, and, in some cases, staff positions are frozen. Frequently, cases are more complex than they were 25 years ago, reflecting a greater number of individuals with challenging behavioral problems, substance abuse issues, and severe mental illnesses, problems requiring a higher degree of staff oversight and interaction.

Some of the focus group and interview respondents revealed high frustration with the overload of vulnerable individuals in dire need and the program's limited ability to respond adequately. Some reported "staff burnout," "judges not sympathetic to the high caseload problem," "more labor-intensive cases," "not enough time to do proper accounting," "not enough time to see wards often enough," "triaging cases," "moratoriums on case acceptance," "too few restoration petitions," and "prohibitively high caseloads preventing a focus on individual needs." Eleven states estimated the additional funding that would be required to support adequate staff, with their figures ranging from $150,000 to $20 million.[8]

17. Although some public guardianship programs use ratios to cap the number of clients, most serve as guardians of last resort without limits on intake. Statutes in seven states (i.e., Florida, New Jersey, New Mexico, Tennessee, Vermont, Virginia, and Washington) provide for a ratio of staff to IPs served. These laws either require a specific statutory ratio or that administrative procedures or contracts set out a ratio. However, most public guardianship programs serve as true last resort and must accept cases, based on judicial appointment, regardless of their staffing level. This puts programs in an intractable position and places clients in jeopardy. The conundrum is that public guardianship was originally intended to fulfill the role of guardian of last resort, taking all comers with nowhere else to go, an essential part of the public safety net. Without sufficient funding, programs are stretched to the breaking point and fail to provide any real benefit to the individuals they are obligated to serve.

18. Funding for public guardianship is from a patchwork of sources, none of which is sufficient. In the prior 1981 study, state statutes were typically silent on public guardianship funding. Today, although almost half of the state statutes reference authorization for state or county monies, the actual appropriations are frequently insufficient or not forthcoming. Funding for public guardianship is often provided by a patchwork of sources. Most states that reported their funding sources named multiple channels, with state general funds as the leading source, followed by the fees collected from clients with assets.

Perhaps the most striking finding from the 2004 survey regarding funding was that the social service model, unlike the other models, pulled from all resources (i.e., state funds, client fees, county funds, federal funds, Medicaid funds, estate recovery, grants/foundations, and private donations). Fifteen states used client fees as a reimbursement for services. In particular, seven states used Medicaid dollars to fund the establishment of guardianship or for guardianship services. Some states list guardianship in their Medicaid plan. At least one state (Illinois) uses an administrative claiming model to access Medicaid funds in which the federal government provides a match for the state funds used to pay for the guardianship services that help incapacitated individuals to apply for Medicaid funds. At least one state (Kentucky) bills Medicaid for guardianship services under its targeted case management program. Washington uses Medicaid dollars to supplement funding for guardians, including the certified guardian providers approved under the 2007 legislation.

19. Data on costs per case are sparse, but estimates were in the range of $1,850 per year. The Los Angeles Public Guardianship Program estimated the cost per case for a "probate conservatorship" at approximately $1,897 per year and for an "LPS conservatorship" as about $1,433 per year. The Maricopa County Office of the Public Fiduciary estimated a yearly cost of $1,850, as did the Kentucky public guardianship program in the Phase I study. Additional data would facilitate the planning and funding of programs. (See #16 and the accompanying references above.)

20. The Supreme Court Olmstead decision provides a strong impetus to support public guardianship. The landmark 1999 U.S. Supreme Court *Olmstead* decision requires states to fully integrate people with disabilities into community settings when appropriate, rather than utilizing institutional placements. Often, individuals require surrogate decision makers to prevent institutionalization or to facilitate discharge and establish community supports. People with disabilities may languish unnecessarily in mental hospitals, in intermediate care facilities for people with developmental disabilities, or in nursing homes because they lack the assistance of a guardian. Thus, *Olmstead* serves as an impetus for states to address the unmet need by establishing and more fully funding public guardianship programs. For example, Virginia's 2007 strategic plan for *Olmstead* implementation includes "surrogate decision making" as one of seven "critical success factors" in advancing community integration of people with disabilities.[9]

Public Guardianship As Part of a State Guardianship System: Due Process Protections and Other Reform Issues

21. Very little data exist on public guardianship. Many states have insufficient or uneven data on adult guardianship in general,[10] and specifically on public guardianship, including: client characteristics, referral sources, costs, actions taken, and time spent by staff. For a majority of the questions in the 2004 national survey, a significant number of states were unable to respond. In some cases, data are kept locally and are not compiled regularly or consistently. While some state programs are developing computerized databases, public guardianship information systems in many jurisdictions remain rudimentary. One site in Arizona used a standardized computer data system, but staff members found it difficult to extract meaningful information. Moreover, no state maintains outcome data on changes in clients over the course of guardianships. Without uniform, consistent data collection, without the evidence-based practice that exists in other fields, such as medicine, practitioners and policymakers are working in the dark.

22. Courts rarely appoint the public guardian as a limited guardian. In the 2004 national survey, there were 11 times more plenary than limited guardianships of property and 4 times more plenary than limited guardianships of the person. In focus groups and interviews, estimates of the proportion of limited appointments ranged from 1 percent to 20 percent, with many reporting that plenary appointments are made as a matter of course. This is in accordance with observations about limited guardianship from other sources.[11]

Limited guardianship maximizes the autonomy and independence of the individual and is predicated on the principle of the least restrictive alternative. The vast majority of state guardianship laws urge the court to use limited orders, and some jurisdictions state a preference for limited, rather than plenary, orders. Moreover, statutes in 9 states clearly specify that the public guardianship program may serve as limited guardian. However, petitioners often do not request it, and judges are often reluctant to craft tailored orders that reflect the specific capacities of the AIP.

23. The guardian ad litem system, as currently implemented, can be an impediment to effective public guardianship services. Based on the in-depth interviews with key informants and various groups during all the site visits, flaws were revealed in the use of GALs. First, little training for GALs exists, and thus, their function as the eyes and ears of the court is compromised. While some GALs faithfully exercise their duties (visiting the AIP, explaining the guardianship process, and even providing follow-up assistance to the individual), others never visit the person, do not investigate the appropriateness of guardianship, make ageist assumptions concerning functional capabilities, and provide the court with incomplete information. In some states, such as Delaware, respondents admitted that the role was ambiguously defined in the statute, such that it was difficult for attorneys to determine whether they worked in the best interest of the client or as a zealous advocate of what the client would want if legally competent.[12] Efforts were underway to better define the role.

Payment to the GALs is abysmal and frequently ignores their potentially time-consuming efforts. Thus, GALs are often inexperienced, and qualified persons serving in this capacity are regularly deterred from doing so. Reportedly, GALs were often ultimately appointed as guardians, which appears to be a conflict of interest in terms of roles.

There is an important movement toward "increasing the reliability of outcomes in cases involving guardians *ad litem*."[13] An adequately staffed and funded

GAL system akin to the public defender system should be established. This would result in uniformity in the state and similar across states.

24. Oversight and accountability of public guardianship are uneven.
Monitoring of public guardianship can be assessed at two levels: internal programmatic auditing procedures and court oversight. State public guardianship programs that are responsible for local or regional offices show great variability in their monitoring practices. In several states, strong internal monitoring is a work in progress, with both computerized systems and procedural manuals underway. State programs generally receive at least basic information on clients from local entities, and, in some cases, conduct random file reviews. However, uniform internal reporting forms are generally lacking. In many states, there is no state-level entity coordinating public guardianship, thus leaving localities that perform public guardianship functions adrift.

Most public guardianship programs are subject to the same provisions for judicial oversight as private guardians and must submit regular accountings and personal status reports on the IPs they serve.[14] Public guardianship statutes in 18 states provide specifically for court review or for special additional court oversight. Most interview respondents found no difference between court monitoring of public and private guardians, frequently pointing out the need for stronger monitoring of both. Notwithstanding the large caseloads and chronic understaffing, most judges did not report additional oversight measures for public guardianship cases.

Court Cases Involving Public Guardianship

25. Litigation is an important but infrequently used strategy for strengthening public guardianship programs. The 1981 study found that litigation in the public guardianship area was "a recent phenomenon" and that its impact on programs was "not clear." The Schmidt study predicted a rapid expansion of persons needing this service. More recently, lawsuits were used effectively, but surprisingly sparingly, to improve public guardianship program functioning and to improve conditions for public guardianship clients. A significant number of cases have clarified public guardianship appointment, powers and duties, and removal (see public guardianship case law summary in Phase I report, 48–59). A 1999 class action suit in Washoe County, Nevada, was unique in directly challenging a public guardianship program's widespread failures in serving IPs. The OPG in Cook County, Illinois, brought multiple high-visibility lawsuits in order to enforce the rights of IPs in various arenas. In general, however, litigation is not often used to confront deficiencies in public guardianship programs, or by public guardianship programs to provide for their clients. The *Olmstead* case may open the door to more litigation challenges on both fronts.

RECOMMENDATIONS

As with the conclusions, the study recommendations are presented in the organizational framework derived from the 1981 study. These 29 recommendations gleaned from findings in both Phase I and Phase II of the study offer a blueprint for practitioners, policymakers, and researchers in the years to come, as the aging and disability populations swell and the need for effective public guardianship systems escalates. These recommendations are followed by a summary list of "Hallmarks of an Efficient, Effective, and Economical Program of Public Guardianship."

Individuals Served

1. States should provide adequate funding for home- and community-based care for individuals under public guardianship. Public guardianship clients need basic services, as well as surrogate decision making. Public guardians can advocate for client needs, but without funding for community services, such as transportation, in-home care, home-delivered and congregate meals, attendant care, and care management, as well as supportive housing, public guardianship is an empty shell. The *Olmstead* case offers a powerful mandate for funding such services to integrate individuals with disabilities into the community.

Program Characteristics

2. States should consider the program characteristics in the Model Public Guardianship Act in this study, adopt or adapt the Model Act legislatively, and implement it rigorously. Model public guardianship acts were proposed in the 1970s and by the Schmidt study in 1981. Since that time, guardianship law has undergone a paradigm shift, and public guardianship populations have changed. Many state legislatures are grappling with public guardianship provisions. The study's updated model act with commentary (Chapter 5) offers critical guidance on the effective administrative structure and location, staffing, powers and duties, data collection, and evaluation.

3. States should avoid the social services agency model. In 2007, 32 states had a social services agency model of public guardianship, with its inherent conflict of interest. At stake is the inability of the public guardian program to effectively and freely advocate for its clients. If the public guardian program is housed in an entity that is also providing social services, then the public guardian cannot advocate for, or objectively assess, services, nor bring lawsuits against the agency on behalf of IPs. For example, in Cook County, Illinois (county model), the Office of Public Guardian effectively uses its ability to sue to increase the quantity and quality of service provided to IPs.

Guardianship of Person and Property: The Functions of Public Guardianship Programs

4. State public guardianship programs should establish standardized forms and reporting instruments. To achieve consistency and accountability, state public guardianship programs should design, and require local entities to use, uniform forms (e.g., intake, initial client assessment and periodic re-assessment, care plans, reports on the personal status of IPs, staff time and activity logs, and values histories)[15] and should provide for the electronic submission of this information for periodic compilation at the state level. These standardized forms have long been used in mental health treatment plans, social services, and educational plans.

5. Individuals should not be accepted into public guardianship programs on the basis of funding. In order to survive, some programs have developed a priority system for accepting clients. The priority systems investigate cases from certain entities (e.g., APS, hospitals) on a fast track over others and, in actual practice, sometimes served as mechanisms to select cases with funds, rather than to screen out cases that were not appropriate for the office. This approach is problematic. The selection of cases on the basis of funding, or any proxy for such a scheme, presents a clear conflict of interest and compromises the last resort function.

6. Public guardianship programs should limit their functions to best serve individuals with the greatest needs. Currently, public guardianship programs serve a broad array of functions for their guardianship clients, and many also serve clients other than those for whom they are appointed as guardian.

Public guardianship programs should not provide direct services to their clients because this puts the programs in a conflicted position in seeking to monitor those very services and determine whether those services are, in fact, best suited to meet the individual's needs. The Second National Guardianship Conference (Wingspan) recommendations urged that "Guardians and guardianship agencies [should] not directly provide services such as housing, medical care, and social services to their own wards, absent court approval and monitoring."[16]

In addition, providing guardianship, representative payee, or other surrogate decision-making services to individuals other than public guardianship clients dilutes the program's focus on the most vulnerable individuals, who have no resources and no other resort. When programs are inadequately staffed and funded, as indicated by nearly every program surveyed, programs should only perform public guardianship and public guardianship services.[17] (Note that a study of this issue is listed below as part of the future research agenda.)

7. Public guardianship programs should adopt minimum standards of practice. Some, but not all, public guardianship programs have written policies and procedures. Programs need written standards on the guardian's relationship with the incapacitated individual, decision making, using the least restrictive alternative, confidentiality, medical treatment, financial accountability, property management, and more. Written policies, as well as training on these policies, will provide consistency over time and across local offices. A clearinghouse of state policies and procedures manuals will encourage replication and raise the bar for public guardianship performance.

8. Public guardianship programs should not petition for their own appointment. Because of the inherent conflicts involved, public guardianship programs should not serve as both petitioner and guardian for the same individuals.[18] Petitioning is an important potential role for the attorney general's office. Indeed, under the concept of *parens patriae*, on which guardianship is historically based, the state has a duty to care for those who are unable to care for themselves, and this could include bringing a petition for the court to appoint a guardian. Additionally, bar association pro bono programs may include this critical function. (Some legal services programs petition for guardianship, but many view their primary role as advocating for the AIP, and see petitioning as incompatible.)

9. Public guardianship programs should develop and monitor a written guardianship plan setting forth short-term and long-term goals for meeting the needs of each IP. This recommendation is taken from the NGA Standards of Practice (Standard #13). In addition, a number of state laws include requirements for the submission of guardianship plans to the court.[19] Such a plan should address medical, psychiatric, social, vocational, education, training, residential and recreational needs, as well as financial plans within the scope of the order.[20]

10. Public guardianship programs should routinely and periodically perform client reassessment and develop an updated guardianship plan. Because the capacity and needs of IPs can change rapidly, programs should have internal protocols for regular, functional re-evaluation of client capacity, addressing whether a guardianship continues to be necessary, whether the scope of the order should be limited, and whether the program's plan for services should be changed. An analogy can easily be drawn with the Minimum Data Set assessments required by the Centers for Medicare and Medicaid Services (CMS) for nursing home residents. For nursing home residents, CMS requires reassessment on a quarterly basis or more frequently if there is a significant change in the resident. Considering that the majority of public guardianship clients are long-term care facility residents and that conditions for individuals under public guardianship are becoming increasingly complex, assessments and plans should be performed on a biannual basis, such as in Maryland.

11. Public guardianship programs should ensure that decision-making staff personally visit clients at least twice a month. The NGA *Standards of Practice* require that the guardian visit monthly [Standard #13(V)]. Some state laws (such as those of Alaska and Florida) require quarterly visits and Washington requires monthly visits,[21] but most laws are silent regarding the frequency of visits. Because needs and circumstances can change rapidly, because IPs are by nature dependent and vulnerable, and because guardians are charged with the high fiduciary duty of "living the decisional life of another," this study recommends bimonthly visits. In addition, this will promote the regular participation of guardians in nursing home and assisted living care planning meetings for clients, as well as in other key facility events.

12. Public guardianship programs should establish and maintain relationships with key public and private entities to ensure effective guardianship services. The study's site visits identified numerous instances in which clients fell through the cracks because of a lack of communication or a misperception between the public guardianship program and community entities, such as APS, mental health agencies, area agencies on aging, disability advocacy agencies, and others. It is critical that the public guardianship program maintain regular and open lines of communication with community agencies and groups that might affect the lives of IPs.

A number of state laws provide that the public guardianship program must "establish and maintain relationships with governmental, public and private agencies, institutions, and organizations to assure the most effective guardianship or conservatorship program" for each client.[22] The 2001 Second National Guardianship Wingspan Conference recommended that "state and local jurisdictions [should] have an interdisciplinary entity focused on guardianship implementation, evaluation, data collection, pilot projects, and funding."[23] Public guardianship programs should be key players in such interdisciplinary working groups.

13. Public guardianship programs at the local and state level would benefit from regular opportunities to meet and exchange information. In some states, such as California, there are conferences for the county public guardian programs, while others offer no such opportunities. Although the NGA holds a yearly conference, there is no specific focus on the unique needs of public guardianship programs. A yearly or biyearly forum or confederation on the local, state, or regional level focused solely on the issues of public guardianship would be an excellent avenue for the exchange of promising practices, relevant research, and networking. Effective but less expensive means of meeting might be created through teleconferencing, interactive Web meetings, and listserves.

14. Public guardianship programs should maintain and regularly analyze key data about clients and cases. Regular internal and external program evaluation requires the consistent collection and aggregation of key data elements, including at least the annual number of guardianship and conservatorship cases for which the office was appointed as guardian or conservator, the total number of open cases, the number of cases terminated and their disposition, the age and condition of clients, and the number institutionalized. Other data elements, such as the number of limited guardianships, size of the estates, paid professional staff time spent on each client, referral sources, and more, would shed additional light on the operation of the program. The state court administrative office, state public guardianship program, or similar entities should ensure the uniformity of local program data collection, perhaps through the same computerized database (see below).

15. Public guardianship programs should track cost savings to the state and report that amount regularly to the legislature and the governor. Only one state (Virginia) has adequately tracked cost savings, although one additional state (Washington) now includes such a mandate in its statute.[24] While the moral imperative for public guardianship is the unmet need for guardians, the fiscal imperative is cost-savings.

The presentation of cost-savings figures in the Commonwealth of Virginia provided justification for the establishment of the programs in 1998. The external evaluation (see below) conducted in 2001 and 2002, where data were collected in a more sophisticated and systematic manner, revealed even greater savings from more programs (over $5,625,000, largely from the discharge of individuals from psychiatric hospitals to less restrictive environments).[25] At that time, the public guardianship programs were in peril and in a fiscal struggle for their very existence. The provision of information on cost-savings effectively supported statewide funding for the program and the need to increase the number of local programs. Each state should begin collecting this information, using the Virginia model as a reference. It can be a crucial argument for, and defense of, public guardianship for any legislative entity.

16. Public guardianship programs should undergo regular, periodic external evaluations and financial audits. Some states (i.e., Utah, Virginia, and Washington) and some localities (i.e., Washoe County, Nevada) have incorporated periodic evaluation into their statutes and settlement agreements, respectively. Several states have undergone one-time audits by outside entities when practices have come into question. Information from more than one site visit revealed that such audits, in addition to achieving fact-finding, are sometimes politically motivated. Thus, the auditing entity may slant the manner in which the audit is conducted to encourage the removal of an official or the closure of a program. Regular audits over time may serve as a defense against a one-time, and potentially troubling, audit (such as the one that was in progress in Los Angeles during the site visit).

Public guardianship involves a highly complex function of government. Audits conducted by individuals or entities that are not highly knowledgeable of the system and its requirements may produce more harm than good. Thus, periodic external evaluations are recommended to encourage input from guardianship stakeholders and evaluators alike. The states mentioned above might serve as models for conducting evaluations. Periodic evaluation (also recommended in 1981) is made far more feasible by the computerized data collection systems that are now available.

Funding and Staffing of Programs

17. Public guardianship programs should be staffed at specific staff-to-client ratios. The recommended ratio is 1:20.[26] The 1981 book strongly endorsed the use of staff-to-client ratios, indicating that a 1:30 ratio best enables adequate individualized client attention.[27] Since 1981, seven states have provided for ratios by statute (see commentary to Model Act, Chapter 5), either mandating a specific ratio in the statute or requiring an administratively specified ratio.

The recommendation for a staff-to-client ratio is as important today as it was 25 years ago. At some tipping point, chronic understaffing means that protective intervention by a public guardianship program simply cannot be justified as being in the best interests of the vulnerable individual. Based on the site visits and observations of Phase I and Phase II, a guardian-to-client ratio of no more than 1:20 is recommended. States could begin with pilot programs to demonstrate the client outcomes achieved through such a specified ratio, and the costs saved in terms of timely interventions that prevent crises, as well as to demonstrate the increased use of community settings.

In computing a staffing ratio, staff should be defined as "paid professional staff exercising decision-making authority for IPs." Such staff members clearly stand in a fiduciary relationship to the individual, a surrogate relationship with a high duty of trust, confidence, and substituted judgment. Such a staff person is truly living the decisional life of another, one of society's most demanding and important professional roles, akin to a parent-child relationship. This role is unique, differing starkly from that of a case manager, who coordinates services and advises on options, but is not a surrogate. The public guardian has legal authority over an individual whose basic rights are severely compromised, and who, therefore, deserves the state's highest level of knowledge and attention. If, according to the landmark 1988 Associated Press report, guardianship "unpersons" an individual, it is up to the state to ensure the necessary level of attention and care.[28]

18. States should provide adequate funding for public guardianship programs. Each state should establish and periodically revise a minimum-cost-per-IP. State funding should enable public guardianship programs to operate with specified staff-to-client ratios. Funding for public guardianship can result in significant cost savings for the taxpayer through sound management of client finances, the prevention of crises, timely and appropriate medical care, the use of the least restrictive alternative setting, avoiding the use of unnecessary emergency services, and the identification of client assets and such incipient benefits as federal entitlements (see above on tracking the cost savings to the state).

19. The public guardian (or director of the public guardianship office) has a duty to secure adequate funding for the office. The head of a public guardianship office will face multiple daunting challenges: a swelling population in need of surrogate services, pressure from the court and community agencies to accept cases, the need to enhance judicial understanding about IPs, the responsibility of directing a professional staff with a range of skills, the demands of disability and aging advocates, and the politics of long-term care. However, one of the foremost duties is to aggressively seek adequate funding for the office. To have a grasp of funding sources, the director must have solid knowledge of Medicaid, knowledge of the local and state budget process, and contacts with state legislators, local elected officials, and city and/or county managers. The public guardian must advocate for the appropriate level of funding for the program so that the individuals served by it do not suffer or die due to inattention from overwhelmed staffers. Some programs studied have used litigation, a strike, and a moratorium to convince funding bodies that the programs have a limit beyond which it is not safe to operate.

Public Guardianship As Part of a State Guardianship System: Due Process Protections and Other Reform Issues

20. State court administrative offices should move toward the collection of uniform, consistent basic data elements on adult guardianship, including public guardianship. The GAO supported the uniform collection of data on guardianship in a recent study.[29] An excellent place to implement uniform data collection is public guardianship, where data are inconsistently maintained. Much of this information is not captured and yet is necessary for program operation, and, more importantly, for the provision of excellent services for IPs.

The establishment of a uniform standard of minimum information for data collection is recommended, using the information requested for this national public guardianship study as a baseline and guide. Even in an age where failing to keep computerized records is inexcusable,[30] some states are, in fact, not doing so. Computer records are necessary for all public programs, and data should be entered, checked, and aggregated regularly. Data on guardianship will facilitate much-needed accountability and will bolster arguments for necessary increases in staffing and funding, as well.

21. Courts should exercise increased oversight of public guardianship programs. Public guardianship is a basic public trust. Yet, many public guardianship programs are underfunded and understaffed, laboring under high caseloads that may not permit the individual attention required. Courts should establish additional monitoring procedures for public guardianship beyond the regular statutorily mandated review of accountings and reports required of all guardians. For example, courts could require an annual program report (as currently required by at least four states), conduct regular file reviews (such as in Delaware, where court review of public guardianship cases is statutorily required every six months), and meet periodically with program directors.

22. Courts should increase the use of limited orders in public guardianship. Given the high volume of cases, courts should use public guardianship programs to implement forward-looking approaches, including the regular use of limited orders to maximize the autonomy of the individual and implement the least restrictive alternative principle. The routine use of limited orders could be enhanced by check-off categories for authorities on the petition form, directions to the court investigator to examine limited approaches, and templates for specific kinds of standard or semi-standard limited orders.[31]

23. Courts should waive costs and filing fees for indigent public guardianship clients. Indigent individuals in need of services from the public guardianship program have no other recourse and should have access to a court hearing and appointment. Court fees set up an obstacle that is not consistent with the function of serving a societal, last-resort function. The use of fees also causes a bottleneck of at-risk individuals with no decision maker, which ultimately could cost the state unnecessarily to address crises that the public guardianship program could have averted more economically or addressed itself. The Washington provision that "the courts shall waive court costs and filing fees in any proceeding in which an IP is receiving public guardianship services" could serve as a model for other states.

Recommendations for Public Guardianship Research

24. The effect of public guardianship services on incapacitated individuals over time merits study. Although some guardianships are still instituted primarily for third-party interests,[32] the purpose of guardianship is surrogate decision making to provide for the needs of the IP, maintain or improve the person's functioning, and conserve the assets of those unable to care for themselves.[33] If the functioning of the IP is not improved, maintained, or at least safely protected from undue restraint, there is little substantive due process purpose to institute guardianship.[34]

Research on guardianship is in its infancy, but the available research suggests that public guardianship produces a significant cost savings.[35] The moral imperative, effective surrogate decision making for an incapacitated and vulnerable individual, is more elusive to capture; attempts to do so have barely scratched the surface. What is truly needed to improve public guardianship is to ascertain the benefit of this governmental service for incapacitated individuals. Accurate social and medical information at the baseline is required, followed by a longitudinal study. Outcome studies and comparisons should be made within states and between models.

25. Research should analyze the role of public guardianship for individuals with mental illnesses. Schmidt noted that the basis for a provision prohibiting the office from committing an IP to a mental facility was Maryland law. Today, a significant number of states bar guardians from such commitments, except if they are following the specific provisions of the commitment laws.[36] Civil commitment laws derive from the state's police power (and *parens patriae* authority), and generally provide that a person is subject to involuntary commitment if the person is severely mentally ill and, as a result, is a danger to self or others. States set out strict procedural protections in the commitment process. This may leave guardians with mentally ill IPs in a quandary: the individual is declining, behaviorally difficult, and at risk, and appears in clear need of mental health treatment, but has not yet reached the required level of severity and dangerousness. The guardian, then, is left to stand by and wait until the individual declines sufficiently for treatment.

The Arizona guardianship law allows the court to authorize a guardian to give consent for an IP to receive inpatient mental health care and treatment, based on clear and convincing evidence that "the ward is incapacitated as a result of a mental disorder [as defined by state commitment law] and is currently in need of inpatient mental health care and treatment."[37] The statute provides for access to counsel for the individual, the right to petition for discharge, and time limits, and requires that the placement be the least restrictive alternative. Such statutes bear further scrutiny in balancing the liberty rights of the incapacitated individual with the need for treatment.

26. Research should analyze the operation, costs, and benefits of review boards or committees for public guardianship programs. At least two states have developed entities for the independent expert review of public guardianship cases. Under Maryland law, local review boards composed of community experts hold face-to-face hearings attended by the IP (if possible), his or her attorney, and the public guardian to discuss the person's condition, services, and treatment, and the necessity for the continuation or modification of the guardianship.[38] Virginia law provides for multi-disciplinary panels to review cases handled by the public guardianship program. Review boards may serve as an important check on the office, and as an aid for judicial review, especially in complex and ethically challenging cases. Such review boards have potential and merit further examination.

27. Research should examine the costs and benefits of allowing public guardianship programs, once adequately staffed and funded, to provide additional surrogate services that are less restrictive than guardianship. A public guardianship issue that is frequently debated is whether the office should focus its generally limited resources solely on those individuals with the most dire need, namely those adjudicated as incapacitated by the court but without anyone to serve as guardian, or whether it should serve in a broader surrogate role for individuals who are not under guardianship. Should the office serve as an agent under health care or durable powers of attorney? Should it serve as the representative payee for government benefits for clients other than guardianship clients? For example, the Iowa statute creates an office of substitute decision maker that serves as guardian, conservator, representative payee, agent under a power of attorney, and personal representative for a decedent's estate.[39] The Washington law provides for a study on "how services other than guardianship services, and in particular services that might reduce the need for guardianship services, might be provided" through the public guardianship program.[40]

28. Research should explore state approaches to using Medicaid to fund public guardianship. This study demonstrated that an increasing number of states are using Medicaid funds to help support public guardianship services, and that states use different mechanisms to access Medicaid funds. Medicaid is a complex federal-state program with wide variations in state plans and policies within the bounds of federal guidance. The extent and creative use of various Medicaid provisions for guardianship merits further examination and would be a useful resource for public guardianship programs.

29. Courts should examine the role of guardians ad litem and court investigators, especially as they bear on the public guardianship system. The role of a GAL or court investigator in examining less restrictive alternatives, the suitability of the proposed guardian, and the available resources for the respondent or IP are critical and bear directly on the cases coming into the public guardianship programs. There is wide variability in the interpretation and performance of the GAL role, which merits critical evaluation.

POSTLUDE

Recognize guardianship for what it really is: the most intrusive, non-interest serving, impersonal legal device known and available to us and as such, one which minimizes personal autonomy and respect for the individual, has a high potential for doing harm and raises at best a questionable benefit/ burden ratio. As such, it is a device to be studiously avoided.[41]

Based on an expansive and thorough study of public guardianship after 25 years, it is clear that there have been significant improvements in the law, yet chasms in the law's implementation remain. Funding levels are egregiously and unconscionably low for a population of IPs that, based on the acknowledgment of all of the commentators, is growing increasingly complex and includes persons with greater incidences and combinations of physical and mental health problems. Even if funding and staffing levels remain static, as have those of many programs, they are actually operating in a deficit mode. The ratios, while generally lower than those found 25 years ago, are still far too high, and only two states (Virginia and Washington) have public guardians practicing with a 1:20 public guardian-to-client ratio. Even this ratio is at risk because the specified number is not written into statute in Virginia, but left for inclusion in regulation, the approval of which was pending nearly 10 years after the programs were statutorily authorized. Schmidt and Teaster revised the 1981 established ratio of 1:30 10 years before the 2007 study due to increasing case complexity.[42]

The majority of the states were unable to produce any meaningful data. While this was a disturbing finding in the 1981 study, it is inexcusable in 2007. Some states admitted that they had data systems, but they were unable to readily retrieve a range of data queries. If even the most rudimentary information is inaccessible, then practitioners and policymakers are working in the dark. At a minimum, states should enhance their data systems to produce answers to the relatively simple questions asked in the national survey for the 2005 report, questions largely taken from the survey sent to states in 1979.

Three basic elements of information for IPs were suggested in the early 1980s: assessments, care plans, and time logs.[43] Still, this basic file information is often lacking due to inadequate funding and staffing of the office. Such tools are long-established in the arenas of medicine, social work, and education. The tasks of public guardianship are analogous to those required in these disciplines.

Attorney intervention or program noncooperation in the research process was present in three cases. In 1981, none of the attorneys questioned the validity of the study and all sites cooperated with the researchers during their site visits and analysis of findings. In 2007, the landscape had changed, and attorneys were brought into the research at three different sites. First, the Alameda County Office of the Public Guardian (one of the original research sites and a site that handwrote a letter of support and willingness to participate), declined to participate when its administration was contacted to finalize plans for the visit. As discussed earlier in this book, an e-mail message was sent indicating that county counsel advised the office to decline participation. The researchers were told that county counsel had sent them a message to this effect, but no message was found in the electronic communications of either the principal investigator or the project director.

A second case of attorney intervention concerned the interviews of IPs under public guardianship in San Bernardino County. A standard methodology of the original study and both phases of this study, permission to interview IPs under public guardianship at this site was denied.

A third case of noncooperation occurred with the Wyoming Guardianship Corporation when the "Public Guardianship Survey" was not completed and the executive director declined consent to participate.

Finally, as indicated in previous scholarship,[44] research revealed that guardianship is sometimes instituted for third-party interests, rather than the best interests of IPs. Public guardianship clients are still living in environments that are too restrictive for many due to funding inadequacies, residual ageism and sanism,[45] and other societal biases. The banner of least restrictive intervention should be held high: limited guardianships should be sought, guardianships should be avoided or terminated when possible, and individuals with diminished capacity should be consulted and their wishes maximized.

Guardianship is not social work, although it involves important elements of social work. Conversely, guardianship, a product of the courts, is not completely law. Guardianship is an amalgam of many disciplines: law, medicine, social work, and psychology. Most importantly, guardianship deals directly with human beings—society's most vulnerable human beings. Yet, those under the care of the state are often still not afforded basic considerations. Living the decisional life for these unbefriended[46] people is perhaps the most important and complex state function. Guardianship remains shrouded in mystery for most of the public, yet the public guardian performs a highly significant state function for the most at-risk population, composed of individuals who deserve no less than excellence from public servants. Public guardians must have sufficient tools to perform the essential function of living the decisional life of another person. Poorly executed public guardianship does greater harm than no public guardianship at all.

NOTES

1. Olmstead v. L.C., 527 U.S. 581, 119 S.Ct. 2176 (1999).
2. Ibid., 598.
3. Winsor Schmidt and Pamela Teaster, "Criteria for Choosing Public or Private (Contracting Out) Models in the Provision of Guardian of Last Resort Services," Appendix H in Winsor Schmidt, Pamela Teaster, Hillel Abramson, and Richard Almeida, *Second Year Evaluation of the Virginia Guardian of Last Resort and Guardianship Alternatives Demonstration Project*, Virginia Department for the Aging (1997).

4. But see cf. Washington Certified Professional Guardian Board, Ethics Advisory Opinion 2005–001-Professional Guardian Petitioning for Appointment, http://www. courts.wa.gov/committee/?fa=committee.display&item_id=644&committee_id=127 ("The practice of nominating oneself as guardian automatically raises the appearance of self-dealing.")

5. Elder Law Section of the Washington State Bar, *Report of the Public Guardianship Task Force to the WSBA [Washington State Bar Association] Elder Law Section Executive Committee* (August 2005).

6. Karen Roberto, Joy Duke, N. Brossioe, and Pamela Teaster, *The Need for Public Guardians in the Commonwealth of Virginia*, Report to the Virginia Department for the Aging (2007). See also Hightower et al., "Elderly Nursing Home Residents' Need for Public Guardianship Services in Tennessee"; Schmidt and Peters, "Legal Incompetents' Need for Guardians in Florida."

7. See http://www.guardianship.org/. The minimum education requirements for Center for Guardianship Certification (CGC) certification as a "registered guardian" include high school graduation or GED (General Equivalency Diploma) equivalent. See the Application Process for Registered Guardian Certification, http://www.guardianshipcert.org/pubevents.cfm. See also Schmidt et al., "The Relationship Between Guardian Certification Requirements and Guardian Sanctioning," 641 ("83.3% of [General Equivalency Diploma] or [high school] graduates are likely to have more severe sanctions compared to 76.4% undergraduate or higher education, and 47.7% with an [Associate of Arts] or [Technical] degree, respectively. Guardians with an A.A. or Tech degree are 0.28 times less likely to have more severe sanctions than guardians with an undergraduate degree or higher education ($p < 0.01$).") The state of Washington recently increased minimum education requirements for certification to an associate's degree, http://www.courts.wa.gov/committee/?fa=committee.display&item_id=601&committee_id=115. The Adult Guardianship Service Standards of the Council of Accreditation (a New York-based "international, independent, not-for-profit, child- and family-service and behavioral healthcare accrediting organization") recently adopted minimum educational qualifications for guardianship workers of a bachelor's degree with two years relevant experience or an advanced (Master's level) degree in a relevant field, http://www.coastandards.org/standards.php?navView=private&core_id=1278

8. While there is little research on cost per case, estimates are about $2,600 to $3,000 per case. A 2003 estimate in Virginia was $2,955 per case annually. Teaster and Roberto, *Virginia Public Guardian and Conservator Programs*. See also Schmidt et al., "A Descriptive Analysis of Professional and Volunteer Programs for the Delivery of Guardianship Services" ($2,857.08 per client); Teaster et al., *The Florida Public Guardian Programs* ($2,714 in Florida in 2008); Teaster et al., "Staff Service and Volunteer Staff Service Models for Public Guardianship and 'Alternatives' Services."

9. Community Integration Implementation Team and Community Integration Advisory Commission, *Virginia's Comprehensive Cross-Governmental Strategic Plan to Assure Continued Community Integration of Virginians with Disabilities: 2007 Update and Progress Report* (draft) at http://www.olmsteadva.com/downloads/052507StrategicPlan.doc.

10. U.S. Government Accountability Office, *Guardianships: Collaboration Needed to Protect Incapacitated Elderly People*. See also Erica Wood, State-Level Adult *Guardianship Data: An Exploratory Survey* (ABA Commission on Law and Aging, for the National Center on Elder Abuse: August 2006); and Karp and Wood, *Guardianship Monitoring: A National Survey of Court Practices* (2006).

11. Norman Fell, "Guardianship and the Elderly: Oversight Not Overlooked," *University of Toledo Law Review* 25 (1994): 202–203; Lawrence Frolik, "Plenary Guardianship: An Analysis, A Critique and a Proposal for Reform," *Arizona Law Review* 23, no. 2 (1981): 599–660; Frolik, "Promoting Judicial Acceptance and Use of Limited Guardianship"; Sally Hurme, "Limited Guardianship: Its Implementation Is Long Overdue," *Clearinghouse Review* 28, no. 6 (1994): 660–670; Schmidt, "Assessing the Guardianship Reform of Limited Guardianship"; Quinn, *Guardianships of Adults*.

12. Cf., e.g., Winsor Schmidt, "Accountability of Lawyers in Serving Vulnerable, Elderly Clients," *Journal of Elder Abuse and Neglect* 5, no. 3 (1993): 39–50.

13. Margaret Dore, "The *Stamm* Case and Guardians *Ad Litem*," *Washington State Bar Association Elder Law Section Newsletter* (Winter 2004–2005): 3, 6–7. Dore cites sources concerning the elimination of GALs from court proceedings in the child custody context, a position consistent with some commentary, and with court decisions or guidelines in Florida, Montana, Nebraska, Pennsylvania, South Carolina, Vermont, and Washington.

14. For an overview of the status of guardianship monitoring, see Karp and Wood, *Guardianship Monitoring*; Karp and Wood, *Guarding the Guardians*.

15. See Schmidt, "The Evolution of a Public Guardianship Program"; Schmidt et al., "A Descriptive Analysis of Professional and Volunteer Programs for the Delivery of Guardianship Services"; Teaster et al., "Staff Service and Volunteer Staff Service Models for Public Guardianship and 'Alternatives' Services"; Teaster and Roberto, *Virginia Public Guardian and Conservator Programs*.

16. Symposium, Wingspan Conference recommendation 47.

17. Separate funding and staffing of representative payee services are endorsed. Cf. Committee on Social Security Representative Payees, *Improving the Social Security Representative Payee Program: Serving Beneficiaries and Minimizing Misuse*, Washington, DC: National Academies Press (2007): http://nationalacademies.org/morenews/20070730. html. In the 2007 state of Washington legislation, it is noted that the public guardianship office must report to the legislature by December 2009 on "how services other than guardianship services, and in particular services that might reduce the need for guardianship services, might be provided . . . [including] but not limited to, services provided under powers of attorney given by the individuals in need of the services" (S.B. 5320).

18. For an ethics opinion on the inherent conflict of interest when a professional guardian petitions for him/herself as guardian, see Washington Courts, Opinion 2005–001, "Professional Guardian Petitioning for Appointment" (March 13, 2006): http:// www.courts.wa.gov/committee/?fa=committee.display&item_id=644&committee_id=127, See also Council on Accreditation, *Adult Guardianship Service Standards*: "The organization only petitions the court for its own appointment as guardian when no other entity is available." http://www.coastandards.org/standards.php?navView=private&core_id=1273

19. Hurme and Wood, "Guardian Accountability Then and Now"; Karp and Wood, *Guarding the Guardians*. See also Schmidt, et al., "A Descriptive Analysis of Professional and Volunteer Programs for the Delivery of Guardianship Services"; Teaster et al., "Staff Service and Volunteer Staff Service Models for Public Guardianship and 'Alternatives' Services."

20. Such a plan is similar to requirement for Social Security Administration representative payees. See Social Security Administration, *Guidebook for Representative Payees*, SSA Pub. No. 05–10076 (SSA Feb. 2006), at www.ssa.gov/pubs/10076.html. See also Council on Accreditation, *Adult Guardianship Service Standards*: "Individuals participate in the development and ongoing review of an assessment-based guardianship plan that: (a) is the basis for delivery of guardianship services; and (b) provides a method for regularly reviewing the quality and effectiveness of guardianship services." http://www.coastandards.org/standards.php?navView=private&core_id=1272

21. Washington public guardianship law, S.B. 5320. See §4(4) at http://www.leg.wa.gov/pub/billinfo/2007-08/Pdf/Bills/Session%20Law%202007/5320-S.SL.pdf. See also Council on Accreditation, *Adult Guardianship Service Standards*: "In-person contact with the individual occurs monthly, and more frequently as needed . . .", http://www.coastandards.org/standards.php?navView=private&core_id=1274

22. See, e.g., Alaska Statute §13.26.380.

23. Symposium, Wingspan Conference recommendation 6.

24. S.B. 5320 (Washington 2007), §4(13). See also Teaster et al., *The Florida Public Guardian Programs*.

25. Teaster and Roberto, *Virginia Public Guardian and Conservator Programs*. See also Teaster et al., "Staff Service and Volunteer Staff Service Models for Public Guardianship and 'Alternatives' Services."

26. Schmidt, et al., *Second Year Evaluation of the Virginia Guardian of Last Resort and Guardianship Alternatives Demonstration Project*, 23 ("The ward to guardian ratio should be 20:1.") Schmidt et al., cite the substantial empirical literature since 2000 on the relationship between specific nurse-to-patient ratios, patient mortality, and other hospital quality of care measures. Schmidt et al., "The Relationship Between Guardian Certification Requirements and Guardian Sanctioning," 651, note 53. See also Council on Accreditation, *Adult Guardianship Service Standards*: "Generally speaking, the staff to client ratio should be set at 1:20 to eliminate situations in which there is little to no service being provided to an individual." http://www.coastandards.org/standards.php?navView=private&core_id=1270

27. Schmidt et al., *Public Guardianship and the Elderly*, 174, 193 ("No office of public guardian shall assume responsibility for any wards beyond a ratio of thirty wards per professional staff member.")

28. For a substantive due process constitutional analysis of this quid pro quo theory, see Winsor Schmidt, "Law and Aging: Mental Health Theory Approach" in *Theories on Law and Ageing: The Jurisprudence of Elder Law*, edited by Israel Doron (Berlin Heidelberg: Springer, 2009), 137–139.

29. U.S. Government Accountability Office, *Guardianships*.

30. For an account of the Dade County Grand Jury investigation of inadequate record keeping, see Schmidt, "The Evolution of a Public Guardianship Program."

31. Frolik, "Promoting Judicial Acceptance and Use of Limited Guardianship."

32. Alexander and Lewin. *The Aged and the Need for Surrogate Management*, 136.

33. Schmidt et al., *Public Guardianship and the Elderly*.

34. Schmidt, "Law and Aging," 137–139. Cf. Youngberg v. Romeo, 457 U.S. 307 (1982); Americana Healthcare Corp. v. Schweiker, 688 F.2d 1072, 1086–1087 (7th Cir.), *cert. denied*, 459 U.S. 1202 (1983) (Youngberg standards apply to nursing home residents).

35. Teaster and Roberto, *Virginia Public Guardian and Conservator Programs*. See also Teaster et al., "Staff Service and Volunteer Staff Service Models for Public Guardianship and 'Alternatives' Services"; Teaster et al., *The Florida Public Guardian Programs*.

36. See, e.g., Florida Statutes Annotated §744.704(7).

37. Arizona Revised Statutes §14-5312.01.

38. Vicki Gottlich and Erica Wood, "Statewide Review of Guardianships: The California and Maryland Approaches," *Clearinghouse Review* 23, no. 4 (1989): 426–432; Hurme and Wood, "Guardian Accountability Then and Now," 912–913.

39. Iowa Code §§231E.1 through 231E.13, Iowa Substitute Decision-Maker Act.

40. S.B. 5320 (Washington 2007), §4(9).

41. Elias Cohen, Protective Services and Public Guardianship: A Dissenting View (address at 31st Annual meeting of the Gerontological Society, Dallas, Texas, November 20, 1978), quoted in Schmidt et al., *Public Guardianship and the Elderly*, 11.

42. Schmidt et al., *Second Year Evaluation of the Virginia Guardian of Last Resort and Guardianship Alternatives Demonstration Project*, 23 ("The ward to guardian ratio should be 20:1.").

43. Schmidt et al., "A Descriptive Analysis of Professional and Volunteer Programs for the Delivery of Guardianship Services."

44. Alexander and Lewin, *The Aged and the Need for Surrogate Management*, 136.

45. Michael Perlin, "On Sanism," *Southern Methodist University Law Review* 46 (1992): 373–407; Michael Perlin, "Things Have Changed: Looking at Non-Institutional Mental Disability Law Through the Sanism Filter," *New York Law School Law Review* 46 (2002–2003): 535–545; Michael Perlin and Deborah Dorfman, "Sanism, Social Science, and the Development of Mental Disability Law Jurisprudence," *Behavioral Sciences and the Law* 11 (1993): 47–66. See also Schmidt, "Law and Aging," 131–132 ("Sanism as a Mental Health Theory Approach to Law and Aging").

46. Karp and Wood, *Incapacitated and Alone: Health Care Decision-Making for the Unbefriended Elderly*.

Chapter 5

MODEL PUBLIC GUARDIANSHIP ACT

INTRODUCTORY OVERVIEW

Intent and Derivation of Model Statute

The Model Public Guardianship Act is intended to translate the findings and recommendations of this study into law and policy. The key themes of the study reflected in the Model Act are the independence of the public guardianship function, the avoidance of conflict of interest, the use of the least restrictive alternative form of intervention, emphasis on the self-determination and autonomy of IPs to the greatest extent possible, quality assurance, and public accountability.

The Model Act incorporates not only the findings and recommendations of the study (including the 2005 Phase I report),[1] but also stands as a distillation and compilation of existing state statutes and a series of earlier model public guardianship statutes. Some 44 states currently have statutory provisions on public guardianship or guardianship of last resort, and 27 of these states have explicit provisions establishing an office or program of public guardianship. Existing state language serves as a rich resource for the Model Act.

In addition, the Model Act uses the Model Public Guardianship Statute from the 1981 public guardianship study by Schmidt et al.[2] as a base. This statute, in turn, relied upon Regan and Springer's Model Public Guardianship Act from the 1977 report to the U.S. Senate Special Committee on Aging on Protective Services for the Elderly,[3] and an earlier statute prepared by Legal Research and Services for the Elderly in 1971.[4] Other model guardianship statutes that offer useful background and frameworks include the UGPPA[5] and the Model Guardianship and Conservatorship Statute published by the American Bar Association Developmental Disabilities Project of the Commission on the Mentally Disabled in 1982,[6] as well as principles derived from the *National Probate Court Standards*,[7] the National Guardianship Conference (Wingspread),[8] and the Second National Guardianship Conference (Wingspan).[9]

In 1981, the introductory comments to the model statute by Schmidt et al. asserted that:

The public guardian, and the public guardian process, do not exist in isolation. It would be difficult, misleading, and unrealistic to draft a statute
addressing only the office of the public guardian. The public guardian is
an end point in the process of guardianship, which itself seems to exist in a
continuum of protective services and civil commitment. In fact, the success
of a public guardian seems to be quite dependent upon the quality of the
state's guardianship statute.[10]

This language is confirmed and endorsed. It stands as true today as it did
in 1981. Ultimately, the key to good public guardianship, along with sufficient
funding and governmental support, is good guardianship. The nature of the
state's guardianship and conservatorship law and practice is directly determina-
tive of the quality of the public guardianship program. Public guardianship programs are shaped by the overall contours of state guardianship statutes, which
determine the procedures for appointment, the definition of incapacity, the powers and duties of guardians, and the mechanisms for judicial oversight. This was
abundantly evident in the study site visits and interviews.

In the intervening 26 years since the study by Schmidt et al., state guardianship law has undergone a sea change. When Schmidt et al. wrote the 1981
model statute, most state laws lacked effective procedural protections, included
no recognition of limited guardianship or use of the least restrictive alternative,
and based the determination of capacity largely on the respondent's medical condition, or on generalized labels that served as poor or discriminatory proxies
(such as advanced age or mental disability). As of 2007, over half the states have
made complete or very substantial revisions to their guardianship codes, and
almost all of the remaining states have made significant changes, as well.[11] These
changes have focused on strengthening procedural protections, such as the right
to counsel, the presence of the respondent at the hearing, and meaningful notice;
a more cognitive and functional definition of incapacity; the encouragement of
limited orders tailored to the needs and abilities of the individual; and enhanced
monitoring. A major need for reform would be satisfied by the implementation
of the statutes currently in place.

Thus, in 1981, Schmidt et al., as well as Regan and Springer in 1977, were com-
pelled to include basic guardianship procedural protections in the model public
guardianship statute because few such protections existed. Today, there may well be
a sufficient statutory basis, which is not always translated into practice, upon which
to build. Therefore, the current Model Act offers two options in this regard.

Alternative A, for states with strong protections already built into their law,
concentrates on the important programmatic aspects of a public guardianship office, as described throughout this study.

Alternative B retains the procedural protections and definitions set out
in the 1981 model.

Comments on Statutory Sections

Sections 1 and 2. Declaration of Policy and Legislative Intent. This
section sets out the basic *parens patriae* concept that the state has a responsibility
toward IPs (the duty as general guardian to take care of people who cannot take
care of themselves), and should furnish guardianship services if there is no one
else to provide, nor funds to purchase, such services. The first paragraph is based
on Schmidt et al., as derived from the Regan and Springer model. The intent is
to provide for partial or limited guardianship, and to serve all IPs in need, rather
than taking a categorical approach toward eligibility. The Model Act consciously
avoids financing mechanisms that are dependent upon fee generation because of
the resulting inducements to serve wealthier clients at the expense of persons with
low incomes and to seek guardianship for wealthy individuals in inappropriate
circumstances. At the same time, the Model implicitly provides for services to
moderate-income persons without willing and responsible family members or
friends who can afford private guardianship.

The second paragraph is based largely on Schmidt, as derived from the ABA
Developmental Disabilities Project model. The intent is to honor the individual's
volition as much as possible, to highlight that the purpose of public guardianship
is the restoration or development of capacity, that public guardianship is not a
life sentence or a facilitator of others' interests, and that these objectives should
be achieved by the least drastic means. The section also includes language from
recent Washington state legislation.

Section 3. Definitions

Alternative A incorporates by reference definitions from the state's general
guardianship code.

Alternative B incorporates state definitions, but also retains the definitions in the 1981 model act.

Section 4. Establishment of Office. In 1977, Regan and Springer's Model
Public Guardian Act offered four alternatives for the location of the public
guardian: (1) within the court; (2) within the state executive branch as an
independent entity; (3) within the state's Office on Aging, Department of Social
Services, or Department of Health and Mental Hygiene; or (4) within each county.
Schmidt et al. chose the county level, and the current Model Act endorses this
approach. While location at the county level is not necessarily without problems,
as evidenced by the site visits, it appears to be most in accord with the study
recommendations. Schmidt explained the selection in 1981:

> The least attractive location is one of the state's social service agencies, be-
> cause of the serious conflict of interest. There could not be a worse location
> for the office of the public guardian than the very agency that often fosters

the need for advocacy and protection of the ward. The courts are a tempting location, but the judges, who recognized a need for public guardianship, themselves voiced discomfort with the potential conflict of interest
and responsibility for administrative activity. An independent state office
under the governor is also tempting, especially considering the overwhelming success enjoyed by such an analogous agency as New Jersey's Department of the Public Advocate. However, the intent of the office of public
guardian is to deliver individual, personalized guardianship services. This
would be geographically precluded in all but the very smallest states, which
could utilize a public guardian at least as effectively at our location choice,
the county level.[12]

The Model Act prohibits the public guardianship function from being contracted out. According to public administration sources,[13] contracting out for
services may be appropriate for discrete services, such as repairing potholes, but
is generally not for highly complex services involving substantial judgment, as
with public guardianship, where clear lines of governmental authority are necessary. Additionally, the Act specifies that the paid professional staff must be public
employees, thus maintaining this direct line of authority and accountability.

The remaining parts of this section are intended to ensure the independence
of the public guardian from service-providing agencies, the avoidance of any conflict of interest, and the limitation of the scope of the office to a serviceable and
manageable number of clients. It is vital that the office of public guardianship not
be part of any county social-service-providing agency. The office must be able to
represent an IP as independently as a private guardian.

In addition, the primary reason for problems in any public guardian office is
that the office and professional staff members have responsibility for too many
IPs. Understaffing hinders access to rights, benefits, and entitlements, and the
provision of guardianship services. The best public guardian offices require and
appreciate an explicit statutory staffing limitation to forestall the inevitable pressure to accept more cases, stretching staff too thinly. As Schmidt emphasized,
these considerations are so important that without them, IPs would be better off
with no public guardianship.

Seven states now provide for a staffing ratio. The Florida statute provides for
a 1:40 ratio of professional staff to IPs. New Jersey law indicates that the public guardianship office must determine the maximum caseload it can maintain,
based upon funding, and when such a maximum is reached, the office may decline additional appointments. In New Mexico, the contract of the state public
guardianship office with guardianship services providers must include a maximum caseload. In Tennessee, the Commission on Aging must certify a maximum
caseload based upon a review of documentation by the district public guardianship programs. In Vermont, the Department of Aging and Disabilities may adopt
rules, including standards on maximum caseload. In Virginia, the Department

on Aging must adopt regulations including "an ideal range of staff to client ratios" for local and/or regional programs. In the recent Washington legislation, no public guardianship service provider may serve more than 20 IPs per certified professional guardian. The implementation of the ratios and their effect on the quality of care in these states merits study as a model for other jurisdictions.

The 1981 statute provided for a 1:30 ratio of paid professional staff to clients. The current statute reduces the ratio to 1:20, based on the available research[14] and on interviews and site visit observations across jurisdictions. The requirement for court notification upon reaching the ratio is derived from Virginia and New Jersey law.

Sections 5 and 6. Appointment of the Public Guardian.

This section is derived from the 1981 Schmidt et al. model. A difficult issue is whether, upon court appointment as guardian or conservator, the fiduciary responsibility falls on the office as an entity or on the individual who serves as the head of the office. Appointment of the entity allows for needed continuity, and may encourage broader court oversight of the office as a whole, while appointment of the director as an individual ("the public guardian") puts a strong onus of personal accountability on the holder of this position. The 1981 act named an individual as public guardian, but included language seeking to provide for continuity of services. The current Model Act places the locus of authority in the office, implemented by the public guardian as director and the professional staff.

The 1981 Model Act indicates that consultation with advocates might assist the county in its selection of the public guardian. While consultation with appropriate aging and disability advocacy agencies and others might benefit the county [board of supervisors; council] in identifying the individual to serve and might be a useful practice, it is not included in the statute, as it might inappropriately be interpreted as giving a veto power to the advocacy groups, hampering the independence of the office.

The Model Act requires the director of the office, the public guardian, to be a licensed attorney. Lawyers are agents of the court, bound to carry out fiduciary duties, and trained in the meaning of fiduciary standards. Lawyers are licensed by the bar, must conform to the requirements of legal ethics, and any deviations are heard by the bar's disciplinary committee. The Act also acknowledges the importance of a background in human development, sociology, psychology, and business, a provision derived from a combination of state public guardianship laws.

The office files a general bond, in lieu of the bond required of an individual guardian or conservator, in an amount fixed by the board of supervisors or council. The bond also functions in lieu of the liability insurance that might be required or recommended for private guardianship agencies.[15]

Section 7. Powers and Duties.

The Act provides for the appointment of the office of public guardian by the court, pursuant to the guardianship and conservatorship law of the state. Any provisions related to the office of public guardian or the IP that are not included in the Act, such as notice requirements, should be considered by referencing the state's guardianship and conservatorship law. (However, Alternative B specifies additional hearing protections, as outlined in the 1981 model.)

The office of public guardian has the same powers and duties as those of a private guardian. The Act's Section 7, Alternative B allows the public guardian, as director of the office, to delegate decision-making functions to paid professional staff, with the proviso that such staff have a college degree and a degree in law, social work, or psychology.[16] In addition, a growing number of states are establishing guardian-certification programs, and it behooves a public guardianship office to require the certification of decision-making staff by such a state program if one exists.

Duties

The initial source for language concerning powers and duties was Schmidt, but the current Act separates duties from powers, and makes significant additions to both, based on multiple state statutes. Highlights of the duties include:

Use of substituted judgment. Reflecting the intent of the act to promote the autonomy and self-determination of the incapacitated individual, this section directs the office to use the "substituted judgment" standard of surrogate decision making, in which the guardian "steps into the shoes" of the individual, using the individual's values and preferences as a guide (i.e., what the IP would have done if competent).

Individualized plan and reports. A growing number of state guardianship statutes,[17] as well as specific public guardianship statutes, such as those of Indiana and Utah, require the guardian to file an individualized, forward-looking plan with the court, which the court can later compare with the report to hold the guardian accountable. Personal and financial plans foster good care and management, and thus the Act requires the office to file such plans, based on assessments of individual needs and abilities. The requirements for a values history survey, annual functional assessment, and decisional accounting reports are derived from the Virginia public guardianship law.[18] While it may be difficult for the office to complete a values history for an unbefriended individual with no family or other contacts and little indication of past preferences, the office should attempt to investigate and fill in the values history to the greatest extent possible.

Required visitation. The bimonthly visitation duty is based on the project's interviews and site visits, which underscored the need for continuous, consistent contact with the public guardianship program's clients. The requirement for visiting prospective facilities was taken from Vermont law.

Prohibition of direct services. Public guardianship programs should not provide direct services to their clients because this would put them in a conflicted position in seeking to monitor those very services and to determine whether those services are in fact best-suited to meet the individual's needs. Public guardianship statutes in Illinois, Iowa, and other states include this prohibition, which is also emphasized in both the Wingspread and Wingspan national guardianship recommendations.

Standards of practice. A number of public guardianship programs have adopted or adapted the NGA Standards of Practice and Code of Ethics, or have fashioned their own set of standards, policies, and procedures.[19] It is critical for an office of public guardian to go through such a process and to clearly articulate the practices it will follow

Independent audit. Independent financial monitoring, in addition to court oversight through the review and possible investigation of accounts, is critical to public guardianship accountability. Florida requires an independent audit at least every two years.

An additional duty considered, but not included in the Model Act, is the establishment and operation of a public guardian review board. The concept of a review board is taken from Maryland law, where local review boards have functioned for over 20 years. In Maryland, review boards composed of community experts hold face-to-face hearings attended by the IP (if possible), his or her attorney, and the public guardian to discuss the person's condition, services, and treatment, as well as the necessity for the continuation or modification of the guardianship.[20] In addition, Virginia law provides for multi-disciplinary panels to review cases handled by the public guardianship program. Review boards or screening committees could serve as important checks on the office, as well as aids for judicial review, and could represent important resources for the office, especially regarding complex and ethically challenging cases. A review board or panel is an innovative practice with promise that merits further evaluation. (See Recommendation 27.)

Powers

The Model Act next lists powers, beginning with a prohibition against the office petitioning for its own appointment as guardian or conservator, as this would subject it to a clear conflict of interest. For example, if the office budget is dependent on the number of individuals served, it may have the incentive to petition more frequently, regardless of individual needs, or it might petition too readily for individuals who are the easiest or least costly and time-consuming to serve at the expense of others.

However, if the office does not petition, there may be a backlog of cases in which at-risk individuals in need are simply not served, or in which preventable emergencies could have been avoided. Advocates have voiced concern about legal services programs petitioning for guardianship, especially legal services for elders under the Older Americans Act, since their primary role is generally to represent the alleged IP (AIP). Under the *parens patriae* concept, the attorney general could fill the role of petitioning for those in need of public guardianship, on behalf of the state. Another approach for petitioning might be the development of a pro bono initiative by the bar association.

The Act relies on the 1981 model statute in providing for the responsibility of office intervention in private guardianship proceedings involving a respondent or IP and based on non-fulfillment of guardian duties, disproportionate waste through costs, or the individual's best interests. Such intervention should function as a necessary monitor and check on the growing private professional guardianship market, as well as on family guardianships.

Schmidt noted that the basis for the provision prohibiting the office from committing an IP to a mental facility was Maryland law. Today, a significant number of states bar guardians from such commitments, except if they are following the specific provisions of the commitment laws.[21]

The Act also articulates other powers, including the following.

Representative payment. Many public guardianship clients will also require a Social Security representative payee, a Veterans Affairs fiduciary, or payee for other public benefits, and it is efficient for the public guardianship office to apply for and serve in these capacities for its guardianship clients. Whether it also should serve in such roles for individuals who do not need a guardian is a question for debate and further research, but the study recommends against this expansion until programs are fully staffed and funded.

Arrangements after death. Generally, guardianship terminates upon the death of the IP, yet public guardianship programs may be left with deceased, unbefriended clients with no one to make arrangements for the disposition of the body. Hence, this Act and a number of existing state laws provide this power.

Section 8. Persons Eligible for Services. As stated above, the intent of this act, based on the 1981 Schmidt model, is to serve all incapacitated adults in need, rather than taking a categorical approach toward eligibility.

Section 9. Appointment and Review Procedure. As stated above, Alternative A does not include this section, as it is aimed at states that recently have enacted strong procedural protections in their adult guardianship code and are now focused on creating or upgrading a pubic guardianship program.

Alternative B generally retains the provisions of the 1981 Model Act and, accordingly, accompanying text by Schmidt et al., is quoted below:

The model statute departs, as recommended by all of the recent model guardianship statutes, from the traditional indefinite term for guardianship and places the burden on the petitioner to secure successive appointments at one year intervals or less after the initial appointment for six months or less. The criteria for appointment [are] stated, including a precondition that necessary, beneficial services are available. Such a precondition is the quid pro quo for the stigma, deprivation of liberty and autonomy, and exacerbation of disability that otherwise accompanies guardianship.

The suggested standard of proof is "clear, unequivocal, and convincing" evidence. Such a standard is intended to inform the fact-finder that the proof must be greater than for other civil cases. While it might be argued that an individual suffering from [incapacity] is not [him or herself] at liberty or free from stigma, we are quite comfortable with our assessment that it is much better at this time for [such] a person to be free of public guardianship than for a person to be inappropriately adjudicated a ward of the public guardian. The provision of functional, rather than causal or categorical, criteria should facilitate the use of the standard. The clear, unequivocal, and convincing evidence standard is utilized in such analogous proceedings as deportation, denaturalization, and involuntary civil commitment [reference omitted]. Public guardianship is easily conceptualized as the denaturalization or deportation of an individual's legal autonomy as a citizen.

The provisions for accounting and review of the appointment are adopted from Regan and Springer. They incorporate by reference appropriate sections of the state's guardianship and conservatorship law.

The hearing subsection is a synthesis from Regan and Springer and the Suggested Statute on Guardianship (ABA Developmental Disabilities Law Project). The provision requiring the presence of the proposed ward is taken from the California probate code. The subsections relating to counsel, trial by jury, and evaluation are from Regan and Springer. The public guardianship process is designed to be adversarial. The significance of effective, adversarial counsel for both the process and the proposed ward cannot therefore be overemphasized. Any failure of guardianship processes can be attributed in large measure to inappropriately paternalistic and condescendingly informal proceedings facilitated by counsel, whose real client is too seldom the proposed ward.

The second evaluation paragraph, relating to the rights of silence and of observers, is an adaptation from the Suggested Statute on Guardianship. The provisions for the right to present evidence and the duties of counsel are from Regan and Springer. The provisions for expert testimony under the rules of evidence subsection and for psychotropic medication are from the Suggested Statute on Guardianship. The Developmental Disabilities Legislative Project is the source for the first rules of evidence paragraph and for the appeal provision.[22]

Section 10. Allocation of Costs. This section is derived directly from the 1981 Schmidt model, based on Regan and Springer's earlier Model Public Guardian Act. Schmidt notes that:

> The financial ability test is intended to afford some flexibility in income or asset eligibility, inclusive of some moderate income persons who cannot afford private guardianship, but with encouragement of court zealousness in concern with asset depletion, rather than short-run overprotection of public funds.
>
> Explicit provision for a reimbursement claim upon the estate at death is not made, so as to avoid any express incentive to perpetuate the guardianship to death or to preserve assets for any other than the ward's benefit. It seems clear that the intended purpose of such a provision—to discourage courts from requiring immediate costs payment or reimbursement—is adequately provided elsewhere.[23]

In addition, the Act allows for court waiver of any court costs and filing fees for public guardianship cases, as in the 1981 model and a number of state laws, such as Florida.[24]

Section 11. Right to Services. The source for the right to services is the 1981 Schmidt model, taken from the ABA Developmental Disabilities Law Project. This concept has not been tested and has not been enacted in any state public guardianship law. Schmidt explains that "The subsection codifies the constitutional right justified either as a quid pro quo for the loss of autonomy and freedom, as a fulfillment of the state purposes in public guardianship (restoration or development of capacity), or as the less restrictive alternative to indefinite or unnecessarily long guardianship."[25]

Today, the subsection on right to services is also rooted in the *Olmstead* decision of the Supreme Court, providing under the Americans with Disabilities Act that

> states are required to place persons with mental disabilities in community settings rather than in institutions when the state's treatment professionals have determined that community placement is appropriate, the transfer from institutional care to a less restrictive setting is not opposed by the affected individual, and the placement can be reasonably accommodated, taking into account the resources available to the state and the needs of others with mental disabilities.[26]

Section 12. Duties of the State Court Administrative Office. As indicated above, this Model Act endorses the approach of the 1981 model in locating the office of public guardian at the county level, where it can best "deliver individual, personalized guardianship services." However, extensive interviews and site visits conducted throughout this study found that states with local offices (whether county offices or local programs funded through state offices) are uneven in quality and often lack consistent practices and data collection. Local offices may benefit from state level functions in:

Providing training for local office staff;
  Establishing uniform formats for data collection;
  Developing forms and instruments as a resource for local offices;
  Promoting the exchange of information and promising practices among
the local offices; and
  Evaluating the local offices.

These functions, along with adequate appropriations, could be carried out by the state court administrative office, bringing consistency to the offices and providing for a clear state-level snapshot over time, without stifling local flexibility or creativity.

The provision for an evaluation is taken from Virginia law,[27] Utah law,[28] and recent Washington legislation.[29] The evaluation includes an analysis of costs and "off-setting savings to the state." The Virginia evaluation included such an analysis in practice,[30] which was critical in securing additional support for the program. The 2007 Washington legislation provides for the tracking of cost savings. (The Washington evaluation also includes an examination of whether surrogate decision-making services for individuals who are not under guardianship, such as the services of agents under powers of attorney and representative payees, should be provided by the office, as authorized, for instance, in the Iowa statute.[31])

Section 13 and 14. Statewide Public Guardianship Advisory Committee; Authorization of Appropriations; Effective Date. The study recommendations cited the development of an advisory council as a hallmark of a good system. Statewide advisory committees are included in a number of existing state laws[32] and have functioned to institutionalize the regular and healthy exchange of perspectives on public guardianship by the aging, disability, mental health, legal, judicial, and policymaking bodies at the state level. This section is an amalgam of state provisions, and elevates the importance of the members by making them gubernatorial appointments.

MODEL PUBLIC GUARDIANSHIP ACT

Section 1. Title

This Act shall be known as the Public Guardianship Act.

Section 2. Declaration of Policy and Legislative Intent

The legislature of the state of _____ recognizes that some persons in the state, because of incapacity, are unable to meet varying essential requirements for their health or personal care or to manage varying essential aspects of their financial resources. The legislature finds that private guardianship is inadequate where there are no willing and responsible family members or friends to serve as guardian, and where the IP does not have adequate income or wealth for the compensation of a private guardian and payment of court costs and fees associated with the appointment proceeding. The legislature intends through this Act to establish the office of public guardian to furnish guardianship services at reduced or no cost for individuals who need them and for whom adequate services otherwise may be unavailable.

The legislature intends to treat liberty and autonomy as paramount values for all state residents and to authorize public guardianship only to the minimum extent necessary to provide for health or safety, or to manage financial affairs, when the legal conditions for appointment of a guardian are met. The legislature intends to establish public guardianship that permits IPs to participate as fully as possible in all decisions that affect them; that assists such persons to regain or develop their capacities to the maximum extent possible; and that accomplishes such objectives through the use of the least restrictive alternatives. This Act shall be liberally construed to accomplish these purposes.

Section 3. [Alternative A] Definitions

(a) The definitions found in [state guardianship and conservatorship law] shall apply to this Act.
(b) "Court" means [the local or county court or branch having jurisdiction in matters relating to adult guardianships].
(c) "Office" means the office of public guardian.
(d) "Paid professional staff" refers to an individual employed by the office of public guardian who exercises decision-making authority for the IPs the office is serving as guardian.
(e) "Public guardian" means the director of the office of public guardian.
(f) "Values history survey" refers to a form documenting an individual's values about health care.

Section 3. [Alternative B] Definitions

As used in this Act:

(a) "Court" means [the local or county court or branch having jurisdiction in matters relating to adult guardianships].

(b) "Lack of capacity to make informed decisions about care, treatment, or management services" refers to the inability, by reason of mental condition, to achieve a rudimentary understanding, after conscientious efforts at explanation, of the purpose, nature, or possible significant benefits of the care, treatment, or management services to be provided under public guardianship; provided that a person shall be deemed incapable of understanding such purpose if, due to impaired mental ability to perceive reality, the person cannot realize that his or her recent behavior has caused or has created a clear and substantial risk of serious physical injury, illness, or disease or of gross financial mismanagement or manifest financial vulnerability to oneself; and provided further that a person shall be deemed to lack the capacity to make informed decisions about care, treatment, or management services if the reason for refusing the same is expressly based on either the belief that he or she is unworthy of assistance or the desire to harm or punish oneself.

(c) "Office" means the office of public guardian.

(d) "Paid professional staff" refers to an individual employed by the office of public guardian who exercises decision-making authority for the IPs the office is serving as guardian.

(e) "Psychotropic medication" means any drug or compound affecting the mind, behavior, intellectual functions, perception, moods, and emotions, and includes antipsychotic, antidepressant, antimanic, and antianxiety drugs.

(f) "Public guardian" refers to the director of the office of public guardian.

(g) "Severe mental disorder" means a severe impairment of emotional processes, the ability to exercise conscious control of one's actions, or the ability to perceive reality or to reason or understand, with the impairment manifesting as instances of grossly disturbed behavior or faulty perceptions.

(h) "Unable . . . to manage one's financial resources" means unable to take those actions necessary to obtain, administer, or dispose of real or personal property, intangible property, business property, benefits, or income so that, in the absence of public guardianship, gross financial mismanagement or manifest financial vulnerability is likely to occur in the near future. For the purposes of this Act, any such inability must be evidenced by recent behaviors causing such harm or creating a clear and substantial risk thereof, and at least one incidence of such behavior must have occurred within 20 days of the filing of the petition for public guardianship, except that such inability shall not be evidenced solely by isolated incidents of negligence or improvidence.

The requirement of the preceding sentence shall not apply in the cause of a petition for renewal of guardianship.

(i) "Unable to meet essential requirements for one's physical health or safety" means unable, through one's own efforts and through the acceptance of assistance from family, friends, and other available private and public sources, to meet one's needs for medical care, nutrition, clothing, shelter, hygiene, or safety so that, in the absence of public guardianship, serious physical injury, illness, or disease is likely to occur in the near future. For the purposes of this Act, any such inability must be evidenced by recent behaviors causing such harm or creating a clear and substantial risk thereof, and at least one incidence of such behavior must have occurred within 20 days of the filing of the petition for public guardianship. The requirement of the preceding sentence shall not apply in the case of a petition for renewal of public guardianship.

(j) "Values history survey" refers to a form documenting an individual's values about health care.

Section 4. Establishment of Office

(a) Establishment of office. Each county within the state shall establish an independent office of public guardian. The office may not be established by contract. Paid professional staff shall be county public employees.

(b) Conflict of Interest. The office of public guardian shall be independent from all service providers and shall not directly provide housing, medical, legal, or other direct, non-surrogate decision-making services to a client.

(c) Authority. The office of public guardian is authorized to take any actions on behalf of an IP that a private guardian may take, except as otherwise provided in this Act.

(d) Effectiveness; Staffing Ratio. No office of public guardian shall assume responsibility for any IPs beyond a ratio of 20 IPs per one paid professional staff. When this ratio has been reached, the office of public guardian may not accept further appointments. The office shall adopt procedures to ensure that appropriate notice is given to the court.

Section 5. Appointment of Public Guardian

(a) Appointment. The county [board of supervisors; council] shall appoint a public guardian to administer the office of public guardianship. The public guardian shall be appointed for a term of five years. The public guardian shall be a licensed attorney, shall be hired based on a broad knowledge of law, human development, sociology, and psychology, and shall have business acuity.

(b) Part-time Appointments. If the needs of the local jurisdiction do not require that a person hold only the position of public guardian, the county [board of supervisors; council] may appoint an individual as public guardian on a part-time basis with appropriate compensation, provided that no other part-time position occupied by such individual may present any conflict of interest.

(c) Compensation. The county [board of supervisors; council] shall fix the compensation for the position of public guardian.

(d) Succession in office. When a person is appointed as public guardian, he or she succeeds immediately to all rights, duties, responsibilities, powers, and authorities of the preceding public guardian.

(e) Continuation of Staff Activities. When the position of public guardian is vacant, staff employed by the office shall continue to act as if the position were filled.

(f) Time Limit to Fill Vacancy. When the position of public guardian becomes vacant, the county [board of supervisors; council] shall appoint a successor in office within 45 days.

Section 6. Bond Required

(a) General Bond. The office of public guardian shall file with the clerk of the court in which the office is to serve a general bond in the amount fixed by the county [board of supervisors; council], payable to the state or to people of the county in which the court is seated, and issued by a surety company approved by the [chief judge; presiding judge] of the court. The bond shall be conditioned upon the faithful performance by the office of public guardian of duties as conservator or guardian.

(b) Nature of Bond. The general bond and oath of the public guardian is in lieu of the bond and oath required of a private conservator or guardian.

Section 7. [Alternative A] Powers and Duties

(a) Appointment by Court. The office of public guardian may serve as guardian and/or conservator, after appointment by a court pursuant to the provisions of the [guardianship and conservatorship law of the state].

Section 7. [Alternative B] Powers and Duties

(a) Appointment by Court. The office of public guardian may serve as guardian and/or conservator, after appointment by a court pursuant to the provisions of the [guardianship and conservatorship law of the state], provided that the AIP has had the opportunity for the hearing prescribed in Section 9 of this Act.

(b) Same Powers and Duties. The office of public guardian shall have the same powers and duties as a private guardian or conservator, except as otherwise limited by law or court order.

(c) Delegation of Powers and Duties. The public guardian may delegate to members of the paid professional staff powers and duties in making decisions as guardian or conservator and such other powers and duties as are created by this Act, although the office of public guardian retains ultimate responsibility for the proper performance of these delegated functions. All paid professional staff with decision-making authority at least shall have graduated from an accredited four-year college or university; have a degree in law, social work, or psychology; [and be certified by the state guardian certification entity].

(d) Other Duties. The office of public guardian shall:

(1) Use the substituted judgment principle of decision making that substitutes as the guiding force in any surrogate decision the values of the IP, to the extent known.

(2) Establish criteria and procedures for the conduct of and filing with the court for each IP of: a values history survey, annual functional assessment, decisional accounting reports, and such other information as may be required by law.

(3) Prepare for each IP within 60 days of appointment and file with the court an individualized guardianship or conservatorship plan designed from a functional assessment.

(4) Personally visit each IP at least twice a month; and maintain a written record of each visit, to be filed with the court as part of the guardian's report to court.

(5) Visit any facility in which an IP is to be placed if outside his or her home.

(6) Have a continuing duty to seek a proper and suitable person who is willing and able to serve as successor guardian or conservator for an IP served by the office.

(7) Develop and adopt written standards of practice for providing public guardianship and conservatorship services.

(8) Establish record-keeping and accounting procedures to ensure (i) the maintenance of confidential, accurate, and up-to-date records of all cases in which the office provides guardianship or conservatorship services; and (ii) the collection of statistical data for program evaluation, including annually the number of guardianship and conservatorship cases open, the number handled by the office and their disposition, the age and condition of clients, and the number institutionalized.

(9) Establish and provide public information about procedures for the filing, investigation, and resolution of complaints concerning the office.

(10) Prepare a yearly budget for implementation of the Act.

(11) Contract for an annual independent audit of the office by a certified public accountant.

(12) Prepare an annual report for submission to the county [board of supervisors; council] and the state court administrative office.

(e) Other Powers: The office of public guardian may:

(1) Not initiate a petition of appointment of the office as guardian or conservator.

(2) On motion of the office, or at the request of the court, intervene at any time in any guardianship or conservatorship proceeding involving an AIP or an IP by appropriate motion to the court, if the office or the court deems such intervention to be justified because an appointed guardian or conservator is not fulfilling his or her duties, the estate is subject to disproportionate waste, or the best interests of the individual require such intervention.

(3) Employ staff necessary for the proper performance of the office, to the extent authorized in the budget for the office;

(4) Formulate and adopt policies and procedures necessary to promote the efficient conduct of the work and general administration of the office, its professional staff, and other employees.

(5) Serve as representative payee for public benefits only for persons for whom the office serves as guardian or conservator.

(6) Act as a resource to persons already serving as private guardian or conservator for education, information, and support.

(7) Make funeral, cremation, or burial arrangements after the death of an IP served by the office if the next of kin of the IP does not wish to make the arrangements or if the office has made a good faith effort to locate the next of kin to determine if the next of kin wishes to make the arrangements.

(8) Not commit an IP to a mental health facility without an involuntary commitment proceeding as provided by law.

Section 8. Persons Eligible for Services

(a) Eligible persons. Any IP residing in the state who cannot afford to compensate a private guardian or conservator and who does not have a willing and responsible family member or friend to serve as guardian or conservator is eligible for the services of the office of public guardian where the individual resides or is located.

Section 9. [Alternative A] Appointment and Review Procedure

[Alternative A does not include this section.]

Section 9. [Alternative B] Appointment and Review Procedure

(a) Appointment. The initial appointment by a court of the public guardian as guardian or conservator shall be for no longer than six months, after the court determines by clear, unequivocal, and convincing evidence that the individual is incapacitated; cannot afford to compensate a private guardian; does not have appropriate, willing, and responsible family members or friends to serve as guardian; and lacks the capacity to make informed decisions about proposed care, treatment, or management services and that necessary services are available to protect the person from serious injury, illness, or disease, or from gross financial mismanagement or manifest financial vulnerability. Successive appointments for a term no longer than one year may be made by the court after the same determinations.

(b) Accounting and Review of Appointment. No later than 30 days prior to the expiration of his or her term as guardian or conservator, the public guardian shall file with the court an inventory and account in accord with the provisions of (section _____ of the guardianship and conservatorship law of the state), which shall be subject to examination pursuant to the provisions of (section _____ of the guardianship or conservatorship law of the state). At the same time, the public guardian shall file a statement setting forth facts that indicate at least: (1) the present personal status of the IP; (2) the public guardian's plan for regaining, developing, and preserving the person's well being and capacity to make informed decisions about care and treatment services; and (3) the need for the continuance or discontinuance of the guardianship or conservatorship or for any alteration of the powers of the public guardian.

(c) Hearing. The court shall hold a hearing to determine the findings set forth in subsection (a), above, concerning the appointment, or renewal of the appointment of the public guardian, unless the court dismisses the petition for lack of substantial grounds.

(d) Presence of Alleged IP. The AIP shall be present at the hearing unless he or she is medically incapable of being present to the extent that attendance is likely to cause serious and immediate physiological damage. Such a waiver for medical incapability shall be determined on the basis of factual information supplied to the court by counsel, including at least the affidavit or certificate of a duly licensed medical practitioner.

(e) Counsel. The AIP has the right to counsel whether or not the person is present at the hearing, unless the person knowingly, intelligently, and voluntarily waives the right to counsel. If the AIP cannot afford counsel or lacks the capacity to waive counsel, the court shall appoint counsel who shall always be present at any hearing involving the person. If the person cannot afford counsel, the state shall pay reasonable attorney's fees as customarily charged by attorneys in this state for comparable services.

(f) Trial by Jury. The AIP shall have the right to trial by jury.

(g) Evaluation. The AIP has the right to secure an independent medical and/or psychological examination relevant to the issues involved in the hearing at the expense of the state if the person is unable to afford such examination and to present a report of this independent evaluation or the evaluator's personal testimony as evidence at the hearing. At any evaluation, the AIP has the right to remain silent, the right to refuse to answer questions when the answers may tend to incriminate the person, the right to have counsel or any other mental health professional present, and the right to retain the privileged and confidential nature of the evaluation for all proceedings other than proceedings pursuant to this Act.

(h) Right to Present Evidence. The AIP may present evidence and confront and cross-examine witnesses.

(i) Duties of Counsel. The duties of counsel representing an AIP at the hearing shall include at least: a personal interview with the person; counseling the person with respect to his or her rights; and arranging for an independent medical and/or psychological examination as provided in subsection (g) above.

(j) Rules of Evidence. Except where specified otherwise, the rules of evidence and rules of procedure, including those on discovery, that are applicable in civil matters shall govern all proceedings under this Act. Any psychiatrist or psychologist giving testimony or reports containing descriptions and opinions shall be required to provide a detailed explanation as to how such descriptions and opinions were reached and a specification of all behaviors and other factual information on which such descriptions and opinions are based. Such witnesses shall not be permitted to give opinion testimony stating the applicable diagnostic category unless the AIP raises the issue through cross-examination or in the presentation of evidence.

(k) Psychotropic Medication. The AIP shall be entitled upon request to have the court and the jury, if any, informed regarding the influence of any psychotropic medication being taken by the person and its effect on his or her actions, demeanor, and participation at the hearing.

(l) Appeal. The AIP shall have the right to appeal adverse orders and judgments as prescribed in [the Rules of Civil Procedure], and the right to appellate counsel, who shall be compensated as provided in subsection (e) above.

Section 10. Allocation of Costs

(a) Determination of Costs. If the office is appointed guardian or con-servator for an IP, the administrative costs of the public guardianship services and the costs incurred in the appointment procedure shall not be charged against the income or the estate of the IP, unless the court determines at any time that the person is financially able to pay all or part of such costs.

(b) Financial Ability. The ability of the IP to pay for administrative costs of the office or costs incurred in the appointment procedure shall be measured according to the person's financial ability to engage and compensate a private guardian. The ability is dependent on the nature, extent, and liquidity of assets; the disposable net income of the person; the nature of the guardianship or conservatorship; the type, duration, and the complexity of the services required; and any other foreseeable expenses.

(c) Investigation of Financial Ability. The office shall investigate the finan-cial status of a person for whom a court is considering the appointment of the office. In connection with such investigation, the office may re-quire the AIP to execute and deliver written requests or authorizations to provide the office with access to records of public or private sources, otherwise confidential, needed to evaluate eligibility. The office may obtain information from any public record office of the state or of any subdivision or agency thereof upon request, without payment of any fees ordinarily required by law.

(d) In any proceeding for appointment of the office, or in any proceed-ing involving an individual for whom the office has been appointed conservator or guardian, the court may waive any court costs or filing fees.

Section 11. Right to Services

(a) Right to Services. Each IP served by the office has the right to prompt and adequate personal and medical care, treatment, and rehabilitative services to meet needs for protection from physical injury, illness, or disease, and for restoration of the abilities to care for oneself and to make one's own informed decisions about care and treatment services.

(b) Petition for Order to Provide Services. If the office is unable to secure such services out of funds available from the IP's estate and income and other private and governmental benefits to which he or she is entitled, the office or the IP may petition the court for an order requiring the [state and/or county] to provide necessary funds for services that would implement the individual's right to services. Such petition shall provide complete details concerning funds and other benefits at the public guardian's disposal and justification for the necessity and appropriateness of the services for which finances are unavailable. Upon receipt of the petition, the court shall schedule the matter for a hearing within 20 days and cause the petition and notice of the hearing to be served upon the public guardian, the IP, the person's attorney, and [appropriate state and/or local officials]. In preparation for the hearing, the [appropriate state and/or local officials] shall have access to relevant care and treatment records of the individual. At the hearing, the burden of proof by a preponderance of the evidence shall be upon the petitioning party.

(c) Order. At the conclusion of the hearing, the court shall enter an order dismissing the petition or requiring the [state and/or county] to provide the necessary funds for any services to which the individual has a right under subsection (a).

Section 12. Duties of State Court Administrative Office

(a) The state court administrative office shall provide training and support for the local offices of public guardian; encourage consistency in data collection, forms, and reporting instruments; and facilitate the exchange of information and promising practices.

(b) The state court administrative office shall contract with an appropriate research or public policy entity with expertise in gerontology, disabilities, and public administration for an evaluation of the local offices of public guardian.

(1) The evaluation shall include an analysis of costs and offsetting savings to the state, and other benefits from the delivery of public guardianship services.

(2) An initial report is due two years following the effective date of this Act and thereafter reports with recommendations are due to the governor and the legislature four years following the effective date of the Act.

Section 13. Statewide Public Guardianship Advisory Committee

(a) The governor shall establish a public guardianship advisory committee consisting of the following members:

(1) Two persons designated by the Supreme Court;

(2) Two senators and two members of the House of Representatives from the state legislature;

(3) One person from the state agency on aging, and one person from the area agency on aging;

(4) One person from the state protection and advocacy system, and one person from the state developmental disabilities council;

(5) One person from the state long-term care ombudsman;

(6) One person from the state guardianship association; and

(7) One person from the state bar association.

(b) Members of the committee shall each serve a three-year term, subject to renewal for no more than one additional three-year term, except that the first appointments to the committee shall be for terms of varying duration, as specified by the governor. A vacancy occurring other than by expiration of term shall be filled for the unexpired term.

(c) Members shall receive no compensation for their services, but may be reimbursed for travel and other expenses incurred in the discharge of their duties.

(d) The purpose of the committee shall be to report to and advise the governor and the legislature on the means for effectuating the purposes of this Act.

(e) The meetings of the advisory committee shall be open to the public, with agendas published in advance, and minutes available to the public. The public notice of all meetings shall indicate that accommodations for disability will be available on request.

Section 14. Authorization of Appropriations

To carry out the purposes of this Act, there is authorized to be appropriated $ _____ for the fiscal year ending _____, $ _____ for the fiscal year ending _____, and $ _____ for the fiscal year ending _____.

Section 15. Effective Date

This Act takes effect _____.

Notes

1. Pamela Teaster et al., *Wards of the State: A National Study of Public Guardianship*.
2. Schmidt et al., *Public Guardianship and the Elderly*, 179–203.
3. Regan and Springer, *Protective Services for the Elderly: A Working Paper*.
4. Legal Research and Services for the Elderly, National Council of Senior Citizens,

Legislative Approaches to the Problems of the Elderly: A Handbook of Model State Statutes (Washington, DC.: National Council of Senior Citizens, 1971).

5. National Conference of Commissioners on Uniform State Laws, *Uniform Guardianship and Protective Proceedings Act* (1982).

6. Bruce Sales, D. Matthew Powell, Richard Van Diuzend, and ABA Commission on the Mentally Disabled, *Disabled Persons and the Law: State Legislative Issues* (New York: Plenum Press, 1982).

7. Commission on National Probate Court Standards, *National Probate Court Standards* (National Center for State Courts, 1993, 1999).

8. American Bar Association Commission on the Mentally Disabled and Commission on Legal Problems of the Elderly, *Guardianship: An Agenda for Reform.*

9. Symposium, Wingspan Conference.

10. Schmidt et al., *Public Guardianship and the Elderly*, 179.

11. Erica Wood in Quinn, *Guardianships of Adults*. See state statutory charts on adult guardianship, as well as the annual update, on the Web site of the ABA Commission on Law and Aging at http://www.abanet.org/aging/legislativeupdates/home.shtml.

12. Schmidt et al., *Public Guardianship and the Elderly*, 183.

13. Winsor Schmidt and Pamela Teaster, "Criteria for Choosing Public or Private (Contracting Out) Models in the Provision of Guardian of Last Resort Services," Appendix H in Schmidt et al., *Second Year Evaluation of the Virginia Guardian of Last Resort.*

14. Schmidt et al., *Second Year Evaluation of the Virginia Guardian of Last Resort*, 23 ("The ward to guardian ratio should be 20:1.") Schmidt et al., cite the substantial empirical literature since 2000 on the relationship between specific nurse-to-patient ratios, patient mortality, and other hospital quality-of-care measures. Schmidt et al., "The Relationship Between Guardian Certification Requirements and Guardian Sanctioning," 651, note 53. See also Council on Accreditation, *Adult Guardianship Service Standards*: "Generally speaking, the staff to client ratio should be set at 1:20 to eliminate situations in which there is little to no service being provided to an individual." http://www.coastandards.org/standards.php?navView=private&core_id=1270

15. The Wingspread National Guardianship Conference recommended that "guardianship agencies should limit the impact of liability through insurance, as it becomes available," and that "states should be encouraged to facilitate the development of insurance coverage for guardianship agencies." ABA Commission on the Mentally Disabled (currently the Commission on Mental and Physical Disability Law) and the Commission on Legal Problems of the Elderly (currently the Commission on Law and Aging), *Guardianship: An Agenda for Reform*, recommendation VI-F (ABA 1988). On January 8, 2007, the Washington Courts Certified Professional Guardian Board voted to adopt a regulation requiring liability insurance effective January 31, 2008, http://www.courts.wa.gov/committee/?fa=committee.child&child_id=50&committee_id=117

16. Cf. Schmidt et al., "The Relationship Between Guardian Certification Requirements and Guardian Sanctioning," 641 ("83.3% of [General Equivalency Diploma] or [high school] graduates are likely to have more severe sanctions compared to 76.4% undergraduate or higher education, and 47.7% with an [Associate of Arts] or [Technical] degree, respectively. Guardians with an A.A. or Tech degree are 0.28 times less likely to have more severe sanctions than guardians with an undergraduate degree or higher education ($p < 0.01$).") The Adult Guardianship Service Standards of

the Council of Accreditation recently adopted minimum educational qualifications for guardianship workers of a bachelor's degree with two years relevant experience or an advanced (Master's level) degree in a relevant field, http://www.coastandards.org/standards. php?navView=private&core_id=1278

17. See state statutory charts on adult guardianship, as well as the annual update, on the Web site of the ABA Commission on Law and Aging at http://www.abanet.org/aging/ legislativeupdates/home.shtml.

18. The values history requirement in Virginia law stems from the New Mexico values history model. See Pam Lambert, Joan McIver Gibson, and Paul Nathanson, "The Values History: An Innovation in Surrogate Medical Decision-Making," *Journal of Law, Medicine, and Ethics* 18, no. 3 (1990): 202–212.

19. See also, e.g., state of Washington Certified Professional Guardian Board: Duties and Responsibilities of a Certified Professional Guardian, Rules and Regulations, Standards of Practice, Ethics Advisory Opinions, Filing a Grievance Against a Certified Professional Guardian at http://www.courts.wa.gov/programs_orgs/guardian/index.cfm. See also Council on Accreditation, *Adult Guardianship Service Standards*, http://www. coastandards.org/standards.php?navView=private&section_id=154

20. Gottlich and Wood, "Statewide Review of Guardianships; Hurme and Wood, "Guardian Accountability Then and Now," 912–913.

21. See, e.g., Florida Statutes Annotated §744.704(7).

22. Schmidt et al., *Public Guardianship and the Elderly*, 186–187.

23. Ibid., 185.

24. Florida Statutes Annotated §744.705(2).

25. Schmidt et al., *Public Guardianship and the Elderly*, 188.

26. Olmstead v. L.C., 527 U.S. 581, 602-04 (1999).

27. Virginia Code Annotated §2.2-712(B)(9).

28. Utah Code Annotated §62A-14-112.

29. S.B. 5320 (Washington 2007), §4(13).

30. Teaster and Roberto, *Virginia Public Guardian and Conservator Programs*. See also Teaster et al., *The Florida Public Guardian Programs*.

31. Iowa Code §§231E.1 through 231E.13, Iowa Substitute Decision-Maker Act.

32. See, e.g., Utah Code Annotated §62A-14-106; Virginia Code Annotated §2.2-2411 and 2412. Note that the recent Washington legislation originally included an advisory committee, but the governor vetoed this section (S.B. 5320).

Appendix A

STATE PUBLIC GUARDIANSHIP STATUTORY CHARTS

Table 1: Statutory Authority and Type of Program

State	Adult Guardianship Statute	Public Guardianship or Last Resort Provisions	Type of Public Guardianship— Implicit or Explicit	Public Guardian Subjects	Public Guardian Scope— Governs Property & Person
AL	Ala. Code §26A	Ala. Code §§26-2-26 & 26-2-50	I	Incapacitated persons	Property only
AK	Ak. Stat. §§13.26.050 through 13.26.320	Ak. Stat. §§13.26.360 through 13.26.410	E	Incapacitated persons or minors who need guardians	X
AZ	Ariz. Rev. Stat. §§5101 through 5433	Ariz. Rev. Stat. §§14-5601 through 14-5606	E	Persons or estates who need guardians	X
AR	Ark. Code Ann. §§28-65-101 through 28-65-603	Ark. Code Ann. §§5-28-307 & 309	I	Maltreated adults receiving court-ordered adult protective services	Person only

Table 1 *(continued)*

State	Adult Guardianship Statute	Public Guardianship or Last Resort Provisions	Type of Public Guardianship— Implicit or Explicit	Public Guardian Subjects	Public Guardian Scope— Governs Property & Person
CA	Cal. Probate Code Ann. §§1400 through 2955	Cal. Govt. Code Ann. §§27430 through 27436; Cal. Prob. Code §§2920 through 2944; Welf. & Inst. Code Ann. §5354.5	E	Persons domiciled in county who need guardians; gravely disabled persons	X
CO	Colo. Rev. Stat. §§15-14-101 through 15-14-433	Colo. Rev. Stat. §15-14-110	I		X
CT	Conn. Gen. Stat. §§45a-644 through 45a-663	Conn. Gen. Stat. §45a-651	I	Incapacitated persons 60+ who need guardians and whose assets are not over $1,500	X
DE	Del. Code Ann. §§12-3901 through 12-3997	Del. Code Ann. §§12-3991 through 3997	E	Disabled adults who need guardians	X
DC	D.C. Code Ann. §§21-2001 through 21-2077	No provision			

Table 1 *(continued)*

State	Adult Guardianship Statute	Public Guardianship or Last Resort Provisions	Type of Public Guardianship— Implicit or Explicit	Public Guardian Subjects	Public Guardian Scope— Governs Property & Person
FL	Fla. Stat. Ann. §§744.101 through 744.715	Fla. Stat. Ann. §§744.701 through 744.709	E	Incapacitated persons who need guardians, primarily those of limited financial means	X
GA	Ga. Code Ann. §§29-1-1 through 29-10-11	Ga. Code Ann. §§29-10-1 through 29-10-11	E	Adults in need of guardians	X
HI	Haw. Rev. Stat. §§560:5-101 through 560:5-432	Haw. Rev. Stat. §§551A-1 through 551A-9; 551-21	E	Incapacitated persons who need guardians	X
ID	Idaho Code §§15-5-101 through 15-5-603	Idaho Code §§15-5-601 through 15-5-603	I	Persons who need guardians	X
IL	755 Ill. Comp. Stat. §§5/11a-1 through 5/11a-23	20 Ill. Comp. Stat. §§3955/1 through 3955/5 & 3955-30 through 3955-36; 755 ILLS §§5/13-1 through 5/13-5	E	(a) Disabled adults who need guardians for estates worth $25,000 or less; (b) disabled adults who need guardians for estate over $25,000	X

175

Table 1 *(continued)*

State	Adult Guardianship Statute	Public Guardianship or Last Resort Provisions	Type of Public Guardianship— Implicit or Explicit	Public Guardian Subjects	Public Guardian Scope— Governs Property & Person
IN	Ind. Code §§29-3-1-1 through 29-3-13-3	Ind. Code §§12-10-7-1 through 12-10-7-9	E	Incapacitated indigent adults	X
IA	Iowa Code §§633.551 through 633.628	Iowa Code §§231E.1 through 231E.13; 217.13; 135.28 & 135.29	E	Adults who need guardians & non-adjudicated persons who elect for voluntary conservator & no one to serve	X
KS	Kan. Stat. Ann. §§59-3051 through 59-3096	Kan. Stat. Ann. §§74-9601 through 74-9606	E	Adults who need guardians & non-adjudicated persons who elect for voluntary conservator & there is no one to serve	X
KY	Ky. Rev. Stat. Ann. §§387.500 through 387.990	Ky. Rev. Stat. Ann. §210.290	I	Residents adjudged partially disabled or disabled who need guardians	X
LA	La. Civ. Pro. Code Ann. art. 389 through 426; art. 4541 through 4569	No statutory provision			

Table 1 *(continued)*

State	Adult Guardianship Statute	Public Guardianship or Last Resort Provisions	Type of Public Guardianship—Implicit or Explicit	Public Guardian Subjects	Public Guardian Scope—Governs Property & Person
ME	Me. Rev. Stat. Ann. 18-A 5-101 through 18-A 5-614	Me. Rev. Stat. Ann. 18-A 5-601 through 18-A 5-614	E	Mentally retarded; other incapacitated persons	X
MD	Md. Est. & Trusts Code Ann. §§13-101 through 13-107 & 13-201 through 13-908	Md. Fam. Law Code Ann. §§14-102,14-203, 14-307, 14-401 through 14-404; Est. & Trusts §13-707	E	Individuals requiring adult protective services who are unwilling or unable to accept services voluntarily	Person only
MA	Mass. Gen. Laws Ann. Chp. 201	No statutory provision			
MI	Mich. Comp. Laws Ann. §§700.5301 through 700.5433	No statutory provision			
MN	Minn. Stat. Ann. §§524.5-101 through 524.5-502	Minn. Stat. Ann. §§252A.01 through 252A.21 & 524.5-3-3; 524.5-502; 626.557	E; I	Mentally retarded persons who need guardian; incapacitated adults who need guardians; maltreated vulnerable adults	X

Table 1 *(continued)*

State	Adult Guardianship Statute	Public Guardianship or Last Resort Provisions	Type of Public Guardianship— Implicit or Explicit	Public Guardian Subjects	Public Guardian Scope— Governs Property & Person
MS	Miss. Code Ann. §§93-13-1 through 93-13-281	Miss. Code. Ann. §§93-13-21 & 93-13-129	I	Ward who has property	X
MO	Mo. Rev. Stat. §§475.010 through 475.480	Mo. Rev. Stat. §§473.730 & 750; 475.055	I		X
MT	Mont. Code Ann. §§72-5-101through 72-5-439	Mont. Code Ann. §§72-5-312(5) & 72-5-415	I		X
NE	Neb. Rev. Stat. §§30-2601 through 30-2661	No statutory provision			
NV	Nev. Rev. Stat. §§13-159.013 through 13-159.325	Nev. Rev. Stat. §§20-253.150 through 20-253.250	E	State residents who need guardians; lack sufficient assets	X
NH	N.H. Rev. Stat. Ann. §§464-A:1 through 464-A:47	N.H. Rev. Stat. Ann. §§547-B:1 through 547-B:8	E	Persons who need guardian nominated by commissioner in mental health services system or administrator of services for developmentally disabled; others in need if funds available	X

Table 1 *(continued)*

State	Adult Guardianship Statute	Public Guardianship or Last Resort Provisions	Type of Public Guardianship— Implicit or Explicit	Public Guardian Subjects	Public Guardian Scope— Governs Property & Person
NJ	N.J. Stat. Ann. §§3B:12-1 through 3B:12-78	N.J. Stat. Ann. §§52:27G-20 through 52:27G-32	E	Elderly state residents 60+ who need guardians	X
NM	N.M. Stat. Ann. §§45-5-101 through 45-5-432	N. M. Stat. Ann. §§28-16B-1 through 28-16B-6	E	Income-eligible incapacitated persons	
NY	N.Y. Mental Hyg. Law §§81.01 through 81.43	N.Y. Mental Hyg. Law §§81.03(a) & 81.19; Social Services Law 473d	I	Persons receiving adult protective services & living outside hospital or residential facility	X
NC	N.C. Gen. Stat. §§35A-1101 through 35A-1361	N.C. Gen. Stat. §§35A-1213 & 35A-1270 through 1273	E	Incapacitated persons for whom six months have elapsed from discovery that the person's property has no guardian	
ND	N.D. Cent. Code §§30.1-28-01 through 30.1-28-15	N.D. Cent. Code §30.1-28-11	I		
OH	Ohio Rev. Code Ann. §§21111.01 through 21111.51	Ohio Rev. Code Ann. §§21111.10 & 5123.55 through 5123.59	I	Persons with mental retardation or developmental disabilities	X

Table 1 *(continued)*

State	*Adult Guardianship Statute*	*Public Guardianship or Last Resort Provisions*	*Type of Public Guardianship— Implicit or Explicit*	*Public Guardian Subjects*	*Public Guardian Scope— Governs Property & Person*
OK	30 Okla. Stat. §§1-101 through 6-102	30 Okla. Stat. §§6-101 & 102; 22 Okla. Stat. §1175.6b	E	Persons who need guardian; persons who are mentally retarded and dangerous in criminal proceedings	
OR	Or. Rev. Stat. Ann. §§125.005 through 125.730	Or. Rev. Stat. Ann. §§125.700 through 125.730	E	Persons who need guardians	X
PA	20 Pa. Stat. Ann. §§5501 through 5555	20 Pa. Stat. Ann. §5511	I	Incapacitated persons who need guardians & have no less restrictive alternative	X
RI	R. I. Gen. Laws §§33-15-1 through 33-15-47	No statutory provision			
SC	S.C. Code §§62-5-101 through 62-5-624	S.C. Code §62-5-105	I	Patients of state mental health facility	Property only (not over $10,000)
SD	S. D. Codified Laws §§29A-5-101 through 29A-5-509	S.D. Codified Laws §§29A-5-110	I	Protected persons	
TN	Tenn. Code Ann. §§34-1-101 through 34-7-105	Tenn. Code Ann. §§34-7-101 through 34-7-105	E	Disabled persons 60+ who need guardian	X

180

Table 1 *(continued)*

State	Adult Guardianship Statute	Public Guardianship or Last Resort Provisions	Type of Public Guardianship— Implicit or Explicit	Public Guardian Subjects	Public Guardian Scope— Governs Property & Person
TX	Tex. Prob. Code Ann. §§601 through 905	Tex. Hum. Res. Code §§48.209; & 161.101 through 161.113	E	Elderly or disabled persons in state of abuse, neglect, or exploitation	X
UT	Utah Code Ann. §§75-5-101 through 75-5-433	Utah Code Ann. §§62A-14-101 through 62A-14 112	E	Incapacitated persons who need guardian	X
VT	Vt. Stat. Ann. §§14-2602 through 14-3096	Vt. Stat. Ann. §§14-3091 through 14-3096	E	Mentally disabled persons 60+ who need guardian	
VA	Va. Code Ann. §§37.2-1000 through 37.2-1029	Va. Code Ann. §§2.2-711 through 2.2713 & 2.2-2411	E	Incapacitated persons who need guardian, but do not have sufficient financial resources	X
WA	Wash. Rev. Code Ann. §§11.88.005 through 11.92.190	Wash Rev. Code Ann. [New chapter in Title 2]	E	Adults who need guardianship services & for whom services are otherwise unavailable, income not over 200% of poverty level, or receiving long-term Medicaid care	X

Table 1 *(continued)*

State	Adult Guardianship Statute	Public Guardianship or Last Resort Provisions	Type of Public Guardianship— Implicit or Explicit	Public Guardian Subjects	Public Guardian Scope— Governs Property & Person
WV	W. Va. Code §§44A-1-1 through 44A-5-9	W. Va. Code §§44A-1-8(g) & (h)	I		
WI	Wisc. Stat. §§54.01 through 54.988	Wisc. Stat. §54.15(7)	I		
WY	Wyo. Stat. §§3-1-101 through 3-3-1106	No provision			

Table 2: Procedural Due Process Safeguards in Guardianship

State	Potential Petitioners in Guardianship Proceedings	Notice & Hearing	Right to Counsel	Free Counsel to Indigents	Right to Jury Trial	Cross-Exam	Standard of Proof	Appeal/ Review
AL	Incapacitated person or any person	Yes	Court shall appoint attorney who may act as guardian *ad litem*		Yes	Yes		Yes
AK	Any person		Entitled to attorney	Court shall appoint Office of Public Advocacy if no funds	Yes	Yes	Clear & convincing	
AZ	Alleged incapacitated person or any person		Court shall appoint		Yes	Yes	Clear & convincing	
AR	Any person		Right to counsel			Yes	Clear & convincing	Yes
CA	Proposed ward, relatives, domestic partners, any other interested person		Right to counsel	Yes	Yes		Clear & convincing	Yes
CO	Individual or person interested in individual's welfare		Right to request court appointed counsel	If court directs		Yes	Clear & convincing	
CT	Any person		Court shall appoint	Yes	Yes		Clear & convincing	

Table 2 *(continued)*

State	Potential Petitioners in Guardianship Proceedings	Notice & Hearing	Right to Counsel	Free Counsel to Indigents	Right to Jury Trial	Cross-Exam	Standard of Proof	Appeal/ Review
DE	Any person (by rule)		Entitled to representation					
DC	Incapacitated person or any person		Court shall appoint			Yes	Clear & convincing	Yes
FL	An adult person		Court shall appoint			Yes	Clear & convincing	Yes
GA	Any interested person, including proposed ward		Right to counsel; court shall appoint unless retained				Clear & convincing	Yes
HI	Individual or person interested in the individual's welfare		Court shall appoint if requested, recommended by visitor (kokua kanawai), or court determines need			Yes	Clear & convincing	
ID	Incapacitated person or any person interested in welfare		Court shall appoint		Yes, for removal of guardian	Yes	If court satisfied	

IL	A reputable person or the alleged disabled person	Entitled to representation; court may appoint; shall appoint if respondent requests or position adverse to guardian *ad litem*		Yes		Clear & convincing	Yes
IN	Any person	Court may appoint			Yes		
IA	Any person	Court shall appoint	Yes	Yes, if demanded	Yes	Clear & convincing	
KS	Any person	Court shall appoint		Yes	Yes	Clear & convincing	Yes
KY	Any interested person or individual needing guardianship	Court shall appoint	Yes	Yes, mandatory	Yes	Clear & convincing	Yes
LA	Any person	Court shall appoint			Yes	Clear & convincing	Yes

Table 2 (*continued*)

State	Potential Petitioners in Guardianship Proceedings	Notice & Hearing	Right to Counsel	Free Counsel to Indigents	Right to Jury Trial	Cross-Exam	Standard of Proof	Appeal/Review
ME	The incapacitated person or any person interested in welfare		Court shall appoint one or more of: attorney, guardian *ad litem* or visitor. Must appoint attorney if respondent objects to petition.			Yes		
MD	Interested person; alleged disabled person (by rule)		Court shall appoint	Yes	Ward's option in guardianship; no jury trial in protective proceedings.	Yes	Clear & convincing	Yes
MA	Parent, relatives, nonprofit corporation, mental health agency, human services, welfare department; alleged incompetent							

State	Who may petition	Appointment of guardian ad litem				Standard of proof	
MI	An individual on own behalf or any person	Court shall appoint if person contests petition or proposed guardian or seeks limited order, or if guardian *ad litem* recommends	Yes	Yes	Yes	Clear & convincing	
MN	Individual or person interested in welfare	Court shall appoint unless individual waives in meeting with court visitor			Yes	Clear & convincing	Yes
MS	Interested party	Court may appoint guardian *ad litem*					Yes
MO	Any person	Court shall appoint		Yes	Yes	Clear & convincing	Yes

Table 2 (continued)

State	Potential Petitioners in Guardianship Proceedings	Notice & Hearing	Right to Counsel	Free Counsel to Indigents	Right to Jury Trial	Cross-Exam	Standard of Proof	Appeal/ Review
MT	Incapacitated person or any person interested in person's welfare		May have counsel of own choice or appointed counsel; or court may order public defender to assign counsel	Court may order public defender to assign counsel	Yes	Yes	If court satisfied	
NE	Alleged incapacitated person or any person		Court may appoint	Yes		Yes	Clear & convincing	Yes
NV	Proposed ward, governmental agency, nonprofit corporation, or any interested person		Court shall appoint if proposed ward requests	Court shall appoint legal aid attorney or private attorney			Clear & convincing	Yes
NH	Any relative, public official or interested person, or any individual in own behalf		Absolute and unconditional right to counsel	Yes			Beyond reasonable doubt	Yes

State							
NJ		Attorney appointed by court for temporary guardianship		Yes, if demanded by alleged incapacitated person		Clear & convincing	Yes
NM	Any interested person	Court shall appoint if not represented		Upon request by petitioner or alleged incapacitated person	Rules of evidence apply	Clear & convincing	Yes
NY	Alleged incapacitated, presumptive distributee, executor or administrator, trustee, person or facility with whom resides, any other person concerned with welfare	If requested, wishes to contest, not consent to move, need major medical decision, temporary appointment requested, evaluator conflict, if helpful	Yes, mental hygiene lawyers	Yes, if demanded	Yes	Clear & convincing	Yes
NC	Any individual, corporation, or disinterested public agent	Court shall appoint unless retains own counsel	Yes	Yes, upon request	Yes	Clear, cogent & convincing evidence	Yes

Table 2 *(continued)*

State	Potential Petitioners in Guardianship Proceedings	Notice & Hearing	Right to Counsel	Free Counsel to Indigents	Right to Jury Trial	Cross-Exam	Standard of Proof	Appeal/Review
ND	Any interested person		Court shall appoint attorney to act as guardian *ad litem*			Yes	Clear & convincing	Yes
OH	Court or any interested party		Right to be represented; right to have counsel appointed at court expense if indigent	Yes			Clear & convincing	
OK	Any person interested in welfare or partially incapacitated person		Court may appoint attorney, may be public defender; if respondent present & requests attorney or if court determines in best interest, court shall appoint	Yes		Yes	Clear & convincing	Yes
OR	Any person interested in welfare		Right to be represented	Notice refers to free or low-cost legal services for eligible individuals		Yes	Clear & convincing	

PA	Any person interested in welfare	Right to have counsel appointed if court deems appropriate	Yes	Yes, if requested	Yes	Clear & convincing	Yes
RI	Any person	Court shall appoint if respondent wishes to contest, limit powers, objects to person nominated	Yes		Yes	Clear & convincing	Yes
SC	Incapacitated person or any person interested in welfare	Court shall appoint unless person has own counsel			Yes	If court satisfied that appointment is necessary	
SD	Relative, responsible entity, any interested person	Court shall appoint if requested, contested, needed		Entitled to demand jury trial	Yes	Clear & convincing	
TN	Any person with knowledge of circumstances	Court shall appoint attorney *ad litem* if recommend- ed by guardian *ad litem* or if necessary to protect rights or interests				Clear & convincing	Yes

Table 2 *(continued)*

State	Potential Petitioners in Guardianship Proceedings	Notice & Hearing	Right to Counsel	Free Counsel to Indigents	Right to Jury Trial	Cross-Exam	Standard of Proof	Appeal/Review
TX	Any person; court, if probable cause		Court shall appoint attorney *ad litem*	Yes	Entitled on request in contested proceeding		Clear & convincing	Yes
UT	Incapacitated person or any person interested in welfare		Court shall appoint attorney unless person has counsel of own	If ward indigent, public guardianship office makes efforts to secure *pro bono* services	Yes	Yes		
VT	Any person interested in welfare		Court shall appoint counsel	Court maintains list of *pro bono* counsel, used before appointing legal services		Yes	Clear & convincing	Yes
VA	Any person		Court may appoint counsel on request of respondent or guardian *ad litem*, or if court determines needed	Yes	Entitled on request	Yes	Clear & convincing	

WA	Any person or entity	Right to be represented; court shall appoint when cannot afford	Yes	Yes		Clear, cogent & convincing	Yes
WV	Individual alleged to need guardian, person responsible for care or custody, any other person	Court shall appoint counsel			Yes	Clear & convincing	Yes
WI	Any person	Right to counsel if proposed ward requests, ward opposes petition, or court determines required		Right to jury trial if demanded		Clear & convincing	Yes
WY	Any person	Right to counsel if ordered by court		May demand jury trial		Preponderance of evidence	

Table 3: Assessment; Civil Liberties; Selection of Guardian

State	Medical Examination	Psychological Exam	Other Exam	Civil Liberties Preserved	Who Serves as Guardian—General Probate Priority	Input by Incapacitated Person
AL	Physician or other qualified person		Court representative interviews respondent		Yes	Yes, nomination in durable power of attorney
AK	Physician or registered nurse		Expert with expertise in alleged incapacity; court visitor	Yes	Yes; competent person, public guardian, private association, or nonprofit	Yes, nomination
AZ		Psychologist			Yes	Yes, nomination
AR			Professional with appropriate expertise	Yes	Suitable person who is resident of state, corporation	
CA	Physician	Psychologist	Religious healing practitioner. Court investigator	Yes	Yes, with court's discretion	Yes, nomination; & express statements reported to court investigator
CO	Physician	Psychologist	Other qualified individual appointed by court		Yes, person nominated, agent, probate priority	Yes, nomination
CT	One or more physicians	Psychologist	Social work, other		Request of respondent; any qualified person, authorized public official, or corporation in best interest	Yes, request or nomination
DE						

	Medical	Psychological	Social, other			
DC				Yes	In accordance with respondent's stated wishes; general probate priority (beginning with spouse or domestic partner)	Yes, in accordance with incapacitated person's stated wishes
FL	Psychiatric or other physician	Psychologist	Registered nurse, nurse practitioner, social worker, gerontologist, other	Yes	Any person qualified; preference for relative; persons with relevant experience	Yes, consider wishes
GA	Physician	Psychologist	Licensed clinical social worker	Yes	Individual; DHR; no conflict of interest; no long-term care facility serving ward	Yes, nomination
HI	Physician	Psychologist	Other qualified individual		Yes	Yes, nomination
ID	Physician	Psychologist	Other qualified person—mental health professional, psychiatrist, licensed social worker, or counselor		Person preferred by incapacitated person, general probate priority	Yes, person preferred by incapacitated person
IL	Physician		One or more independent experts	Yes	Person capable of providing active & suitable program of guardianship	Yes, may designate
IN					Consider request by respondent, relationship & best interest; probate priority	Yes, nomination
IA					Qualified and suitable person	
KS	Physician	Psychologist	Psychiatrist; other professional		Nominee of proposed ward; nominee of spouse, adult child, family member; nominee of petitioner	Yes, nomination

Table 3 *(continued)*

State	Medical Examination	Psychological Exam	Other Exam	Civil Liberties Preserved	Who Serves as Guardian—General Probate Priority	Input by Incapacitated Person
KY	Physician	Psychologist	Social worker	Yes	Any person or entity capable of conducting active guardianship program	Yes, preference or designation in power of attorney
LA	Physician (for temporary & preliminary interdiction)	Psychologist (for temporary & preliminary interdiction)	Examiner with training & experience in type of infirmity alleged	Yes	Person best able to fulfill duties; probate priority	Yes, person designated by defendant in writing
ME	Physician	Psychologist			Probate priority; includes domestic partner	Yes, nomination
MD	Physician	Psychologist		Yes	Probate priority	Yes, nomination
MA	Physician	Psychologist	Certified psychiatric nurse, clinical specialist, expert in mental illness	Rights of freedom of religion & religious practices	Court may not appoint person or entity with conflict of interest	
MI	Physician		Mental health professional		Person named by ward; probate priority	Yes, named by ward
MN			County social service agency may create screening committee to determine if less restrictive alternative	Yes	Agent appointed under health care advance directive; probate priority	Yes, agent named under advance directive

196

MS	Physician	Psychologist (for conservatorship petition)				
MO	Physician	Psychologist	Other appropriate professional	Yes	Person nominated by ward; probate priority	Yes, nomination
MT	Physician		Visitor trained in law, nursing, social work, medical care, mental health care, pastoral care, education, or rehabilitation	Yes	Person nominated by ward; probate priority	Yes, nomination
NE	Physician		Court visitor trained in law, nursing, social work, mental health, mental retardation, gerontology or developmental disabilities	Yes	Person nominated by ward; probate priority	Yes, nomination
NV	Physician		Any other qualified person		Person nominated by ward; probate priority	Yes, nomination
NH	Physician			Yes	Any competent person who agrees	Yes, nomination
NJ	Physician	Psychologist			Spouse or domestic partner, heirs, friends	Yes, as designated in power of attorney, health care proxy or advance directive

Table 3 *(continued)*

State	Medical Examination	Psychological Exam	Other Exam	Civil Liberties Preserved	Who Serves as Guardian—General Probate Priority	Input by Incapacitated Person
NM		Psychologist	Qualified health care professional; also visitor may be a psychologist, social worker, developmental incapacity professional, physical and occupational therapist, educator, rehabilitation worker	Yes	Person nominated; probate priority	Yes, nomination
NY	Physician	Psychologist	Court evaluator, including mental hygiene legal services, not-for-profit corporation, attorney, physician, psychologist, accountant, social worker, or nurse		Person nominated, any suitable individual, corporation, social services official, public agency	Yes, nomination
NC	Medical	Psychological	Social worker; professional in education, vocational rehabilitation, occupational therapy, vocational therapy, psychiatry, speech-and-hearing, communications disorders	Yes	An adult individual, corporation, or disinterested public agent	
ND	Physician	Psychologist	Visitor in nursing or social work	Yes	Any competent person, person nominated by ward; probate priority	Yes, nomination

State					
OH	Physician	Other qualified persons	Yes	Person nominated by ward; others	Yes, nomination
OK	Physician	Psychologist	Social worker; other expert	Court must make specific determinations on right to vote, other rights, for limited guardianship	Individual nominated; probate priority	Yes, nomination
OR	Physician	Psychologist	Visitor with training or experience to evaluate functional capacity & needs, communicate with respondent	Yes	Most suitable person, desire of respondent, relationship by blood or marriage	Yes, desire of respondent considered
PA			Individuals qualified by training & experience in evaluating incapacities	Yes	Any qualified individual or corporation	If appropriate, court give preference to nominee
RI	Physician			Yes	Relatives & friends, financial institutions, nonprofit corporations	Court consider wishes of incapacitated person

Table 3 (continued)

State	Medical Examination	Psychological Exam	Other Exam	Civil Liberties Preserved	Who Serves as Guardian—General Probate Priority	Input by Incapacitated Person
SC	Physician		Visitor trained in law, nursing or social work, or court appointee		Any competent person or suitable institution; person nominated by incapacitated person; probate priority	Yes, nomination
SD	Physician	Psychologist	Psychiatrist		Person who will act in best interests; lists factors to consider	Yes, nomination
TN	Physician	Psychologist		Yes	Person designated by alleged disabled person; probate priority	Yes, designation
TX	Physician	Psychologist; psychological & intellectual testing records	Court visitor	Yes	Best interests of individual; probate priority	Yes, court consider preference of incapacitated person
UT	Physician		Court visitor trained in law, nursing or social work, or appointee of court		Any competent person or suitable institution, person nominated by individual; probate priority	Yes, nomination
VT			Qualified mental health professional	Yes	Competent individuals; court consider ward preference, location, relationship, guardian ability, financial conflicts of interest	Yes, court consider preference of ward

State						
VA	Physician	Psychologist	Professionals skilled in assessment & treatment of alleged conditions			
WA	Physician	Psychologist	Advanced registered nurse practitioner	Yes	Any suitable person. For professional guardian any individual or guardianship service that meets certification requirements.	Yes, nomination
WV	Physician	Psychologist			Any adult capable of providing active & suitable program of guardianship; nonprofit corporations. Consider location, familial relationship; ability.	Yes, nomination
WI	Physician	Psychologist		Yes	Court consider opinions of proposed ward & family, conflicts of interest, other factors	Yes, nomination
WY					Any qualified person; no conflict of interest; probate priority	Yes, nomination

Table 4: Powers and Duties of Guardians; Costs

State	Specified Agency as Public Guardian	Conflict Raised/ Remedied	General Probate Powers for public Guardian	Specific Powers for Public Guardian	Public Guardian Funding Specified	Costs Borne by State or County	Costs Borne by Estate
AL	General county conservator or sheriff						
AK	Office of public advocacy in dept. of administration	Yes	Yes	Yes	Yes	Yes	Yes
AZ	County board of supervisors appoint public fiduciary		Yes	Yes	Yes	Yes	Yes
AR	Department of human services	Yes		Yes			
CA	County board of supervisors creates office of public guardian		Yes	Yes	Yes	Yes	Yes
CO	Public administrator or state or county agency	Yes	Yes		Yes		
CT	Commissioner of social services; may contract with public or private agency		Yes	Yes	Yes		
DE	Office of public guardian in judiciary	NA	Yes	Yes	Yes	Yes	Yes
DC		NA	Yes				
FL	Statewide public guardianship office in dept. of elderly affairs. Statewide office establish local offices in counties or judicial circuits	Yes	Yes	Yes	Yes	Yes	

GA	Qualified individuals or private nonprofit entities registered as public guardian and approved by probate court. Division of aging of dept. of human resources maintains list. If none, dept. of human resources. County administrators as ex officio county guardians	Yes	Yes	Yes	Yes	Yes	Yes
HI	Office of public guardian in judiciary, appointed by chief justice. Clerk of court as guardian of property if below $10,000.	NA	Yes	Yes	Yes	Yes	Yes
ID	Board of county commissioners creates board of community guardian	Yes	Yes	Yes	Yes	Yes	Yes
IL	(a) Office of state guardian, in guardianship and advocacy commission; (b) governor appoints suitable person as county public guardian; for counties over one million chief circuit court judge appoints attorney as county guardian	Yes	Yes	Yes	Yes	Yes	Yes
IN	Adult guardianship services program in family & social services administration; contracts with regional nonprofits	Yes	Yes	Yes	Yes	Yes	
IA	State office of substitute decision-maker in dept. of elder affairs; local offices of substitute decision-maker	Yes	Yes	Yes	Yes	Implementation subject to availability of funding	Yes
KS	A public instrumentality with board appointed by governor, including chief justice; coordinates volunteer guardians		Yes	Yes	Yes	Yes	Yes

Table 4 *(continued)*

State	Specified Agency as Public Guardian	Conflict Raised/ Remedied	General Probate Powers for Public Guardian	Specific Powers for Public Guardian	Public Guardian Funding Specified	Costs Borne by State or County	Costs Borne by Estate
KY	Cabinet for health & family services	Yes	Yes		Yes		Yes
LA							
ME	Dept. of behavioral & developmental disabilities, for persons with mental retardation; dept. of human services, for incapacitated persons		Yes	Yes	Yes	Yes	Yes
MD	Secretary of aging or director of area agency on aging for adults 65 or older; director of local dept. of social services for other adults		Yes				
MA		Yes					
MI		Yes					
MN	Commissioner of human services; county contracts for services, & county employee serves	Yes	Yes	Yes	Yes	Yes	Yes
MS	Chancery court appoint clerk of court		Yes		Yes		Yes
MO	County public administrator of each county; social service agencies in counties of designated size	Yes	Yes	Yes			Yes

State		Col 1	Col 2	Col 3	Col 4	Col 5
MT	State or federal agency authorized to provide direct services to incapacitated persons (for guardian); public administrator (for conservator)	Yes	Yes			
NE						
NV	County board of commissioners establish county public guardian program	Yes	Yes	Yes	Yes	Yes
NH	Department of health & human services contracts	Yes	Yes	Yes	Yes	Yes
NJ	Public guardian office in dept. of community affairs; appointed by governor	Yes	Yes	Yes	Yes	Yes
NM	Office of guardianship in developmental disabilities planning council	Yes	Yes	Yes	Yes	
NY	Local dept. of social services; may contract with community guardian program	Yes	Yes	Yes	Yes	Yes
NC	Clerk appoints individual as county public guardian; also, clerk appoints disinterested public agent without conflict of interest to serve as last resort	Yes	Yes	Yes		Yes
ND	Any appropriate government agency unless provides direct care & custody (unless court finds no substantial risk)	Yes				
OH	Dept. of mental retardation & developmental disabilities contract with public or private agency		Yes	Yes	Yes	

Table 4 (continued)

State	Specified Agency as Public Guardian	Conflict Raised/ Remedied	General Probate Powers for Public Guardian	Specific Powers for Public Guardian	Public Guardian Funding Specified	Costs Borne by State or County	Costs Borne by Estate
OK	Office of public guardianship in dept. of human services (subject to funding)		Yes	Yes	Full implementation dependent upon state funding		
OR	County court or board of commissioners create office of public guardian	Yes	Yes	Yes	Yes	Yes	Yes
PA	Guardianship support agencies	Yes	Yes	Yes	Yes	Yes	Yes
RI		Yes					
SC	Director of dept. of mental health or designee. (Also, a "suitable institution" may serve as guardian.)						
SD	Dept. of human services or dept. of social services; also any public agency if provides active & suitable guardianship program						
TN	Program administered by commission on aging; contracts with district agencies		Yes	Yes	Yes	Yes	Yes

State	Program				
TX	Dept. of aging and disability services; may contract with guardianship program or other entity		Yes		
UT	Office of public guardian in dept. of human services	Yes		Yes	Yes
VT	Office of public guardian in dept. of aging & disabilities	Yes		Yes	Yes
VA	Public guardian and conservator program in dept. for the aging; contracts with local/regional programs	Yes	Yes	Yes	Yes
WA	Office of public guardianship in administrative office of courts; contracts with private providers	Yes	Yes	Yes	Yes
WV	Department of health & human resources designates agency under its supervision; county sheriff may be appointed	Yes	Yes		
WI	Nonprofit corporation approved by the dept. of health and family services				
WY		Yes			

Table 5: Additional Guardianship Provisions

State	Provision for Termination	Restoration	Incapacitated Person Petition	Annual Report	Other Reporting Period	Emergency Guardian	Temporary Guardian	Limited Guardian
AL	Yes	Yes	Yes		Report as ordered by court; accounting at least every 3 years	Yes	Yes	Yes
AK	Yes	Yes	Yes	Yes		Yes	Yes	Yes
AZ	Yes	Yes	Yes	Yes		Yes	Yes	Yes
AR	Yes	Yes	Yes	Yes		Yes	Yes	Yes
CA	Yes	Yes	Yes	Yes	Within 6 months of appointment	Yes	Yes	Yes, for developmentally disabled
CO	Yes	Yes	Yes	Yes	Within 60 days of appointment	Yes	Yes	Yes
CT	Yes	Yes	Yes	Yes		Yes	Yes	Yes
DE	Yes	Yes	Yes		Accounting as court requires, not more than biennially; frequency of status report not stated	Yes	Yes	Yes
DC	Yes	Yes	Yes		Accounting at least yearly or on court order; report at least semi-annually or on court order	Yes	Yes	Yes

FL	Yes	Yes	Yes		Yes	Yes	Yes
GA	Yes	Yes	Yes		Yes	Yes	Yes
HI	Yes	Yes	Yes		Yes	Yes	Yes
ID	Yes	Yes	Yes		Yes	Yes	Yes
IL	Yes	Yes	Yes	Report at intervals as indicated by court;	Yes	Yes	Yes
IN	Yes	Yes	Yes	Report as ordered by court; accounting biennially	Yes	Yes	Yes
IA	Yes	Yes	Yes		Yes	Yes	Yes
KS	Yes	Yes	Yes		Yes	Yes	Yes
KY	Yes	Yes	Yes	Accounting biennially	Yes	Yes	Yes
LA	Yes	Yes	Yes		Yes	Yes	Yes
ME	Yes	Yes	Yes	As required by court	Yes	Yes	Yes
MD	Yes	Yes	Yes	County review board conduct review of each public guardianship case every six months	Yes	Yes	Yes
MA	Yes	Yes	Yes		Yes	Yes	Not in statute but by case law.
MI	Yes	Yes	Yes		Yes	Yes	Yes

Table 5 (*continued*)

State	Provision for Termination	Restoration	Incapacitated Person Petition	Annual Report	Other Reporting Period	Emergency Guardian	Temporary Guardian	Limited Guardian
MN	Yes	Yes	Yes	Yes		Yes	Yes	Yes
MS	Yes	Yes		Yes				Yes
MO	Yes	Yes	Yes	Yes		Yes	Yes	Yes
MT	Yes	Yes	Yes	Yes		Yes	Yes	Yes
NE	Yes	Yes	Yes					Yes
NV	Yes	Yes	Yes	Yes		Yes	Yes	Yes
NH	Yes	Yes	Yes	Yes	Status report annually unless court finds not necessary	Yes	Yes	Yes
NJ	Yes	Yes	Yes		At time intervals as ordered by the court	Yes	Yes	Yes
NM	Yes	Yes	Yes	Yes		Yes	Yes	Yes
NY	Yes	Yes	Yes	Yes		Yes	Yes	Yes
NC	Yes	Yes	Yes	Yes	Initial report within six months	Yes	Yes	Yes
ND	Yes	Yes	Yes	Yes		Yes	Yes	Yes
OH	Yes	Yes	Yes		Every two years for status report	Yes	Yes	Yes

State						
OK	Yes	Yes	Yes	Yes	Yes	Yes
OR	Yes	Yes	Every six months for persons who are mentally retarded & dangerous in criminal proceeding	Yes	Yes	Yes	Yes
PA	Yes	Yes	Personal status report at least annually & accounting whenever directed by court	Yes	Yes	Yes	Yes
RI	Yes	Yes	Yes	Yes	Yes	Yes	Yes
SC	Yes	Yes	Yes	Yes	Yes	Yes	Yes
SD	Yes	Yes	Yes	Yes	Yes	Yes	Yes
TN	Yes	Yes	Yes	Yes	Yes	Yes	Yes
TX	Yes	Yes	Yes	Yes	Yes	Yes	Yes
UT	Yes	Yes	As ordered	Yes	Yes	Yes	Yes
VT	Yes	Yes	Yes	Yes	Yes	Yes	Yes
VA	Yes	Yes	Yes	Yes	Yes	Yes	Yes
WA	Yes	Yes	Yes	Yes	Guardian *ad litem* may move for temporary relief from abuse, neglect, or exploitation, or to address other emergency	Yes	Yes

Table 5 *(continued)*

State	Provision for Termination	Restoration	Incapacitated Person Petition	Annual Report	Other Reporting Period	Emergency Guardian	Temporary Guardian	Limited Guardian
WV	Yes	Yes	Yes	Yes	Semi-annually in first year and annually thereafter	Yes	Yes	Yes
WI	Yes	Yes	Yes	Yes		Yes	Yes	Yes
WY	Yes	Yes	Yes	Yes, accounting	Personal status report every six months	Yes	Yes	Yes

STATE PUBLIC GUARDIANSHIP PROFILES

Appendix A is current as of 2007, unless otherwise indicated.

ALABAMA

Statute. Under Alabama law, a general conservator of the county may be appointed as guardian if there is no one else to serve. If there is no general conservator in a county, the sheriff must be appointed. Alabama Code §26-2-50.

Program. In Alabama, the county sheriff serves as a guardian of last resort. Funding is from the estate, if funds are available, and from the sheriff's operating budget. The number of wards served is unknown, as is the extent of unmet need.

ALASKA

Statute. In Alaska, the Office of Public Advocacy, within the Department of Administration, serves as public guardian or conservator. The office must visit each ward or protected person once every quarter, provide public information on guardianship, assist guardians and court-appointed visitors, and maintain a listing of services to assist incapacitated individuals. The office may intervene in a private guardianship or conservatorship proceeding to protect the best interests of a respondent or ward. The office may charge fees from client estates and may make a claim against the estate upon the death of the incapacitated person. Alaska Statutes §§13.26-360 through 410.

Program. The Office of Public Advocacy receives funding from state appropriations, Medicaid, and client fees based on a sliding scale. The office serves as both guardian and conservator, and may serve as agent under health care or financial powers of attorney, trustee, and representative payee for federal benefits for guardianship clients only.

The office has over 800 clients and 15 paid professional staff. Each professional staff has over 60 clients—about half elders and half younger adults with mental illnesses, mental retardation, or developmental disabilities. The great majority are receiving public benefits. About half the wards are Alaskan natives.

ARIZONA

Statute. Each county board of supervisors must establish an office of public fiduciary, and the county must cover the costs of conducting the program. In addition to serving as guardian or conservator, the public fiduciary may serve as a representative payee. The public fiduciary may charge the estate of a ward, protected person, or decedent reasonable expenses and compensation. Arizona Revised Statutes §§14-5601 through 5606.

Program. Arizona has 15 public fiduciary programs, one in each of the counties. The largest program is the Maricopa County Public Fiduciary in Phoenix, followed by the Pima County Public Fiduciary in Tucson. In addition to county funds, the programs also may collect fees from client estates. Public fiduciaries, as well as other professional guardians, must be certified under state law.

ARKANSAS

Statute. Under Arkansas law, no employee of any public agency that provides direct services to an incapacitated person may be appointed guardian of the person or estate of the incapacitated person. Arkansas Code Annotated §28-65-203(h). However, the court may appoint the Department of Human Services as guardian of the person for maltreated adults receiving court-ordered adult protective services from the Department. Arkansas Code Annotated §§5-28-307 & 309.

In 2007, legislation created an Office of Public Guardian for Adults within the Division of Aging and Adult Services. The director of the division must appoint a division employee to serve as public guardian. The 2007 act does not take effect until adequate funding is available, which the Division anticipates may occur in 2010.

Program. The adult protective services program of the Division of Aging and Adult Services serves as guardian of the person only. The program is funded by state appropriations and also uses Medicaid funds. The program does not collect fees from wards. It does petition for appointment as guardian of its own wards. The program serves over 180 APS clients and has a staff of 20 professionals.

CALIFORNIA

Statute. Each county board of supervisors may create an office of public guardian for persons domiciled in the county who need a conservator (a guardian of the person or property for adults). The board may designate the public administrator. The county may pay expenses of the public guardianship program, and may establish a revolving fund to do so. The board may designate a public representative payee. California Government Code Annotated §§27430 through 27436.

The public guardian may apply for appointment, and must apply for appointment if there is an imminent threat to a person's health or safety or estate, or if the court so orders. If there is no one else qualified and willing to act, and if it is in the best interest of the person, the court must appoint the public guardian. If a person is under the jurisdiction of the state Department of Mental Health ("gravely disabled" under the California Welfare and Institutions Code), an application of the public guardian may not be granted without the written consent of the Department. The public guardian must serve as conservator of a mentally ill person found to be "gravely disabled," if the court recommends the conservatorship and no other person or entity is willing and able to serve. Cal. Welf. & Inst. Code Ann. §5354.5.

Program. The state's "probate public guardianship system" is located at the county level. The counties differ in local placement of the program. In some counties, it is an independent county agency, while in others, it is placed under the county Department of Mental Health, Department of Social Services, Aging, district attorney, or elsewhere. The program may be combined with the public administrator, the office on aging, social services, or mental health. The counties, Medicaid, and client fees fund it. County public guardianship programs serve as conservator (guardian of the person or property) for adults. They may also conduct investigations of cases before a petition is filed. The programs may petition for appointment, but often lack the resources to sufficiently serve the unmet need. At least some counties have experienced longstanding underfunding, high caseloads, and demand for services exceeding program capacity.

In addition, the state has a separate public guardianship system under the county departments of behavioral health for individuals with mental illness who are determined "gravely disabled." These cases are called LPS conservatorships, after the Lanterman-Petris-Short authorizing legislation. Under an LPS conservatorship, a client is involuntarily hospitalized for three days based upon a request for evaluation by a mental health professional or police officer. If the client is determined to be a danger to self or others, the client may be hospitalized for an additional fourteen days, and if a physician determines the client remains gravely disabled, the physician may request the appointment of a conservator, and the case may be sent to the public guardian.

COLORADO

Statute. There is no specific statutory provision for public guardianship. The Colorado general guardianship statute is in Colorado Revised Statutes §§15-14-301 through 318, and is based on the Uniform Guardianship and Protective Proceedings Act.

Program. In 2006, 48 of the 64 Colorado county departments of social services provided guardianship. The program has no statutory basis. No funds are designated specifically for guardianship services, but guardianship is covered under federal Title XX block grant funds provided to counties for adult protective services. The county departments of social services act as guardian of the person only. They may also serve as representative payee for federal benefits. The departments may petition for appointment as guardian. The county departments throughout the state serve over 400 individuals annually.

CONNECTICUT

Statute. If no suitable person is found to serve as conservator (guardian of the person or property) for individuals age 60 or older and with assets not exceeding $1,500, then the Commissioner of Social Services shall be appointed. Connecticut General Statutes §45a-651.

Program. The Department of Social Services (DSS) applies to the probate court to serve as guardian (called a "conservator") when there is no one else to serve. The DSS Commissioner may be appointed as conservator of the estate for frail elderly persons age 60 or older who are incapable of managing their own affairs. Regional DSS staff administer the DSS Conservator of Person Program to supervise the personal affairs of incapacitated individuals, and the program is funded through general state funds.

DELAWARE

Statute. The Delaware Code establishes an Office of the Public Guardian within the court system. The chancellor must appoint the public guardian. The General Assembly sets the salary of the public guardian, who is paid from the state's general fund. The office serves as guardian of the person and/or of property for incapacitated adults. Costs may be charged to the general fund, unless the estate can pay.

Delaware Code Annotated §§6-3991 through 3997.

Program. Delaware has had a statewide Office of the Public Guardian since 1974, located within the court system. The budget for the statewide program is over

$400,000, appropriated by the state legislature. The office also collects fees from the estates of incapacitated individuals. The office serves as guardian, conservator, representative payee, trustee, and personal representative of decedents' estates. The office petitions for appointment when necessary. The office serves over 225 incapacitated individuals and has 7 professional full-time staff. Cases come from nursing homes, hospitals, the Court of Chancery, and adult protective services.

DISTRICT OF COLUMBIA

Statute. There is no specific statutory provision for public guardianship or guardianship of last resort. General guardianship statute is District of Columbia Code Annotated §§21-2001 through 21-2077.

Program. Court funds provide for the appointment of attorneys from a fiduciary panel to serve as guardian and/or conservator when there is no one else to serve. Attorneys receive payment from court funds at a set rate.

FLORIDA

Statute. Florida law establishes a Statewide Public Guardianship Office within the Department of Elder Affairs. The statewide office in turn establishes local programs in counties or judicial circuits. The local public guardian programs must maintain a staff or contract with qualified individuals to carry out guardianship functions. The programs must primarily serve incapacitated persons of limited financial means. A professional staff member must see each client at least quarterly. The ratio for professional staff to wards is one professional to forty guardianship clients.

Costs of administration, including filing fees, are paid from the budget of the statewide office. Funds are appropriated by the legislature for the Statewide Public Guardianship Office, but this does not preclude the use of funds raised through the efforts of the office. Florida law also creates a "direct support organization" to support the statewide office. In addition, the legislature established the "Joining Forces for Public Guardianship" matching grant program, although it was not funded. Florida Statutes Annotated §§744.701 through 744.709.

Program. In 1999, the Florida legislature created a Statewide Public Guardianship Office, located in the Department of Elder Affairs, and authorized the creation of local public guardianship programs. There are now 17 local public guardianship programs. The statewide office must appoint each local program. The local programs have varying models of operation, but do not yet cover all of the 67 counties of Florida. The programs serve adults 18 years of age and older, and serve as guardian of the person and property, as well as the Social Security representative payee.

The public guardianship program throughout the state serves over 2,486 wards (as of 2006), and has a total of close to 70 full-time equivalent paid professional staff. Because state law provides for a statutory guardian-to-ward ratio of 1:40, public guardian services are not accessible for some in need in areas where this cap is reached.

A continuing challenge is securing adequate funding. The Department of Elder Affairs in 2004 estimated an unmet need for public guardianship services of between 5,000 and 10,000 persons statewide, and concluded that the average cost of public guardianship is $2,363 per individual.

GEORGIA

Statute. In 2005, the Georgia General Assembly enacted a public guardianship initiative. It provides that any qualified individual may be registered as a public guardian in the probate court of the county in which he or she is domiciled upon approval by the probate court. A qualified private entity also may be registered. Each probate court must maintain a list of registered public guardians in the county. The Division of Aging Services of the Department of Human Resources must maintain a master list of registered public guardians throughout the state. Georgia Code Annotated §§29-10-1 through 29-10-11.

Prior to the enactment of the public guardianship statute in 2005, the law provided for county Department of Family and Children Services directors to serve guardians of last resort. Ga. Code Ann. §§29-8-1 through 29-8-5. Additionally, county administrators are listed in the order of preference for guardians or conservators.

Program. In 2005, the Georgia Legislature enacted a public guardianship initiative providing that any qualified individual or entity may be registered as a public guardian, setting out the qualifications, and designating the Division of Aging of the Department of Human Resources to coordinate the initiative, provide or approve training, and maintain a list of registered public guardians.

To implement this legislation, the Georgia Department of Human Resources, Division of Aging Services, worked with probate courts and the Georgia Council of Probate Court Judges and established an implementation team to develop a registry for public guardians and the required training. The Division of Aging Services hired a coordinator to recruit public guardians, to host community information sessions, to develop and conduct the required training, and to maintain the database. However, as of 2009, there are no funds to support the program. Thus, guardianship of last resort is currently provided by the appointment of the state Department of Human Resources, volunteer public guardians, and county guardians.

Hawaii

Statute. Hawaii law establishes an Office of the Public Guardian in the judiciary. The chief justice appoints a public guardian. The public guardian serves as guardian, limited guardian, testamentary guardian, or temporary guardian of the person for incapacitated persons. The public guardian may file a petition for the public guardian's own appointment, and petitions also may be filed by others.

The public guardian may receive fees for services from the client's estate unless it would endanger the person's independence. No fee is allowed when the ward's primary source of support is from public benefits. Funding for the Office of the Public Guardian is included in the budget of the judiciary. Hawaii Revised Statutes §§551A-1 through 9.

In addition, the court may appoint the clerk of the circuit court as guardian of the property of a protected person whose estate is a "small estate" of less than $10,000. If the estate increases to $16,250, a guardian of the property will be appointed or, at the court's discretion, the clerk may continue to serve. Haw. Rev. Stat. §551-21.

Program. Hawaii has an Office of Public Guardian located in the judiciary. The office has a budget of over $560,000, and is funded with state appropriations. The office has the authority to petition for appointment, but it does not provide this service.

The office serves over 770 clients and has 10 full-time equivalent professional staff serving as guardians statewide, one accountant, and one clerk-typist. The office serves as guardian of the person only, but a different judiciary program provides conservatorship services. The office serves about 35 percent to 40 percent older persons with dementia and about 60 percent to 65 percent younger adults with developmental disabilities, including mental retardation and mental illness.

Idaho

Statute. Local boards of county commissioners may create a board of community guardian, or several counties may jointly create such a board. A board of community guardian consists of 7 to 11 members of community groups involving persons needing guardians or conservators, appointed by county commissioners. A board of community guardian may petition for appointment if there is no other qualified person to serve. The board may be compensated from the estate of the ward, but the court may waive payment of fees. Idaho Code §§15-5-601 through 603.

Program. In 1982, Idaho law specified that the county boards of commissioners could create a board of community guardian, which could provide for guardian services, generally through volunteers. Some counties have established such boards (Ada, Canyon, Kootenai, Bonneville, Twin Falls, and Payette), but others have not. Funding is very limited, almost nonexistent. There is no paid staff in any county except for a recent position in Ada County. Guardians can collect fees from the estates of wards, but most wards have insufficient funds. The board of community guardian petitions, such as for appointment of a volunteer guardian. The boards generally make annual reports to county commissioners or the court.

The boards of community guardian are uneven throughout the state and fall far short of addressing the unmet need. In 2005, Idaho's legislature authorized a committee to study the guardianship and conservatorship system. The legislation authorized the collection of filing fees to establish a Guardianship Pilot Project Fund. The Supreme Court is charged with administering the fund to develop a pilot project in several counties; including consideration of public guardianship needs. As of 2009, a new and more permanent committee is to be appointed with a focus on the entire state, not just the pilot projects.

ILLINOIS

Statute. Illinois law provides for two schemes for public guardianship: the Office of State Guardian for incapacitated individuals with estates under $25,000; and a system of county guardians for those with estates of $25,000 and over.

Office of State Guardian. The Office of State Guardian is within the Illinois Guardianship and Advocacy Commission, and has seven regional offices throughout the state. The office serves as plenary or limited guardian of the person or estate, temporary guardian, testamentary guardian, or successor guardian for individuals with estates under $25,000. The office may file a petition for its own appointment.

The Office of State Guardian must visit and consult with its wards at least four times a year. The office receives state appropriations through the Guardianship and Advocacy Commission. Illinois Compiled Statutes §§20-3955/30 through 33.

County Offices of Public Guardian. The governor, with the advice and consent of the Senate, must appoint in each county a suitable person to serve as public guardian of the county, who is to hold office for four years. For counties with a population over one million (currently only Cook County), the chief judge of the circuit court must appoint a licensed attorney as the public guardian for the county. County public guardians serve individuals with estates of $25,000 and over.

The public guardian may petition the court for payment of fees quarterly. However, in counties with a population over one million, the public guardian is paid an annual salary set by the county board. Expenses of the operation of the office are paid by the county treasury, and all fees collected are paid into the county treasury. Ill. Comp. Stat. §§755-5/13-1 through 5/13-5.

Program. Illinois has two schemes for public guardianship: the Office of State Guardian, for incapacitated individuals with estates under $25,000; and a system of county guardians for those with estates of $25,000 and over.

Office of State Guardian. The Office of State Guardian (OSG), situated within the Illinois Guardianship and Advocacy Commission, serves approximately 5,500 incapacitated individuals through regional offices. Each of the regional offices has a manger and caseworkers, with administration and overall supervision handled from offices in Chicago and Springfield. Many regional offices have an attorney. Each office handles different caseloads with a cross section of clients including elders, as well as younger adults with developmental disabilities or mental illnesses. The OSG budget is over $8,000,000 statewide. Funding sources include assessments against estates (but these are limited), Medicaid, and state general fund dollars.

The Office of State Guardian may petition for its own appointment, but often does not due to extreme limitations of staffing and resources. The OSG has 48 caseworkers, of whom 95 percent are registered guardians certified by the national Center for Guardianship Certification. The office also has support staff, attorneys, and managers for a total of 73 full-time equivalent employees. To address the lack of sufficient staff, OSG has focused heavily on staff training and certification. Clients in institutions are visited once every three months. The OSG may serve as representative payee for its wards.

County Public Guardians. The governor appoints county public guardians for a term of four years for individuals with estates at or above $25,000. Fees collected from client estates fund the system. The system appears uneven throughout the state, and marked by underfunding and understaffing.

By law, the Public Guardian of Cook County is an attorney appointed by the circuit court judge. The county pays costs of the office, which has garnered a strong staff of over 300, including a large number of attorneys, and has leveraged significant funds both from the county and from litigation. The office serves approximately 650 adults and 12,000 children. It petitions for appointment.

INDIANA

Statute. An adult guardianship services program provides services within the limits of the available funding for indigent incapacitated adults. The program is within the Division of Disability, Aging and Rehabilitative Services of the Family and Social Services Administration. An indigent adult is an individual with no appropriate person to serve as guardian, the inability to obtain private guardianship services, and an annual gross income of not more than 125 percent of the federal poverty level.

The division contracts with a nonprofit corporation for guardianship and related services in each region. The provider must have an individualized service plan for each person; and is subject to periodic audit by an independent certified public accountant. Indiana Code §§12-10-7-1 through 9.

Program. The state's public guardianship program was established in 1992, is 100 percent state funded, and is coordinated by the Indiana Family and Social Services Administration, Division of Aging, with regional programs through Indiana's area agencies on aging and mental health associations. The program served approximately 253 individuals in FY 2006. The local programs petition the probate court to establish guardianship. Caseloads per individual guardian ranged from 25 to 46 wards. Clients are visited at least monthly, but those in nursing facilities are seen every 90 days.

IOWA

Statute. In 2005, legislation created a state Office of Substitute Decision-maker and authorized local offices. It directed the Department of Elder Affairs to create and administer a statewide network of substitute decision makers if no other decision maker is available, including personal representative services for estates after an adult's death, as well as guardianship and other less restrictive means of decision making.

Under the law, state office is to act as the decision maker if no local office is available. The state office is also to establish a referral system, develop and maintain a listing of public and private services to aid wards, provide public information, develop education and training, and ensure that the least restrictive decision-making service is used, including representative payment, power of attorney, and limited guardianship or conservatorship.

The local offices are to provide substitute decision making and personal representative services, identify client needs and local resources, and determine the most appropriate form of decision-making required in individual cases.

The implementation of the new law was subject to the availability of funding. Iowa Code §231E.

Code sections existing prior to the 2005 law authorized a statewide system of volunteer guardianship programs. Trained volunteers may serve clients of the Department of Human Services who need guardians and/or conservators, but have no suitable or appropriate decision-maker. Iowa Code §217.13.

In addition, Iowa law provides for a state substitute medical decision-making board and local substitute medical decision-making boards. The state board includes medical professionals and lay persons appointed by the director and the state board of health. Local boards in each county also include medical professionals and lay persons, and may act as substitute decision maker for patients incapable of making their own medical care decisions, if no one else is available. Iowa Code §§135.28 & 29.

Program. Iowa has had separate piecemeal guardianship mechanisms that continue in place, but the 2005 legislation sought to create a new statewide program.

First, some counties serve as guardian of last resort. The county board of supervisors provides funding for guardianship, conservatorship, and representative payee services. The program is staff-based and housed within the county. In other instances, non-profit organizations have developed programs in which persons in need of a decision maker are served through that program.

Second, legislation to allow for statewide volunteer guardianship programs was enacted in 1989, for clients of the Department of Human Services needing guardianship services, but funding was never appropriated. Polk County is one of the few counties to implement a successful volunteer program.

Third, a unique provision in state law enacted in 1989 established a state medical substitute decision-making board operated by the Department of Public Health, and allowed for the creation of local boards, as well. These boards are able to act as medical decision maker of last resort. The boards' ability is confined to one-time medical decisions, and does not include placement decisions. At 1 time, 7 of the state's 99 counties had local boards that could hear cases. In areas where there is no board, the state board can act. Generally, the boards serve a younger adult population, including those with developmental disabilities and mental retardation.

In 2005, legislation created a new state Office of Substitute Decision Maker and authorized local offices. It covers guardianship, other less restrictive means of surrogate decision making (such as the use of advance directives and powers of attorney, as well as representative payment for public benefits), and also personal representative services for estates after an adult's death.

The implementation of the new law was subject to the availability of funding, which was not appropriated in 2005 or 2006. The Department was the recipient of a federal grant to assist in laying the groundwork for the office. State funding was appropriated in 2007 and 2008, but funding was eliminated in 2009.

KANSAS

Statute. Kansas law establishes a statewide volunteer guardianship program. The Kansas Guardianship Program is a public instrumentality with a board appointed by the governor. The program recruits and monitors volunteers to serve as guardians or conservators for incapacitated adults.

The program's board consists of seven members, including the chief justice and six residents of the state, at least one of whom serves as a volunteer in the program. Members serve four-year terms. The board must employ staff; accept and receive gifts, grants, or donations; and report annually on actions to the governor, the legislature, the judiciary, and the public. Funding is from state appropriations. Kansas Statutes Annotated §§74-9601 through 9606.

Program. The Kansas Guardianship Program was initiated in 1979 under Kansas Advocacy and Protection Services, Inc. The 1995 legislature established the program as a separate instrumentality governed by a seven-member board of directors including the chief justice (or designee). It is the only statewide volunteer-based guardianship program in the nation.

The program works collaboratively with the Kansas Department of Social and Rehabilitative Services. The Department identifies individuals in need of guardianship. Adult protective services and the state hospital make referrals. The program screens volunteers, and matches the abilities and interests of the volunteer with the needs of the potential ward or conservatee. Department counsel petitions the court for appointment of the volunteer. The program does not petition.

After a volunteer is appointed, the program contracts with the volunteer for services, requires a monthly report, provides a small monthly stipend, and gives ongoing training and support. The program serves over 1,400 low-income clients. It has a paid staff of 12 full-time equivalent professionals and 830 volunteers. The program has a budget of over $1.2 million, appropriated from the state's general fund. It does not collect fees from clients.

KENTUCKY

Statute. The Cabinet for Health and Family Services may be appointed as the guardian or conservator for incapacitated individuals when no other suitable person or entity is available. The cabinet receives fees for its fiduciary services from the estates of clients who are able to pay. The fees are placed in the state general fund. Funding for the program comes from the general fund. Kentucky Revised Statutes §210.290.

Program. As of 2009, the public guardianship program is administered by the Division of Guardianship, Department for Aging and Independent Living, in the Cabinet of Health and Family Services, and is implemented through field offices. The majority of case referrals come through adult protective services. Usually, adult protective services petitions for a capacity determination, and the public guardianship program petitions for its appointment with the supervisor of the guardianship region in which the individual lives as applicant on behalf of the cabinet. The public guardianship program must accept all cases for which the court makes an appointment. The program is funded from the Social Services Block Grant (Title XX), state general fund appropriations, and Medicaid.

The Division's Fiduciary Services Branch is responsible for issues related to the financial needs of the wards. The Field Support Branch provides information to the public, assists the field offices, and develops training for the staff and the community.

For calendar year 2006, the program served 2,652 wards with 96 percent of all wards served being Medicaid eligible. The caseload average was 63 wards to one staff, with the highest caseload at 107 wards and the lowest at 47 wards per staff. The program was comprised of a total of 72 employees and 9 contract fiduciary staff, 43 of whom are caseworkers. The projected annual budget for FY 2006–07 was $4.03 million.

LOUISIANA

Statute. There is no statutory provision for public guardianship or guardianship of last resort in Louisiana law. The general guardianship law (termed "interdiction") is in La. Civ. Pro. Code Ann. art. 389 through 426, and art. 4541 through 4569.

Program. A private not-for-profit organization, Louisiana Guardianship Services, Inc., provides guardianship (or "curator" services) for approximately 35 older adults and 90 younger adults with developmental disabilities, including mental retardation. Staff curators are trained and certified by the national Center for Guardianship Certification. The agency contracts with the Louisiana governor's Office of Elderly Affairs to serve as the curator for elderly adult protective services for clients in need. It also contracts with the Department of Health and Hospitals to act as the curator for individuals with developmental disabilities. The agency and individuals served were severely affected by Hurricane Katrina in 2005.

MAINE

Statute. The Department of Health and Human Services (DHHS) acts as the public guardian or conservator for incapacitated adults in need of a guardian or conservator. The authority is exercised by the commissioner of health and human services and by any persons delegated by the commissioner, including social workers or others qualified by education or experience. The DHHS Office of Elder Services acts as public guardian and conservator for incapacitated adults except those with mental retardation and/or autism. The DHHS Office of Cognitive and Physical Disability Services acts as public guardian and conservator for incapacitated adults with mental retardation and/or autism.

Any person may nominate the public guardian to serve. Prior to appointment, the Department must accept or reject the nomination within 30 days of notification. If the nomination is accepted, the Department must file a detailed plan, including the proposed living arrangement and how the financial, medical, remedial, and social needs will be met.

The public guardian or conservator receives compensation as allowed by the probate court, allocated to an account from which expenses for filing fees, bond premiums, court costs, and other expenses may be drawn. In some cases, the Department of Health and Human Services must pay for the costs of a guardian *ad litem* or other special costs. Maine Revised Statutes Annotated 18A; §§5-601 through 614.

Program. The budget for the program administered by the Office of Elder Services is approximately $6 million, which includes monies for adult protective services. Funding is primarily from state funds and client fees. The program has a total of 71 paid staff.

Both programs petition for appointment if necessary. These programs serve over 1,500 individuals. Cases are generally referred from private social services agencies, as well as from families, physicians, and others. Nearly half the clients are elders with dementia, and the balance includes younger adults with mental illnesses, mental retardation, and substance abuse issues. Most of the clients are low income (with less than $10,000 in assets).

MARYLAND

Statute. Maryland has two statutory schemes for public guardianship: one for elders and another for younger incapacitated adults. Both provide for guardianship of the person only. For adults under 65 years of age, the director of the local Department of Social Services may serve as guardian, and for adults 65 years old or older, the secretary of aging or the director of the area agency on aging may serve. These officials may delegate guardianship responsibilities to staff whose names and positions are registered with the court. Maryland Code Annotated §13-707(a)(10); §14-203(b); §14-307(b).

Maryland law also establishes a system of public guardianship review boards. There must be at least one review board in each county, but two or more counties may establish a single board. Each board consists of 11 members appointed by the county commissioner—including a professional from a relevant local department, two physicians, including one psychiatrist from a local health department, a representative of a local commission on aging, a representative of a local nonprofit social service organization, a lawyer, two lay individuals, a public health nurse, a professional in the field of disabilities, and a person with a physical disability.

The board must review each public guardianship case at least every six months. Once a year, the review is an in-person review, alternating with a file review. The review board must recommend to the court that the guardianship be continued, modified, or terminated. Md. Code Ann. §§14-401 through 404.

Program. Maryland has two separate public guardianship schemes: one for elders age 65 and over, through the Department of Aging and the area agencies on aging, and one for younger adults in need of guardianship services through local departments of social services (LDSS). These two public programs provide guardianship of the person only. Private attorneys generally serve as guardians of the property.

Funding is from state appropriations from general funds, and additional county funds in some jurisdictions. Some local guardianship programs may collect fees.

The guardianship program for older persons has about 36 paid full-time equivalent professional staff members and about 720 wards, with most residing in nursing homes or assisted living facilities. The LDSS guardianship program for adults age 18–64 has close to 500 wards.

A local public guardianship review board reviews each case every six months, holding an in-person hearing once a year and a file review in between. The incapacitated individual must attend the annual hearing and be represented by an attorney.

MASSACHUSETTS

Statute. Massachusetts has no statutory provision for public guardianship or guardianship of last resort.

Program. In Massachusetts, the Executive Office of Elder Affairs administers a protective services guardianship program through contracts with non-profit agencies for elders who have been abused, neglected, or exploited. The Executive Office of Elder Affairs contracts with 5 non-profit agencies for a total of 150 guardianship slots. The agencies accept appointments as guardians or conservators, subject to Elder Affairs' approval, and seek to keep the elder safe and secure in the least restrictive and appropriate placement. The petition is submitted by the appropriate elder protective services agency, which requests a slot from Elder Affairs. If approved, and if there is a slot available, the case is assigned to a guardianship agency.

MICHIGAN

Statute. Michigan has no statutory provision for public guardianship or guardianship of last resort. The general guardianship law is at Michigan Compiled Laws Ann. §§700.1101 through 5108 and 5301 through 5520. (In addition, Mich. Comp. Laws Ann. §600.880b sets aside certain fees collected by the probate registrar for adult guardianship, including independent evaluations, legal counsel, and periodic review. The provision of guardianship services is not listed.)

Program. While there are no statutory provisions regarding guardianship of last resort, Michigan has a public administrator in almost every county—an attorney appointed by the attorney general's office who can act as a guardian.

The Department of Human Services provides funding for guardianship for adult protective services clients. Approximately $600,000 per year is set aside to fund guardians of last resort for vulnerable people discovered by APS. A guardian can charge $60 per month to provide services with the DHS funds. This funding is insufficient and has not been increased for many years. Michigan has allowed up to $45 per month (as of 2007) to be set aside for guardianship when calculating Medicaid eligibility for care in a nursing facility.

Of the state's 83 counties, less than one-third have some form of public guardianship. Some counties have funded programs with county funds through a special senior millage or through the county's general fund dollars.

MINNESOTA

Statute. Minnesota has two statutory schemes for public guardianship.

Individuals with Mental Retardation. The Commissioner of Human Services may be nominated to act as guardian for individuals with mental retardation. The commissioner must accept or reject the nomination, and the commissioner's acceptance must be affirmed at a judicial hearing. The commissioner must accept the nomination if the evaluation concludes that the person has mental retardation, is in need of supervision and protection by a guardian, and there is no qualified person willing to serve.

If the commissioner accepts a nomination, a local agency designated by the county board of commissioners, human services boards, local social services agencies, or a multi-county local social services agency, petitions on behalf of the commissioner. The commissioner or the parent or relative of the individual also may petition. If the commissioner determines that a conservator should be appointed, the commissioner may petition the court for the appointment of a private conservator.

Minnesota Statutes §§252A.01 through 21.

Incapacitated Adults; Maltreated Vulnerable Adults. If a suitable relative or other person is not available to petition for guardianship or conservatorship for incapacitated adults, a county employee must petition with representation by the county attorney. The county must contract with, or arrange for, a suitable person or organization to provide ongoing guardianship services. If no suitable person can be found, a county employee may serve as guardian or conservator. Minn. Stat. §656.557 Subd. 10(c).

Program. Minnesota has two public guardianship programs.

Individuals with Mental Retardation. For individuals with mental retardation, the Commissioner of Human Services may serve as public guardian through a local human services or social services agency. The department of a local agency may petition if necessary, but does so infrequently. When a petition is filed, there must be a comprehensive evaluation, and an attorney represents the individual at the hearing. The program is funded with state appropriations, although it is described as an unfunded mandate, with the exception of a portion of the salary of the public guardianship administrator.

The department or local agency may petition for appointment of a private conservator, or may serve as conservator if the estate is under $20,000.

The program serves over 3,400 individuals with mental retardation, and has 1 paid full-time equivalent professional staff, but also uses the staff of local agencies.

Incapacitated Individuals. For incapacitated individuals identified through adult protective services, the county must contract with, or arrange for, a suitable person or organization to provide ongoing guardianship services. If the county has made a diligent search and no suitable person is found, a county employee may serve as guardian or conservator.

MISSISSIPPI

Statute. If an individual with property needs a guardian but there is no one who qualifies, it is the duty of the Chancery Court or the chancellor to appoint the clerk of the court. The clerk is entitled to compensation from the estate of the individual—up to 10 percent of the estate when it is finally settled. Mississippi Code Annotated §93-13-21. The court may not appoint the Department of Human Services as guardian. Miss. Code Ann. §43-47-13(4).

Program. Although Mississippi law provides that the court may appoint the clerk as guardian if there is no qualified person to serve, in reality, such appointments are infrequent. The law provides that the court may not appoint the Department of Human Services. The Department of Mental Health is appointed on a few occasions. Otherwise, despite the vast and growing need, there is no public guardianship in the state.

MISSOURI

Statute. Missouri law provides that the county public administrators are to serve as public guardians. Missouri Revised Statutes §§473.730 and 750. In certain counties of a designated size, social service agencies in the county may serve unless they provide residential services to wards, and only if the agency employs a licensed professional with sufficient expertise to meet the needs of the ward. Mo. Rev. Stat. §475.055(1)(3).

Program. According to Missouri law, it is the responsibility of elected county public administrators to act as public guardians or conservators if there is no one else to serve. They may also serve as trustees or representative payees. The only requirements for serving are to be a resident of the county, at least 21 years old, a current registered voter, and have all taxes paid.

There are currently 115 public administrators in the state. There is wide variability in the background and experience of the public administrators, the method of payment, the additional functions they perform, their caseloads, the extent of support from county commissioners and judges, and their petitioning practices. The Missouri Public Administrators Association has voted to adopt the NGA's Code of Ethics and Standards of Practice as a guideline.

A challenge for the public administrators is to work with the county commissioners to obtain sufficient funding to cover the required needs. Another problem is the precarious nature of the elected public guardians. Many of the public administrators have very high caseloads. In 2000, legislation provided that there should be a full-time worker to assist the public administrator for every 50 clients, but the wording was optional rather than mandatory, and sufficient funding to support this staffing level has not been forthcoming. It is not uncommon for one public administrator to have 80 or more wards, without any office help or staff.

MONTANA

Statute. If the court determines there is no qualified person willing to serve as guardian, the court may appoint an agency of the state or federal government (or a designee of the agency) that is authorized or required by statute to provide services to the persons with the incapacitated person's condition. When an agency is appointed, the court also may appoint a limited guardian to represent a special interest of the incapacitated person, with this interest as the sole responsibility of the limited guardian, and the interest is then removed from the responsibility of the agency. Montana Code Annotated §72-5-312(5).

Program. In Montana, APS provides guardianship services. There is no separate line-item funding for public guardianship. The program is funded through the state APS budget, as well as private donations. The program does not collect fees from the estates of clients. The program also may serve as representative payee or agent under power of attorney. The program can petition for appointment. It serves over 360 wards, and has eight paid full-time equivalent professional staff, and ten volunteers. All of the cases come from adult protective services.

NEBRASKA

Statute. There is no statutory provision for public guardianship or guardianship of last resort in Nebraska. The general guardianship law is at Nebraska Revised

Statutes §§30-2601 through 2661. A bill to create an office of public guardianship was introduced in the 2007 legislative session, but did not pass.

Program. Nebraska does not provide public guardianship services. However, there are training sessions on guardianship offered in some counties.

NEVADA

Statute. The board of county commissioners of any county must establish an office of public guardian. The board must appoint a public guardian for a four-year term. The board may: (1) appoint a public guardian for a four-year term; (2) designate a county office to serve; (3) contract with a private professional guardian (unless the county population is 100,000 or more); or (4) contract with the board of county commissioners of a neighboring county in the same judicial district to use its public guardian.

The costs of serving as guardian and the costs incurred in the appointment process are chargeable against the individual's estate with court approval. Payment for the services of the public guardian is allowed as a claim against the estate. Nevada Revised Statutes §§253.150 through 250.

Program. County boards of commissioners have established county public guardianship programs in some counties, which are housed as independent agencies or in the offices of the public administrators or district attorneys. One of the largest programs is the Washoe County Public Guardian, in which staff members are certified by the national Center for Guardianship Certification.

NEW HAMPSHIRE

Statute. New Hampshire law establishes a public guardianship and protection program of the person, estate, or both. The program must serve in three instances: (1) when nominated as guardian by the commissioner in the mental health services system; (2) when nominated by the administrator of services for individuals who are developmentally disabled; and (3) when nominated as guardian by the director of the adult protective services program. In all three cases, payment is from the estate of the client, except in cases of indigence. The law provides for state appropriations.

The Department of Health and Human Services must contract with one or more of the organizations approved by the state Supreme Court for the organization to serve as the public guardian and protection program. The contract must fix the cost per guardianship. The contract may also provide for related surrogate services, such as conservatorship and serving as an agent under the power of attorney or as a representative payee. New Hampshire Revised Statutes Annotated §§547-B:1 through B:8.

Program. The Office of Public Guardian was established as a state agency in 1979. Under legislation enacted in 1983, the office became a free-standing, non-profit corporation approved by the Supreme Court. The New Hampshire Department of Health and Human Services contracts with the office to serve. The Department also contracts with the Tri-County Community Action Program/ Granite State Guardianship Services.

The budget for the program is approximately $1.8 million for services to individuals with mental illnesses, developmental disabilities, or open adult protective services cases. Funding is from: (1) state appropriations, approximately $835,000 in general funds through the Department of Health and Human Services and $33,500 through the Department of Corrections; (2) Medicaid case management funds; (3) Medicaid and Social Security funds; and (4) client fees.

The program serves as guardian, conservator, agent under power of attorney, representative payee, trustee, and occasionally accepts guardian *ad litem* appointments. It also provides private guardianship services. The program does not generally petition for appointment. It serves about 950 individuals.

NEW JERSEY

Statute. New Jersey law establishes an Office of the Public Guardian for Elderly Adults in the Department of Health and Senior Services, but specifies that the office is independent of any control by the Department. The office serves incapacitated adults age 60 or older. The chief executive officer of the office is the public guardian, who is appointed by the governor. The public guardian must administer the office, may serve as guardian or conservator, and may intervene in guardianship or conservatorship proceedings if the appointed fiduciary is not fulfilling his/her duties.

Any elderly state resident without a willing and responsible family member or friend to serve is eligible for public guardian services. After family or friends, the law requires the court to give first consideration to the office of the public guardian. The costs of services and of appointment are charged against the income and estate of the individual. The reasonable value of the guardianship services may be a lien on the estate.

The public guardian has the authority to determine the maximum caseload that the office can maintain, based on the funds available, and when the maximum is reached, may decline appointment.

When the office is not available to serve as guardian, attorneys, professional guardians, or other appropriate persons as determined by the court may serve as guardian. New Jersey Statutes Annotated §§52:27 G-32, et seq.

Program. The Office of the Public Guardian is located in the New Jersey Department of Health and Senior Services, in its Division of Aging and Community Services. It serves incapacitated adults age 60 and over. It employs attorneys, investigators, care managers, accountants, and support staff. The office does not initiate cases. Hospitals, long-term care facilities, adult protective services, and county welfare agencies or other public and private agencies often petition to have the office appointed.

The office has three parts: legal, trust, and care management services.

The budget is approximately $517,000. The office receives state appropriations, and uses Medicaid funds, client fees, and estate recovery. The fee schedule is governed by statute. The office has over 700 clients and has over 50 full- and part-time professional paid staff.

In addition to serving as guardian or conservator, the office serves as agent under powers of attorney and representative payees for its guardianship clients, and is also to administer the state's registration program for private professional guardians.

NEW MEXICO

Statute. New Mexico law establishes the Office of Guardianship in the Developmental Disabilities Planning Council. The council director must hire the director of the guardianship office. The office provides probate guardianship services to income-eligible incapacitated persons. It also provides for the recruitment and training of persons to serve as mental health treatment guardians—guardians who have the authority to make decisions about treatment for consumers of mental health services, including decisions about psychotropic medications, aversive stimuli, convulsive treatment, experimental treatment, and psychiatric services. New Mexico Statutes Annotated §43-1-15.

The office contracts for guardianship services, and must monitor and enforce all contracts. It has access to case records, court filings and reports, and financial and other records maintained by contractors, and may arrange visits with wards served by contract guardians. The law sets out specifications for the contract. N.M. Stat. Ann. §§28-16B-1 through 6.

Program. The New Mexico Office of Guardianship is in the Developmental Disabilities Planning Council. The office contracts with providers of guardianship services, including the Arc (an organization that advocates for the rights of individuals with intellectual and developmental disabilities) of New Mexico for the developmental disability population, and Desert State Life Management for all other populations.

The office is funded with appropriations from the state general fund. It does not collect fees for guardianship services. It serves as guardian of the person only.

NEW YORK

Statute. A local department of social services may serve as guardian, and may contract with a not-for-profit corporation to serve as a community guardian for individuals who are eligible for, and who are receiving, adult protective services, who are without anyone to serve, and who are living outside a hospital or residential facility. If a community guardian client enters a hospital or residential facility on a long-term basis, the program must petition the court for removal as guardian. The community guardian program may receive fees from the estate of clients. New York Mental Hygiene Law §81.03(a); New York Social Services Law §473-d.

Program. While New York law provides for the creation of not-for-profit community guardian programs to serve indigent adult protective services clients in the community, these programs only exist in New York City. The city has three community guardian programs funded through the New York City Human Resources Administration, Adult Protective Services. The remainder of the state provides no public guardianship. Courts and professionals have recognized the need for many years The Vera Institute, working with the New York State Office of Court Administration, has created a guardianship project that acts as a court-appointed guardian for incapacitated individuals in Brooklyn.

North Carolina

Statute. The law provides for the clerk of the superior court in every county to appoint a county public guardian for a term of eight years. The public guardian must apply for and obtain letters of guardian in the following cases: (1) when a period of six months has elapsed from the discovery of any property belonging to any minor or incapacitated person without a guardian; or (2) when any person entitled to letters of guardianship requests in writing, to the clerk, to issue letters to the public guardian. North Carolina General Statutes §35A-1270 through1273.

The law also provides that the clerk of superior court may appoint as guardian "a disinterested public agent." A "disinterested public agent" guardian is defined as the director or assistant director of a local human services agency, or an adult officer, agent, or employee of a state human services agency. N.C. Gen. Stat. §35A-1213.

Program. The statute provides that the clerk of the superior court may appoint a county public guardian. In practice, the public guardian is usually an attorney, who may be appointed to serve as guardian of the person, estate, or as general guardian.

North Carolina law also provides that the clerk of superior court may appoint a "disinterested public agent." In practice, local departments of social services, mental health, public health, and county departments on aging are often appointed to serve as "disinterested public agent" guardians.

NORTH DAKOTA

Statute. In North Dakota, if there is no one else to serve as guardian, an employee of an agency, institution, or nonprofit group home providing care and custody may be appointed if the employee does not provide direct care to the individual and the court finds that the appointment poses no substantial risk of conflict of interest. N.D. Cent. Code §30.1-28-11(1). In addition, in 2005, the legislature provided that the Department of Human Services could create and coordinate a system of volunteer guardians for vulnerable adults ineligible for developmental disabilities case management.

Program. In 2005, legislation allowed the Department of Human Services to create and coordinate a "unified system for the provision of guardianship services to vulnerable adults who are ineligible for developmental disabilities case management services." The legislation provided that the system must include guardian standards, staff competency requirements, and guidelines and training for guardians; and that the Department must require that a contracting entity develop and maintain a system of volunteer guardians for the state. The legislation was only minimally funded, with monies to be used specifically for individuals with mental illnesses.

OHIO

Statute. An agency providing protective services under contract with the Department of Mental Retardation and Developmental Disabilities (MRDD) may be nominated as guardian of a mentally retarded or developmentally disabled person. The agency may charge the client fees for services. There must be a comprehensive evaluation of the individual before the agency is appointed. The agency must review the physical, mental, and social condition of each person for whom it is acting as guardian, and must file these reports with the Department annually. Ohio Code Annotated §§5123.55 through 59.

Program. The Ohio Department of MRDD contracts with a nonprofit agency, Advocacy and Protective Services, Inc., to provide guardianship services for adults with mental retardation and developmental disabilities. In addition, courts often use attorneys or sometimes volunteer as guardian when there is no one else, willing, qualified, and available. The state has a number of volunteer guardianship programs, including Lutheran Social Services of Northwestern Ohio and the Central Ohio Area Agency on Aging.

OKLAHOMA

Statute. Oklahoma law creates an Office of Public Guardian within the Department of Human Services. The legislation also creates a public guardianship pilot program, and specifies that until the pilot is expanded statewide and subject to the availability of funds, the office is to function as a source of information and assistance on guardianship and alternatives for the public. Oklahoma Statutes Annotated §§30-6-101 & 102.

Also, in a criminal proceeding, if a person is found to be incompetent because of mental retardation, and is found by the court to be dangerous, the court must suspend the criminal proceeding and place the person in the custody of the office of public guardian. The office must place any such person in a facility or residential setting, and must report to the court every six months about that person's status. Okla. Stat. Ann. §22-1175.6b.

Program. The Oklahoma Public Guardian law has not been funded. Currently, the Office of Public Guardian serves only criminal defendants who are found, by the district court in which the criminal charges are pending, to be: (1) not competent to stand trial due to mental retardation; and (2) dangerous. The court may place the defendant in the custody of the public guardian, who has complete discretion on placement to meet the safety needs of the ward and the public. The public guardian has 26 wards.

OREGON

Statute. A county court or board of county commissioners may create an office of public guardian and conservator and expend county funds for this purpose. The office may serve as guardian or conservator upon the petition of any person or upon its own petition. The office may employ private attorneys if the fees can be defrayed out of the funds of the estate. The office has a claim against the ward's or protected person's estate for reasonable expenses for guardianship or conservatorship services and for services of the attorney of the office. Oregon Revised Statutes §§125.700 through 730.

Program. While state law provides for an office of public guardian at the county level, such programs exist in only a few regions. For example, in Multnomah County (Portland), the Department of County Human Services provides guardianship services through the area agency on aging, which is also the Medicaid agency. Jackson County (Medford) contracts with legal services. Funding is from the county budgets, as well as Medicaid administrative match monies. In addition, the Multnomah County program charges a fee for services. The Multnomah County program has about 150 clients, the majority of whom are adults with mental retardation, developmental disabilities, or mental illness.

PENNSYLVANIA

Statute. Pennsylvania law provides for the establishment of guardian support agencies to supply guardianship services; assistance in decision making; assistance in securing and maintaining benefits and services; and the recruitment and training of individuals to serve as representative payees, agents under powers of attorney, and trustees. The agencies must charge for services based on the recipient's ability to pay, and the agencies must make an effort to minimize costs through the use of volunteers. 20 Pennsylvania Consolidated Statutes Annotated §§5551 through 5555.

Program. There is no uniform, statewide provision of guardianship services. It varies by county. Some counties have private guardianship support agencies and in others, the judge may assign the area agency on aging to accept cases. In still other counties, there is no guardian of last resort.

Rhode Island

Statute. There is no statutory provision for public guardianship. The probate court may appoint Good Samaritan guardians if the estate of a proposed ward is insufficient to pay for the services of a guardian. A Good Samaritan guardian may not seek fees or compensation for services. Filing fees are waived and surety is not required. The court may waive court fees. Rhode Island General Laws §§33-15-4.1 through 4.5.

Program. Meals-on-Wheels, Inc., coordinates a guardianship of last resort program for frail elders who are cognitively impaired, 60 years of age or older, have assets below $15,000, and are in need of a guardian of the person when there are no other options. The Department of Elderly Affairs contracts with Meals-on-Wheels, and uses volunteers to provide guardianship services. The Department provides oversight of the agency in the recruitment, training, assignment, and support of the volunteers. The program serves 85 to 90 individuals, almost all in nursing homes.

South Carolina

Statute. If a patient of a state mental health facility has no conservator, the director of the Department of Mental Health may act as conservator. South Carolina Code Annotated §62-5-105.

Program. South Carolina has no system of public guardianship, but the probate court attempts to identify a guardian when there is no one willing and qualified to serve.

South Dakota

Statute. Any public agency may be appointed as a guardian, a conservator, or both, if it can provide an active and suitable program of guardianship or conservatorship for a protected person, and if it is not providing substantial services or financial assistance to the protected person. The departments of human services or social services may be appointed as guardian, conservator, or both to individuals under its care or to whom it is providing services or financial assistance, if there is no one else qualified and willing to serve. South Dakota Codified Laws §29A-5-110.

Program. The Department of Human Services (DHS) acts as the guardian of last resort when there are no appropriate family members or others willing and able to serve as guardian for a person with a developmental disability who is 18 years of age or older and who is receiving services or financial assistance from the Department. DHS contracts with people who are located in or near each protected person's community. The Department of Social Services acts as guardian for adult protective services clients, serving approximately 60 such individuals, most of whom are in nursing homes. Funding is derived through Social Services Block Grants, the Older Americans Act, and state monies.

TENNESSEE

Statute. A statewide program administered by the Commission on Aging provides guardianship for the elderly. The law provides for the operation of district public guardians within each developmental district. The commission must provide a coordinator and must contract with grantee agencies in each of the nine development districts, which must hire staff members to serve as district public guardians.

The district public guardians serve as conservator for "disabled persons" who are 60 years of age or older and have no one else to serve, and also may serve as agents under power of attorney. The Commission on Aging, in consultation with the Departments of Human Services and Health, may develop a statewide program to recruit, train, supervise, and evaluate volunteers.

If an individual qualifies for SSI, there is no charge for court costs or for any fees to the estate or to the district public guardianship program. If not, the costs and compensation for the public guardian are handled as in other guardianships.

The district public guardians must submit certification to the court when the maximum caseload is reached and the court then may not assign additional cases. Costs for the public guardianship program are met through an annual appropriation to the Commission on Aging. Tennessee Code Annotated §§34-7-101 through 105.

Program. The Tennessee Public Guardianship for the Elderly Program is coordinated by the Commission on Aging and Disability, and housed in the nine area agencies on aging and disability, providing services in the 95 counties of the state. The program serves persons 60 years of age and older who are unable to manage their affairs and have no one to act on their behalf. The Commission's policies and procedures set out guidelines for the nine district programs, and the quality assurance unit of the commission staff monitors these programs annually.. The programs may collect fees on a sliding scale basis when client resources are sufficient. The statewide program serves over 400 individuals.

TEXAS

Statute. According to statutory changes in 2005, the Department of Family and Protective Services, which houses adult protective services, must refer an elderly or disabled person who has been subject to abuse, neglect, or exploitation and is an alleged incapacitated person to the Department of Aging and Disability Services (DADS). Tex. Hum. Res. Code Ann. §48.209. If DADS determines that guardianship is appropriate for the individual, it must file an application to be appointed as guardian of the person, the estate, or both. Tex. Hum. Res. Code Ann. §161.101. The Department may contract with a political subdivision of the state, a guardianship program, private agency, or another state agency to provide guardianship services, and the Department must establish a monitoring system to ensure the quality of guardianship services provided through contract. Tex. Hum. Res. Code Ann. §§161.101 through 107. A guardianship program is a local, county, or regional program authorized to provide guardianship services. Tex. Hum. Res. Code Ann. §111.001(6).

Program. In 2004, in response to significant problems in the Texas adult protective services system, the governor issued an executive order directing the Health and Human Services Commission to oversee systemic APS reform. The commission issued a report documenting needed improvements, including the transfer of the state guardianship program to DADS. Consequently, the 2005 legislation included substantial changes in the state's guardianship role in addition to major APS revisions.

Four state agencies are currently involved in adult guardianship in Texas. The Department of Family and Protective Services (DFPS) is charged with investigating referrals of abuse, neglect, and exploitation. When an alleged incapacitated has been a victim of abuse, neglect, or exploitation, the Department makes a referral to DADS for an assessment of whether a guardianship or less restrictive alternative service is needed. DFPS is also charged with alerting DADS to make an assessment of alleged incapacitated minors who are aging-out of DFPS conservatorship. Under these two situations, DADS is authorized to apply to be appointed as temporary or permanent guardian. Otherwise, a court may appoint DADS only as temporary guardian of last resort after notice to DADS. A court may not appoint DADS as permanent guardian unless DADS files an application to be appointed or DADS otherwise agrees. The DADS may contract with local guardianship programs for guardianship services for individuals who would otherwise be its wards. Texas law still does not name a guardian of last resort.

The Health and Human Services Commission (HHSC) is the executive branch's lead health and human service agency with authority over both DADS and DFPS. It also provides grants, totaling $400,000 per year, to local guardianship programs.

Local guardianship programs run by non-profit organizations in the state's 254 counties continue to provide the bulk of the public guardianships in Texas annually. They receive limited funding from the state, and may contract with the counties to provide the service.

UTAH

Statute. The Office of Public Guardian (OPG) within the Department of Human Services must develop and operate a statewide program to educate the public about the role and function of guardians and conservators. It may also serve as guardian, conservator, or both when no one else is willing and available, and the office has petitioned for, or agreed in advance to, the appointment.

The office may petition to be appointed as guardian, conservator, or both; develop a volunteer program; and solicit and receive donations to provide guardian and conservator services. The law creates a nine-member board of guardian services to establish policy for the office, and provides for the governance of the board.

Before the office files a petition for appointment, it must conduct a face-to-face assessment to determine the need for guardianship and evaluate the financial resources. The OPG also must determine if conservatorship is needed. The office must prepare an individualized guardianship or conservatorship plan for each client. It may contract with providers of guardianship and conservatorship services, and must monitor those services.

The client's estate must pay for guardian or conservator services, including court costs and attorney fees. If the individual is indigent, the office must serve without charge, and seek to secure *pro bono* legal services. Court costs and attorney fees may not be assessed to the office. Utah Code Annotated §§62A-14-101 through 112.

Program. Established in 1999, the Office of Public Guardian is in the Department of Human Services. The office provides public guardianship and conservatorship services to incapacitated adults who have no one else to serve, and priority is given to those who are in life-threatening situations, or who are experiencing, or are at risk of, abuse, neglect, self-neglect, or exploitation. The office also provides a range of additional services, including information and referral, guardianship assessment, petitioning for guardianship, alternatives to guardianship, and advocacy for the rights of incapacitated persons.

The office receives state appropriations. It contracts a portion of guardianship services to Guardianship Associates of Utah. It serves about 200 individuals and has approximately seven full-time equivalent paid staff. The office accepts and trains volunteers for administrative work, fundraising, and as visitors for clients. The results of a recent study suggest an unmet need for the guardianship of at least 1,100 persons.

VERMONT

Statute. Vermont has two different statutes that establish public guardianship: one that establishes public guardianship for individuals with developmental disabilities and one that establishes public guardianship for individuals age 60 and older. Both programs are the responsibility of the Commissioner of the Department of Disabilities, Aging, and Independent Living.

(1) Public guardianship for individuals with developmental disabilities. Public guardianship is available for individuals with developmental disabilities who have a diagnosis of mental retardation, autism, or pervasive developmental disorder, and who also have substantial deficits in their adaptive behavior. 18 Vermont Statutes Annotated §9320(1). A public guardian may exercise guardianship in the following areas: general supervision, contracts, legal/judicial, and medical. There is no authority to exercise financial guardianship. 18 Vt. Stat. Ann. §9310. A public guardian may be appointed for a person with developmental disabilities who is unable to exercise some or all of these powers and who is not receiving the active assistance of a responsible adult.

In carrying out the powers of public guardianship, the Commissioner must be guided by the wishes and preferences of the individual, and must exercise authority through the least restrictive approach consistent with need for protection. The statute specifically authorizes the commissioner to delegate the powers of guardianship to staff within the Department. 18 Vt. Stat. Ann. §§9310 through 9316.

(2) Public guardianship for individuals age sixty or older. Guardianship is authorized for individuals age 60 or older who are mentally disabled and for whom the court is unable to appoint a guardian from the private sector. The Commissioner may adopt rules including standards relating to the maximum number of appointments that may be accepted by the office. The office of public guardianship may not petition for guardianship.

If an individual under guardianship is going to be placed outside his or her home, the public guardian must visit the proposed residence in advance. The public guardian must monitor the care and progress of each person under guardianship, including at least quarterly personal contact. 14 Vt. Stat. Ann. §§3091 through 3096.

Program. Both types of public guardianship are provided in a unified program in the Office of Public Guardian (OPG), which is located in the Department of Disabilities, Aging, and Independent Living. The Office consists of 25 public guardians who operate out of 12 offices throughout the state, a two-staff representative payee program, an administrative assistant, and program director. Four public guardians have supervisory responsibility as senior public guardians. One public guardian specializes in developing alternatives to guardianship. Some public guardianship staffers have special expertise in working with aging people, while others specialize in working with individuals with developmental disabilities. Public guardians are assigned based on geography and availability. Although authorized to do so, the office does not refuse cases at this time, based upon caseload size. The typical caseloads are 30 and do not ever exceed 35.

VIRGINIA

Statute. Virginia law establishes a statewide public guardian and conservator program within the Department for the Aging. The Department must contract with local or regional public or private entities to provide guardian and conservator services. The Department must adopt regulations proving for requirements for professionals and volunteers, a staff-to-client ratio, and procedures disqualifying any program operating outside the ratio.

The Department must establish record-keeping and accounting procedures for the local and regional programs, and criteria for the programs to file values history surveys, annual decisional accounting and assessment reports, care plans, and priorities for services. The Department must contract with a research entity for a program evaluation every four years, provided the legislature appropriates funds. The local or regional guardian and conservator programs must have a multi-disciplinary panel to screen cases to ensure appropriate appointments and to review cases regularly.

The law establishes a Public Guardian and Conservator Advisory Board to report to and advise the Commissioner of the Department for the Aging. Virginia Code Annotated §§2.2-711 through 713 & 2.2-2411.

Program. The Virginia public guardian and conservator program is located in the Department for the Aging, and is coordinated by a designated Department staff person. It serves both older individuals and younger adults with mental retardation, developmental disabilities, or mental illnesses. The program receives funding through state appropriations, and issues a request for proposals to local and/or regional nonprofit or governmental agencies throughout the state. Currently, there are 15 local and/or regional programs in operation, but these programs do not cover the entire state. In 2006, the program received additional funding through the Department of Mental Health, Mental Retardation, and Substance Abuse Services to serve additional clients with mental retardation and developmental disabilities.

Each local and/or regional program has a multidisciplinary panel to screen cases and assist in case review. The law provides for a program evaluation every four years, if funds are appropriated for that purpose. Two such reviews have been conducted by the Virginia Tech Center for Gerontology, which evaluated the local program activities and characteristics of clients, and found that the public guardianship program saved significant state dollars.

The program has a statutory board of 15 members who meet quarterly to advise the Department. The board prepared a draft regulation, which was approved in 2009, providing for a 1:20 staff-to-client ratio to limit caseloads and ensure quality services.

WASHINGTON

Statute. In 2007, the Washington Legislature created an Office of Public Guardianship. The office is within the administrative office of the courts. The Supreme Court must appoint a public guardianship administrator to direct the office. The office must contract with public or private entities or individuals to provide public guardianship services. Eligible incapacitated individuals include adults with incomes that are not over 200 percent of the federal poverty level or who are receiving Medicaid long-term care services. The office may not petition for appointment. The law specifies a ratio of 1:20 certified professional guardians to incapacitated persons, and requires public guardianship providers to visit each incapacitated person no less than monthly. Washington Revised Code 2.72.005 through 2.72.900.

Program. Until the 2007 law was implemented, Washington had no public guardianship system. However, the law and administrative rules provided, and continue to provide, for maximum fees from Medicaid funds for the establishment and continuation of a guardianship in which the incapacitated person is a client of the Department of Social and Health Services. Under the 2007 law, the fees are used to pay professional guardians who are monitored by the office of public guardianship. All public guardianship providers must be certified under the 2007 law. The legislature appropriated funds for FY 08–09 to establish the office and to develop pilot programs in a minimum of two areas.

WEST VIRGINIA

Statute. Under West Virginia law, a guardian may include any political subdivision or other public agency or public official. A public agency that is not a provider of health care services to the protected person may be appointed as a guardian or conservator or both if it is capable of providing an active and suitable program of guardianship or conservatorship and is not otherwise providing substantial services or financial assistance to the protected person. A nonprofit corporation may be appointed to serve as guardian or conservator if licensed to do so by the secretary of the Department of Health and Human Resources.

The secretary of the Department must designate a division or agency under his or her jurisdiction to serve as guardian if there is no other individual, non-profit corporation, or other public agency to serve. The sheriff of the county may be appointed as conservator if there is no one equally or better qualified and willing to serve. West Virginia Code §44A-1-4(12); §44A-1-8.

Program. Under West Virginia law, the Department of Health and Human Resources may be appointed as guardian as last resort, and the local sheriff may be appointed as conservator if there is no one else qualified and willing to serve. Social services personnel in the Department's district offices provide the decision-making services. Support is from general state funds, but there is no specific budget for guardianship services. The Department provides guardianship services for over 700 clients, including incapacitated persons age 65 and older, and adults age 18 to 64. The Department has a system of ethics consultation to assist staff in making complex life and death decisions. Department program coordinators maintain that staffing is insufficient to fully advocate for incapacitated persons and that additional community support resources are required.

WISCONSIN

Statute. A nonprofit corporation approved by the Department of Health and Family Services to be a "corporate guardian" is qualified to act as the guardian of person or property, or both, if the court finds the corporation a suitable agency to serve. Wisconsin Statutes §54.15(7). In addition, individuals may serve as paid guardians of the person if they have five or fewer unrelated wards or have the permission of the court to have more. There is no limit on the number of unrelated wards for whom an individual may serve as guardian of the estate. Wisc. Stat. §54.15 (9).

Program. Wisconsin has no statewide public guardianship program, but it does have three mechanisms to provide for guardianship of last resort. First, corporate guardians may provide guardianship services with payment by counties or from the estate of the individual, if they are approved by the Department of Health and Family Services and by the court. Second, volunteer guardianship programs are operated by county agencies or nonprofit entities, and originally were funded by small state grants. Third, county-paid or ward-paid guardians of the person serve five or fewer wards, or more if the court so authorizes.

WYOMING

Statute. Wyoming law providing for public guardianship was repealed in 1998. The general guardianship law is at Wyoming. Statutes Annotated §§3-1-101 through 3-6-119.

Program. After the repeal of the state's public guardianship statute in 1998, the cases were assumed by the Wyoming Guardianship Corporation, a private nonprofit entity with over 80 volunteer guardians. In some cases, the director is named individually as guardian and, in other cases, the corporation is named. The Developmental Disabilities Division and the Wyoming State Hospital fund the corporation. The corporation also receives federal funding as a Social Security representative payee and Veterans' Administration fiduciary, and receives fees for private guardianship services. The corporation provides staff and volunteers to serve as guardians for incapacitated persons "when no other appropriate person is willing or able to serve." The director is certified by the national Center for Guardianship Certification.

Appendix C

CLASSIFICATION OF MODELS BY STATE

Court Model	Independent State Office	Within Social Service Agency	County Model	None
Delaware **DE**	Alaska **AK**	Arkansas **AR**	Alabama **AL**	Nebraska **NE**
Hawaii (Large) **HI-L**	Illinois (OSG) **IL**	Colorado **CO**	Arizona **AZ**	**(1 state)**
Hawaii (Small) **HI-S**	Kansas **KS**	Connecticut **CT**	California **CA**	
Mississippi **MS**	New Mexico **NM**	Florida **FL**	Idaho **ID**	
Washington **WA**	**(4 states)**	Georgia **GA**	Illinois (OPG) **IL**	
District of Columbia **(4 states, 6 programs)**		Indiana **IN**	Missouri **(MI)**	
		Iowa **IA**	Nevada **NV**	
		Kentucky **KY**	North Carolina **NC**	
		Louisiana **LA**	North Dakota **ND**	
		Maine **ME**	Oregon **OR**	
		Maryland **MD**	Wisconsin **WI**	
		Massachusetts **MA**	**(11 States)**	
		Michigan **MI**		
		Minnesota **MN**		
		Missouri **MO**		
		Montana **MT**		

(continued)

Court Model	Independent State Office	Within Social Service Agency	County Model	None
		New Hampshire **NH**		
		New Jersey **NJ**		
		New York **NY**		
		Ohio **OH**		
		Oklahoma **OK**		
		Pennsylvania **PA**		
		Rhode Island **RI**		
		South Carolina **SC**		
		South Dakota **SD**		
		Tennessee **TN**		
		Texas **TX**		
		Utah **UT**		
		Vermont **VT**		
		Virginia **VA**		
		Washington **WA**		
		West Virginia **WV**		
		Wisconsin (Volunteer & Corporate Guardian) **WI**		
		Wyoming **WY**		
		(34 states)		

BIBLIOGRAPHY

Alexander, George, and Travis Lewin. *The Aged and the Need for Surrogate Management.* Ithaca, NY: Cornell University Press, 1972.

American Bar Association Commission on Law and Aging, American Psychological Association, and National College of Probate Judges. *Judicial Determination of Capacity of Older Adults in Guardianship Proceedings.* Washington, DC: American Bar Association and American Psychological Association, 2006.

American Bar Association Commission on the Mentally Disabled and Commission on Legal Problems of the Elderly. *Guardianship: An Agenda for Reform—Recommendations of the National Guardianship Symposium and Policy of the American Bar Association.* Washington, DC: American Bar Association, 1989.

Barrett, Peter. "Temporary/Emergency Guardianships: The Clash Between Due Process and Irreparable Harm." BIFOCAL 13 (1992–1993): 3.

Bayles, Fred, and Scott McCartney. *Guardians of the Elderly: An Ailing System.* Associated Press Special Report, September 1987.

Blenkner, Margaret, Martin Bloom, and Margaret Nielsen. "A Research and Demonstration Project of Protective Services." *Social Casework* 52, no. 8 (1971): 483–499.

Blenkner, Margaret, Martin Bloom, Margaret Nielsen, and Ruth Weber. *Final Report: Protective Services for Older People: Findings from the Benjamin Rose Institute Study.* Cleveland, OH: Benjamin Rose Institute, 1974.

Brown, Robert. *The Rights of Older Persons.* New York: Avon Books, 1979.

Center for Social Gerontology. *Guidelines for Guardianship Service Programs.* Ann Arbor, MI: Center for Social Gerontology, 1986.

Center for Social Gerontology. *National Study of Guardianship Systems: Findings and Recommendations.* Ann Arbor, MI: Center for Social Gerontology, 1994.

Center for Social Gerontology. *Utah Office of Public Guardian: Program Evaluation.* Ann Arbor, MI: Center for Social Gerontology, 2001.

Commission on National Probate Court Standards. *National Probate Court Standards.* Washington, DC: National Center for State Courts, 1993, 1999.

Committee on Social Security Representative Payees. *Improving the Social Security Representative Payee Program: Serving Beneficiaries and Minimizing Misuse.* Washington, DC: National Academies Press, 2007. http://nationalacademies.org/morenews/20070730.html.

Community Integration Implementation Team and Community Integration Advisory Commission. *Virginia's Comprehensive Cross-Governmental Strategic Plan to Assure*

Continued Community Integration of Virginians with Disabilities: 2007 Update and Progress Report (draft) at http://www.olmsteadva.com/downloads/052507StrategicPlan. doc.

Conrad, Peter, and Joseph W. Schneider. *Deviance and Medicalization: From Badness to Sickness.* Philadelphia: Temple University Press, 1992.

Council on Accreditation. *Adult Guardianship Service Standards.* http://www.coastan dards.org/standards.php?navView=private&section_id=154

Creswell, John. *Research Design: Qualitative and Quantitative Approaches.* Thousand Oaks, CA: Sage Publications, 1994.

Davis, Robert, and Juanjo Medina-Ariza. *Results from an Elder Abuse Prevention Experiment in New York City.* National Institute of Justice, September 2001.

Dore, Margaret. "The *Stamm* Case and Guardians *Ad Litem.*" *Washington State Bar Association Elder Law Section Newsletter* (Winter 2004–2005): 3, 6–7.

Elder Law Section of the Washington State Bar. *Report of the Public Guardianship Task Force to the WSBA [Washington State Bar Association] Elder Law Section Executive Committee.* Seattle, WA: Washington State Bar Association, August 2005. http://www. wsba.org/lawyers/groups/elderlaw/

Elder Law Section of the Washington State Bar Association. *Report of the Guardianship Task Force to the WSBA Elder Law Section Executive Committee.* Seattle, WA: Washington State Bar Association, August 2009. http://www.wsba.org/lawyers/groups/elderlaw/.

Fell, Norman. "Guardianship and the Elderly: Oversight Not Overlooked." *University of Toledo Law Review* 25 (1994): 189–93.

Fields, Robin. "Adult Caretaker Program Overworked, Underfunded: Report Finds That the County Office That Serves As Conservator for Incapacitated Clients Is Beset by Problems." *Los Angeles Times,* May 12, 2005.

Fields, Robin, Evelyn Larrubia, and Jack Leonard. "Guardians for Profit" (four-part series). *Los Angeles Times,* November 13–16, 2005.

Florida Statewide Public Guardianship Office. *Forgotten Faces of Florida.* 2000.

Frolik, Lawrence. "Plenary Guardianship: An Analysis, A Critique and a Proposal for Reform." *Arizona Law Review* 23, no. 2 (1981): 599–660.

Frolik, Lawrence. "Promoting Judicial Acceptance and Use of Limited Guardianship." *Stetson Law Review* 31, no. 3 (2002): 735–755.

Goffman, Erving. *Asylums: Essays on the Social Situation of Mental Patients and Other Inmates.* Garden City, NY: Anchor Books, 1961.

Gottlich, Vicki, and Erica Wood. "Statewide Review of Guardianships: The California and Maryland Approaches." *Clearinghouse Review* 23, no. 4 (1989): 426–432.

Hightower, David, Alex Heckert, and Winsor Schmidt. "Elderly Nursing Home Residents: Need for Public Guardianship Services in Tennessee." *Journal of Elder Abuse and Neglect* 2, no. 3/4 (1990): 105–122.

Horstman, Peter. "Protective Services for the Elderly: The Limits of *Parens Patriae.*" *Missouri Law Review* 40, no. 2 (1975): 215–236.

Huberman, A. Michael. *An Expanded Sourcebook: Qualitative Data Analysis.* 2nd ed. Thousand Oaks, CA: Sage Publications, 1994.

Hurme, Sally. "Current Trends in Guardianship Reform." *Maryland Journal of Contemporary Legal Issues* 7, no. 1 (1995–1996): 143–189.

Hurme, Sally. "Limited Guardianship: Its Implementation Is Long Overdue." *Clearinghouse Review* 28, no. 6 (1994): 660–670.

Hurme, Sally, and Erica Wood. "Guardian Accountability Then and Now: Tracing Tenets for an Active Court Role." *Stetson Law Review* 31, no. 3 (2002): 867–940.

Johns, Frank. "Guardianship Folly: The Misgovernment of *Parens Patriae* and the Forecast of Its Crumbing Linkage to Unprotected Older Americans in the Twenty-First Century—A March of Folly? Or Just a Mask of Virtual Reality." *Stetson Law Review* 27, no. 1 (1997): 1–93.

Karp, Naomi, and Erica Wood. *Guardianship Monitoring: A National Survey of Court Practices.* Washington, DC: AARP Public Policy Institute, 2006.

Karp, Naomi, and Erica Wood. *Guarding the Guardians: Promising Practices for Court Monitoring.* Washington, DC: AARP Public Policy Institute, 2007.

Karp, Naomi, and Erica Wood. *Incapacitated and Alone: Health Care Decision-Making for the Unbefriended Elderly.* Washington, DC: American Bar Association Commission on Law and Aging, 2003.

Kittrie, Nicholas. *The Right to Be Different: Deviance and Enforced Therapy.* Baltimore: Johns Hopkins Press, 1971.

Kroch, Uri. "The Experience of Being A Dependent Adult (Ward): A Hermeneutic Phenomenological Study." PhD diss., University of Calgary, 2009.

Lachs, Mark, Christianna Williams, Shelly O'Brien, and Karl Pillemer. "Adult Protective Service Use and Nursing Home Placement." *The Gerontologist* 42, no. 6 (2002): 734–739.

Lambert, Pam, Joan Gibson, and Paul Nathanson. "The Values History: An Innovation in Surrogate Medical Decision-Making." *Journal of Law, Medicine, and Ethics* 18, no. 3 (1990): 202–212.

Legal Research and Services for the Elderly, National Council of Senior Citizens. *Legislative Approaches to the Problems of the Elderly: A Handbook of Model State Statutes.* Washington, DC: National Council of Senior Citizens, 1971.

Leoning, Carol. "Misplaced Trust: Special Report." *Washington Post,* June 15–16, 2003: A1.

Lisi, Lauren, Anne Burns, and Kathleen Lussenden. *National Study of Guardianship Systems: Findings and Recommendations.* Ann Arbor, MI: Center for Social Gerontology: 1994.

Mayhew, Michael. "Survey of State Guardianship Laws: Statutory Provisions for Clinical Evaluations." BIFOCAL 27, no. 1 (2005): 1–2, 13–19.

Miller, Kent. *Managing Madness: The Case Against Civil Commitment.* New York: Free Press, 1976.

Mitchell, Annina. "Involuntary Guardianship for Incompetents: A Strategy for Legal Services Advocates." *Clearinghouse Review* 12, no. 8 (1978): 451–468.

Moye, Jennifer, Steven Butz, Daniel Marson, Erica Wood, and the ABA-APA Capacity Assessment of Older Adults Working Group. "A Conceptual; Model and Assessment Template for Capacity Evaluation in Adult Guardianship." *The Gerontologist* 45, no. 5 (2007): 591–603.

Moye, Jennifer, Stacey Wood, Barry Edelstein, Jorge Armesto, Emily Bower, Julie Harrison, and Erica Wood. "Clinical Evidence in Guardianship of Older Adults Is Inadequate: Findings From a Tri-State Study." *The Gerontologist* 47, no. 5 (2007): 604–612.

National Academy of Elder Law Attorneys, National Guardianship Association, and National College of Probate Judges. *2004 National Wingspan Implementation Session: Action Steps on Adult Guardianship Reform.* 2004. http://www.guardianship.org/associations/2543/files/WingspanReport.pdf.

National Conference of Commissioners on Uniform State Laws. *Uniform Adult Guardianship and Protective Proceedings Jurisdiction Act.* 2007. http://www.nccusl.org/Update/.

National Conference of Commissioners on Uniform State Laws. *Uniform Guardianship and Protective Proceedings Act.* 1982. http://www.nccusl.org/Update/.

Olsen, Lise. "New Payment Guidelines Ease Strain Probate Fees Put on Elderly, Disabled." *Houston Chronicle,* September 4, 2007.

Perlin, Michael. "On Sanism." *Southern Methodist University Law Review* 46 (1992): 373–407.

Perlin, Michael. "Things Have Changed: Looking at Non-Institutional Mental Disability Law Through the Sanism Filter." *New York Law School Law Review* 46 (2002–2003): 535–545.

Perlin, Michael, and Deborah Dorfman. "Sanism, Social Science, and the Development of Mental Disability Law Jurisprudence." *Behavioral Sciences and the Law* 11 (1993): 47–66.

Peters, Roger, Winsor Schmidt, and Kent Miller. "Guardianship of the Elderly in Tallahassee, Florida." *The Gerontologist* 25, no. 5 (1985): 532–538.

Phillips, Charyl. "Secrecy Hides Cozy Ties in Guardianship Cases." *Seattle Times,* December 4, 2006.

Quinn, Mary Joy. *Guardianships of Adults: Achieving Justice, Autonomy and Safety.* New York: Springer Publishing, 2005.

Regan, John, and Georgia Springer. U.S. Senate Special Committee on Aging. *Protective Services for the Elderly: A Working Paper.* Washington, DC: GPO, 1977.

Reynolds, Sandra. "Guardianship Primavera: A First Look at Factors Associated with Having a Legal Guardian Using a Nationally Representative Sample of Community-Dwelling Adults." *Aging and Mental Health* 6, no. 2 (2002): 109–120.

Reynolds, Sandra, and L. Carson. "Dependent on the Kindness of Strangers: Professional Guardians for Older Adults Who Lack Decisional Capacity." *Aging and Mental Health* 3, no. 4 (1999): 301–310.

Reynolds, Sandra, and Kathleen Wilber. "Protecting Persons with Severe Cognitive and Mental Disorders: An Analysis of Public Conservatorship in Los Angeles County." *Aging and Mental Health* 1, no. 1 (1997): 87–97.

Roberto, Karen, Joy Duke, N. Brossioe, and Pamela Teaster. *The Need for Public Guardians in the Commonwealth of Virginia.* Report to the Virginia Department for the Aging, 2007.

Sales, Bruce, D. Matthew Powell, Richard Van Diuzend, and ABA Commission on the Mentally Disabled. *Disabled Persons and the Law: State Legislative Issues.* New York: Plenum Press, 1982.

Schmidt, Winsor. "Accountability of Lawyers in Serving Vulnerable, Elderly Clients," *Journal of Elder Abuse and Neglect* 5, no. 3 (1993): 39–50.

Schmidt, Winsor. "Adult Protective Services and the Therapeutic State." *Law and Psychology Review* 10 (1986): 101–121.

Schmidt, Winsor. "Assessing the Guardianship Reform of Limited Guardianship: Tailoring Guardianship or Expanding Inappropriate Guardianships?" *Journal of Ethics, Law and Aging* 2, no.1 (1996): 5–14.

Schmidt, Winsor. "Critique of the American Psychiatric Association's Guidelines for Legislation on Civil Commitment of the Mentally Ill." *New England Journal on Criminal and Civil Confinement* 11, no. 1 (1985): 11–43.

Schmidt, Winsor. "The Evolution of a Public Guardianship Program." *Journal of Psychiatry and Law* 12, no. 3 (1984): 349–372.

Schmidt, Winsor, ed. *Guardianship: Court of Last Resort for the Elderly and Disabled.* Durham, NC: Carolina Academic Press, 1995.

Schmidt, Winsor. "Guardianship of the Elderly in Florida: Social Bankruptcy and the Need for Reform." *Florida Bar Journal* 55, no. 3 (1981): 189–195.

Schmidt, Winsor. "Law and Aging: Mental Health Theory Approach." In *Theories on Law and Ageing: The Jurisprudence of Elder Law.* Edited by Israel Doron. Berlin Heidelberg: Springer, 2009, 121–143.

Schmidt, Winsor. "Quantitative Information About the Quality of the Guardianship System: Toward a Next Generation of Guardianship Research." *Probate Law Journal* 10 (1990): 61–80.

Schmidt, Winsor, Fevzi Akinci, and Sarah Wagner. "The Relationship Between Guardian Certification Requirements and Guardian Sanctioning: A Research Issue in Elder Law and Policy." *Behavioral Sciences and the Law* 25, no. 5 (2007): 641–653.

Schmidt, Winsor, and Kent Miller. "Improving the Social Treatment Model in Protective Services for the Elderly: False Needs in the Therapeutic State." *Journal of Comparative Social Welfare* 1, no. 1 (1984): 90–106.

Schmidt, Winsor, Kent Miller, William Bell, and Elaine New. *Public Guardianship and the Elderly.* Cambridge, MA: Ballinger Publishing Company, 1981.

Schmidt, Winsor, Kent Miller, Roger Peters, and David Loewenstein. "A Descriptive Analysis of Professional and Volunteer Programs for the Delivery of Guardianship Services." *Probate Law Journal* 8, no. 2 (1988): 125–156.

Schmidt, Winsor, and Roger Peters. "Legal Incompetents' Need for Guardians in Florida." *Bulletin of the American Academy of Psychiatry and Law.* 15, no. 1 (1987): 69–83.

Schmidt, Winsor, Pamela Teaster, Hillel Abramson, and Richard Almeida. *Second Year Evaluation of the Virginia Guardian of Last Resort and Guardianship Alternatives Demonstration Project.* Memphis, TN: The University of Memphis Center for Health Services Research, 1997.

Symposium. "Wingspan—The Second National Guardianship Conference." *Stetson Law Review* 31, no. 3 (2002): 573–1055.

Teaster, Pamela. "When the State Takes Over a Life: The Public Guardian as Public Administrator." *Public Administration Review* 63, no. 4 (2003): 396–404.

Teaster, Pamela, Marta Mendiondo, Winsor Schmidt, Jennifer Marcum, and Tenzin Wangmo. *The Florida Public Guardian Programs: An Evaluation of Program Status and Outcomes.* Lexington: University of Kentucky Graduate Center for Gerontology, 2009.

Teaster, Pamela, and Karen Roberto. *Virginia Public Guardian and Conservator Programs: Evaluation of Program Status and Outcomes.* Blacksburg: The Center for Gerontology, Virginia Polytechnic Institute and State University, 2003.

Teaster, Pamela, and Karen Roberto. *Virginia Public Guardian and Conservator Programs: Summary of the First Year Evaluation.* Virginia Department for the Aging, 2002.

Teaster, Pamela, Winsor Schmidt, Hillel Abramson, and Richard Almeida. "Staff Service and Volunteer Staff Service Models for Public Guardianship and 'Alternatives' Services: Who Is Served and With What Outcomes?" *Journal of Ethics, Law, and Aging* 5, no. 2 (1999): 131–151.

Teaster, Pamela, Erica Wood, Naomi Karp, Susan Lawrence, Winsor Schmidt, and Marta Mendiondo. *Wards of the State: A National Study of Public Guardianship.* Lexington: University of Kentucky Graduate Center for Gerontology, 2005.

Teaster, Pamela, Erica Wood, Susan Lawrence, and Winsor Schmidt. "Wards of the State: A National Study of Public Guardianship." *Stetson Law Review* 37, no. 1 (2007): 193–241.

Teaster, Pamela, Erica Wood, Winsor Schmidt, and Susan Lawrence. *Public Guardianship After 25 Years: In the Best Interest of Incapacitated People?: National Study of Public Guardianship Phase II Report.* Lexington: University of Kentucky Graduate Center for Gerontology, 2007.

Topolnicki, Denise. "The Gulag of Guardianship." *Money Magazine,* March 1, 1989.

U.S. Government Accountability Office. *Guardianships: Collaboration Needed to Protect Incapacitated Elderly People.* GAO-04-655, 2004.

U.S. House of Representatives, Select Committee on Aging. *Abuses in Guardianship of the Elderly and Infirm: A National Disgrace.* GPO Committee Publication No. 100–641, 1987.

U.S. Senate Special Committee on Aging. *Guardianship Over the Elderly: Security Provided or Freedom Denied?* GPO Serial No. 108–3, 2003.

Wood, Erica. *State-Level Adult Guardianship Data: An Exploratory Survey.* Washington DC: American Bar Association Commission on Law and Aging, for the National Center on Elder Abuse, August, 2006.

Wood, Erica. *Statement of Recommended Judicial Practices on Guardianship Proceedings for the Aging.* Washington DC: American Bar Association Commission on Legal Problems of the Elderly and National Judicial College, 1986.

Yeoman, Barry. "Stolen Lives." *AARP: The Magazine,* January–February, 2004.

INDEX

About the Authors

PAMELA B. TEASTER, PhD, is a Professor, the Director of the Graduate Center for Gerontology, and Chairperson of the Department of Gerontology at the University of Kentucky (KY). She serves on the editorial boards of *The Gerontologist*, the *Journal of Applied Gerontology*, and the *Journal of Elder Abuse and Neglect*, of which she is a former editor. She is the President of the National Committee for the Prevention of Elder Abuse and is the first president of the Kentucky Guardianship Association. She recently served on the National Academy of Sciences Committee on Social Security and Representative Payees, the American Bar Association Commission on Law and Aging, and the Center for Guardianship Certification. She is a Fellow of the Gerontological Society of America and a recipient of the Rosalie Wolf Award for Research on Elder Abuse. Current research projects include: exploring linkages between poverty and elder abuse (KY Center for Poverty Research), a prevalence study of nursing home abuse (private donors), A Week in the Life of APS in Kentucky (University of KY and the KY Cabinet for Families and Children), and court-focused elder abuse initiatives (The National Institute of Justice). She has recently conducted a national survey of elder and vulnerable adult abuse (National Center on Elder Abuse), public guardianship systems (The Retirement Research Foundation), and the sexual abuse of vulnerable adults in institutions (National Institute on Aging). She is the author of over 70 peer-reviewed articles, reports, books, and book chapters.

WINSOR C. SCHMIDT Jr., JD, LLM, holds the following appointments at the University of Louisville School of Medicine and School of Public Health and Information Sciences in Louisville, KY: Endowed Chair/Distinguished Scholar in Urban Health Policy; Professor of Psychiatry and Behavioral Sciences; Professor of Family and Geriatric Medicine; and Professor of Health Management and Systems Sciences. His previous publications include *Public Guardianship and the Elderly* and *Guardianship: Court of Last Resort for the Elderly and Disabled*, as well as over 50 book chapters and articles on health and mental health law and policy issues. He is a member of the Washington Courts Certified Professional Guardian Board, the National Committee for the Prevention of Elder Abuse, and the District of Columbia Bar.

ERICA F. WOOD, JD, is Assistant Director of the American Bar Association Commission on Law and Aging, where she has focused on issues concerning guardianship, health care decision-making, long-term care, dispute resolution and legal assistance since 1980. She serves on the Virginia Public Guardian and Conservator Advisory Board.

SUSAN A. LAWRENCE, PhD, has just completed a Master's Degree in Social Work at the University of Louisville. She received her PhD from the Graduate Center for Gerontology at the University of Kentucky in 2007. She has had extensive experience working with frail elders in both New York and Kentucky. She was a consultant on the Mayor's Task Force on Long-Term Care, in Lexington, Kentucky. She has received numerous academic honors and is a member of the Gerontological Society of America and the National Association of Social Workers. Her previous publications include articles on aging and mental health, and public guardianship. Her research interests include complexity theory, men and depression, financial abuse of older adults, guardianship, and advocacy issues as they pertain to older adults.

MARTA S. MENDIONDO, PhD, is a biostatistician and Assistant Professor with a faculty appointment in the Department of Biostatistics, College of Public Health at the University of Kentucky. She has worked at the UK Sanders-Brown Center on Aging since 1997, and she has collaborated with Dr. Teaster since 2003 in several projects, such as the Retirement Research Foundation grant, *Wards of the State: A Study of Public Guardianship Programs in Seven Jurisdictions* and the NIA grant, "The Sexual Abuse of Vulnerable Adults in Institutions."